OUTREACH

OUTREACH

EXTENDING COMMUNITY SERVICE IN URBAN AREAS

JOSEPH J. BANNON
University of Illinois

CHARLES C THOMAS · PUBLISHER
Springfield · Illinois · U.S.A.

Published and Distributed Throughout the World by
CHARLES C THOMAS • PUBLISHER
Bannerstone House
301-327 East Lawrence Avenue, Springfield, Illinois, U.S.A.

This book is protected by copyright. No part of it
may be reproduced in any manner without written
permission from the publisher.

© *1973, by* CHARLES C THOMAS • PUBLISHER
ISBN 0-398-02887-7
Library of Congress Catalog Card Number: 73-7536

With THOMAS BOOKS careful attention is given to all details of manufacturing and design. It is the Publisher's desire to present books that are satisfactory as to their physical qualities and artistic possibilities and appropriate for their particular use. THOMAS BOOKS will be true to those laws of quality that assure a good name and good will.

Library of Congress Cataloging in Publication Data

Bannon, Joseph J
   Outreach: extending community service in urban areas.

   1. Recreation leadership. 2. Youth—United States—Recreation. 3. Socially handicapped—United States—Recreation. I. Title.
GV14.5.B33   301.5'7   73-7536
ISBN 0-398-02887-7

Printed in the United States of America
C-1

CONTRIBUTORS

JOSEPH J. BANNON Senior author and Editor in Chief, Office of Recreation and Park Resources, University of Illinois. Dr. Bannon received his bachelor's degree from Ithaca College and his master's and doctorate from the University of Illinois. He has served as superintendent of the Leonia, New Jersey, Recreation Commission, and as general superintendent of the Topeka, Kansas, Recreation Commission. During the past three years, Dr. Bannon has served as project director for the Roving Leader Program and has traveled extensively throughout the United States consulting with metropolitan areas that conduct outreach programs. During 1971, he studied the effectiveness of Roving Leader training programs in New York City. Dr. Bannon is the author of numerous articles on recreation and parks, and recently completed a book entitled *Problem Solving in Recreation and Parks*. He formerly served as chairman of the National Council and is a member of the Board of Trustees of the National Recreation and Park Association.

EDWIN GREENIDGE is deputy administrator of the Housing Development Administration for the City of New York. In this position, he assists the administrator in directing activities in housing and development fields including urban renewal, middle-income housing, code enforcement, rent control, rehabilitation, demolition, and the municipal loan program, as well as residential and commercial relocation. Mr. Greenidge also serves as a consultant, author, and guest lecturer in the fields of urban renewal, poverty, youth, narcotics, and related areas. He is the chief consultant to the University of Illinois Roving Leader Program and is the coauthor of *If Not Now, When?* published in 1969.

MILTON C. DOUGLAS, JR. is Chief of the ACT program, a community-based predelinquent program in Washington, D. C. From 1961-1967, he was a Roving Leader in the D. C. Department of Recreation, working in all areas of the city with gangs, individuals and groups who exhibited delinquent behavior. During 1967-1968, he served as Program Coordinator of the Roving Leader Program, moving into the Deputy Director position in 1968-1969, where he was responsible for field operations and the overall administrative responsibility for field operations and all administrative responsibility during the 1968 April riots. In 1969-1970 he became Director of the Roving Leader Program. He also served as consultant to the National Recreation and Park Association's Model Cities Programs, the U. S. Post Office Institute for Urban Problems, as well as consultant to the Roving Leader Training Program at the University of Illinois. He is a member of several professional organizations and civic clubs, and the recipient of leadership awards for his work with inner-city youth.

JOHN G. WILLIAMS is presently serving as director of parks and recreation in Sunnyvale, California. Prior to this assignment, he served as superintendent of recreation in the City of Baltimore, Maryland, and assistant director of park and recreation in Dade County, Florida. Mr. Williams received his bachelor and master's degrees from the University of Illinois. He brings a great deal of experience in working with urban programs, and in particular with the disadvantaged. Mr. Williams has served as a consultant to the Vice President's Council on Youth Opportunity, consultant to the University of Illinois Roving Leader Program, and as president of the Georgia Park and Recreation Association. He has written articles for professional magazines and recently completed a chapter on "Staff Motivation" for a soon to be published book on recreation and park administration.

PHYLLIS GRUNAUER presently serves as director of training for the Youth Service Agency in the City of New York. She received her bachelor's degree at Hunter College and her master's degree in anthropology from Columbia University. Prior to her present position, she served as community liaison officer for the United Nations Community Development and World Disarmament Committee; program director for the B'nai B'rith; and acting chief of Community Action Programs for the New York City Commission on Human Rights. Mrs. Grunauer has lectured at Fordham University, Adelphi College, and New York University. She has traveled extensively, advising and consulting on inner-city programs. She has also served as a consultant to the University of Illinois Roving Leader Program.

SIDNEY G. LUTZIN is the manager of conferences for the National Recreation and Park Association. He received his bachelor and master's degrees in education from Tufts University, Medford, Massachusetts. An acknowledged expert in the field of recreation, youth, and delinquency prevention, Mr. Lutzin was formerly regional director of the New York State Division for Youth for a number of years. He played a major role in the development of the Roving Leader Program in New York and has written numerous articles on these subjects. In addition, he has served as editor of *Parks and Recreation* magazine, *American Recreation Bulletin,* and the *American Recreation Journal.* He is a charter member of the American Recreation Society, past president of the New York Recreation Society, and formerly served as Vice President and member of the Board of Trustees of NRPA prior to joining the NRPA staff.

DONALD H. PARKIN is director of the Recreation Degree Program, and interdisciplinary degree in the College of Arts and Sciences, University of Colorado. He received bachelor's degrees from Rockmont College, Conservative Baptist Theological Seminary, and the University of Northern Arizona. He received his master's degree and Ph.D. from the University of Colorado. His experience includes: high school teaching; ministry; recreation director in summer camps in Texas, New Mexico, Colorado, Arizona and Oregon; college and university varsity coaching; college athletic director; and university instructor. Dr. Parkin has instituted and is Director of the Inner City Recreation Specialist Program. This is a living-learning experiential multi-institutional program. He is also the Director of the Colorado Institute on Leisure Time Use. He has also experimented in the video-taping of university courses for off-campus distribution, requiring instructor-student interaction through use of a local resource monitor.

JAMES F. MURPHY is presently serving as Assistant Professor of Recreation and Park at San Jose State University, San Jose, California. He received his bachelor's degree at San Francisco State College, his master's at Indiana University, and his Ph.D. at Oregon State University. Dr. Murphy has served in leadership capacity in Sunnyvale, California; Baltimore, Maryland; and Oakland, California. He has written extensively in recreation for the disadvantaged, and most recently co-edited a book on *Recreation and Leisure Services for the Disadvantaged*.

To
ALLEN V. SAPORA
and
GEORGE D. BUTLER

Who have had a profound influence on the professional development of the Editor of this book.

OUTREACH WORKER
   Roving Leader
   Streetclub Worker
   Detached Worker
   Extension Worker
   Satellite Worker
   "Program Pimp"

Is assigned to a specific community to strengthen, extend, and stimulate hard-to-reach youth to participate in wholesome recreation programs. A basic purpose of this outreach service is to help disadvantaged youth use their free time constructively and, at the same time, assist them in effectively using community resources in education, health, employment and related social services.

FOREWORD

THE WAR ON POVERTY is over. But the problems to which that crusade was addressed remain. The decade of the sixties witnessed the greatest concentration on human services since the Depression, yet we entered the seventies with a sense of despondency toward the "benign neglect" that has displaced the more altruistic fervor of the past ten years. Although federal appropriations for social welfare will actually increase during 1973-1974 because of prior legislation, more than fourteen billion dollars have been cut for various projects in education, manpower training, health, ecology, housing, and public assistance, with a further cut of about nineteen billion anticipated for 1975.

The outreach concept was a popular and successful tool of many social service agencies during the 1960's, as it had been during the 1930's. It should continue to be so. Broadly defined, "outreach" is the effort that takes place when a social service agency, such as recreation, reaches out and assists through personal contacts those citizens systematically excluded from, unaware of, or unreceptive to an agency's services or those of related agencies. Since outreach projects are intimately related to the sponsoring agency, it is possible for them to survive while other social-serving projects are stifled, though one should not be complacent about this state of affairs either.

Poverty is rooted in a group of social problems, which includes unemployment, inadequate education, poor health, substandard housing. To attack these problems requires an integrated, broad-scale approach. Recreation is one of the human services that really demands a coordinated approach to the needs of the urban poor. For instance, offering leisure activities to inner-city residents without a comprehension of the *nature* of their leisure is irresponsible; many of them experience enforced leisure from massive unemployment or underemployment. As human service specialists, we have to comprehend such leisure within a broader framework than simply free time or fun and games.

While many of the authors contributing to this book are primarily recreation professionals and practitioners, they represent a broad spectrum of experience. The stress of the book is not intended to be confined to recreation alone. We believe the outreach concept, especially in work with inner-city residents, has applications for other social and human services. In fact, outreach has long been used in various social welfare organizations, and the concepts in this book can most readily be applied to other human services. The experiences of most of the authors in this book have been with the

Roving Leader Program, an outreach program adopted by many recreation agencies throughout the country.

The Roving Leader concept represents a creative approach for providing leadership to hard-to-reach, delinquency-prone youth in the inner cities. The Roving Leader, an outreach worker also known by a variety of other titles– streetclub worker, detached worker, gang worker, etc.–is generally assigned to a specific area within a community for the purpose of attracting youth to organized recreation programs. A basic purpose of this outreach service is to help delinquency-prone or disadvantaged youth use their free time constructively, and at the same time introduce these youth to essential community resources in education, health, employment, and related social services available to them. Although the original intent of outreach was to work with potential delinquents, it has been broadened to include work with citizens in need of special attention and services, from preschoolers to the elderly.

The Roving Leader Program, which is the prime example of outreach work in recreation, has been an ongoing research and development project of the University of Illinois, Office of Recreation and Park Resources. This research was primarily supported through grants from the Department of Health, Education, and Welfare, U. S. Office of Education, Division of Manpower Development and Training. In August 1968, the Office of Recreation and Park Resources contracted with the National Recreation and Park Association to prepare a *Roving Recreation Leader Training Guide,* with funds provided by the Office of Education. This guide, published by HEW in 1971 and appended in its entirety to this book (see Appendix A), represents "how-to" guidelines to facilitate the training of Roving Leaders in the methods and techniques of conducting outreach work in the inner city. The National Recreation and Park Association executive leadership has displayed keen interest and encouragement throughout the entire Roving Leader project.

We are all familiar with the often-deserved criticism of social service workers that they are unable to relate to their clients, especially poor Blacks and other racial minorities in ghetto areas. While we do not wish to traduce social workers, our efforts do reflect a desire to move away from "welfare colonialism." We make little claim that the viewpoints in this volume are any more sensitive to minority needs, or even reflect a more inclusive or accurate social analysis. Nor is it our intention to represent this book as an exhaustive coverage of outreach for recreation. Rather, to the best of our knowledge, this book represents the first attempt to encompass the major considerations affecting outreach work in the inner city. It offers a discussion of both the practical and theoretical concerns of outreach as a social-serving tool, and also represents a variety of viewpoints and approaches to the topic. There was no editorial policy to achieve conformity among the authors; we feel the diversity of insights offered in these readings is itself indicative of the true state of Roving Leader projects.

Chapter I on the history and development of outreach quickly belies the myth that it is a "new" concept. Outreach has been with us since the 1930's; unfortunately, as Sidney Lutzin reminds us, so have the problems with inner-city youth. In fact, in reading this lively chapter one quickly sees the overwhelming similarities in outreach between the 1970's and past decades.

Chapter II on "Community Outreach in Recreation" offers a broad discussion of the philosophy and aspirations of outreach, as well as its rationale in inner-city settings. The chapter also presents a basic foundation on outreach work in various social services over the past decade. In addition, in Chapter II we touch upon several topics which are covered in more detail in subsequent contributions to this volume, especially the various aspects of relating to inner-city residents.

Chapter III focuses on the role and functions of outreach programs, with stress given to the Roving Recreation Leader program. Edwin Greenidge and Milton Douglas give a great deal of attention to inner-city cultures and point out how a Leader can relate to these. Chapter IV, by the senior author, covers program planning in outreach work and presents some further discussion on how to achieve rapport with inner-city youth, as well as on how to design programs that will be relevant for them.

In Chapter V Phyllis Grunauer pinpoints the crucial issues in training outreach workers for inner-city jobs and concretely outlines a series of learning sessions. Because of the general aspects of training covered in this chapter, it can readily be applied to outreach training tasks in other social services. In Chapter VI John Williams considers the administrative problems inherent in undertaking an outreach program. He elaborates on the dilemmas and ambiguities such a concept can raise for everyone involved, including also various responses to such conflicts.

Chapter VII reflects a broad-scale approach to outreach work in recreation. Through referrals to other social agencies, youth are encouraged to obtain services that solve problems which often have a higher priority than their leisure needs. In this chapter, Dr. Donald Parkin presents the how-to of referral work, as well as the variety of agencies an outreach worker needs to be familiar with.

Finally, Chapter VIII covers a crucial component of outreach work–the role of higher education in the inner cities. Since recreation is viewed as a local responsibility, Dr. James Murphy considers colleges and universities in metropolitan areas to be essential to the success of many outreach activities in their locality. Not only do these institutions offer courses designed to train outreach workers effectively, as well as programs to encourage youth to continue their education, but they also can open all their resources to the surrounding community. Their libraries, faculty and student expertise, social facilities, conferences–all have immediate value to the poorer communities.

It is our hope that this volume will stimulate further exploration with outreach both in recreation and other human services. Indeed it is not intended solely for classroom use, but should be of value to practitioners in recreation and parks, to social workers and other human service workers, as well as to urban sociologists and those responsible for outreach training in metropolitan areas. This book is a small attempt to keep the attack against poverty viable in fact as well as in theory. As long as the pervasive social problems of the inner city maintain, no recreation specialist in such areas can ignore them, no matter how "great" a recreation philosophy he or she might have.

JOSEPH J. BANNON

Urbana, Illinois

ACKNOWLEDGMENTS

It would be almost impossible to recognize all the agencies and individuals who made this book possible. No attempt here will do that. It does seem appropriate, however, that those agencies and individuals who made major contributions to this effort should be acknowledged.

Appreciation is extended to Dr. Howard A. Matthews and Orieanna C. Syphax of the Office of Education, Division of Manpower Development and Training, for providing the funds for developing the *Roving Recreation Leader Training Guide*. Thanks is also due to the National Recreation and Park Association staff, particularly Sidney Lutzin and Dr. Don Henkel for their help and assistance in the initial stages of the Roving Leader Project. Mr. Sherwood Dee, of the Illinois Board of Vocational and Technical Education, also provided support throughout the development of the Roving Leader Training Program. Counsel and advice were received from Dr. A. V. Sapora, Department of Recreation and Park Administration, University of Illinois; Dr. Ernest W. Anderson, Professor of Extension Education, University of Illinois; Dr. King McCristal, Dean, College of Physical Education, University of Illinois; Dr. Doyle Bishop, Department of Recreation and Park Administration, University of Illinois; Dr. Roy Jones, Director of Community Studies Center, Howard University; Dr. Edwin J. Staley, Executive Director, Recreation and Youth Services Planning Council, Los Angeles; Stanley J. Anderson, Advisor on Youth Programs, Children's Bureau, Department of Health, Education, and Welfare; George M. Nishi Naka, Executive Director, Special Service for Groups, Inc., Los Angeles, California; Clifford T. Seymour, Chairman, Department of Recreation, Southern University; Donald Hawkins, Professor, Department of Recreation, George Washington University; Lee Carey, Assistant Director, Springfield (Illinois) Recreation Commission; Dr. Charles Pezoldt, Undergraduate Curriculum Director, Department of Recreation and Park Administration, University of Illinois; and Mr. Clarence Pendleton, Jr., Director, Model City Agency, San Diego, California.

Appreciation is extended to the many authors and publishers who have permitted their work to be used to strengthen and support the ideas and suggestions presented in this book.

Of course, no acknowledgment would be complete without recognition of the typist, those who transcribed many of the conference recording tapes and who prepared the preliminary drafts of the book: Barbara Kucera, Carol

Lake, Michelle Mailloux, and Linda Algee. Sincere thanks is extended to Jacqueline Nigg for typing the final manuscript.

A very special note of appreciation is due Mary Kelly Black for editing the final manuscript and providing suggestions for layout and format.

J. J. B.

CONTENTS

	Page
Contributors	v
Dedication	ix
Foreword	xiii
Acknowledgments	xvii

Chapter

I. THE EVOLUTION OF THE OUTREACH PROGRAM—"HOW IT ALL BEGAN"
    Sidney G. Lutzin 3

II. COMMUNITY OUTREACH IN RECREATION—"WE'RE COMING AFTER YOU"
    Joseph J. Bannon 29
    Introduction
    Outreach: A New Strategy
    Some Trends
    Advocacy
    Mobilization for Youth
    The Impact of Community Participation
    Conclusion

III. ROLE AND FUNCTION OF THE OUTREACH PROGRAM—"THE STREET IS MY TURF"
    Edwin Greenidge and *Milton C. Douglas, Jr.* 53
    Social Aspects
    The Outreach Worker's Task
    Needs of Inner City Youth
    The Roving Leader Program
    Some Concluding Thoughts

IV. PROGRAM PLANNING—"MY BAG OF GOODIES"
    Joseph J. Bannon 85
    Establishing Rapport With Youth
    Developing Youth Programs

V. TRAINING FOR THE OUTREACH FUNCTION—"A LITTLE LEARNING WILL HELP US TELL OUR STORY"
    Phyllis Grunauer 103
    Detached Worker Functions

Chapter	Page
Planning	
Design of Outreach Training Program	
Trainer Responsibility	
Content of Training Design	
"How-To" Training Techniques	
Interpretation of Contact	
Outreach Situations of Vignettes	
Some Thoughts on Role Playing	
Summary	
VI. ADMINISTRATIVE PROBLEMS INHERENT IN THE OUTREACH PROGRAMS—"THE BOSS HAD BETTER LOOK OUT"	
John G. Williams	129
VII. THE REFERRAL PROCESS—"OUTREACH'S LITTLE HELPERS"	
Donald H. Parkin	145
Social Systems	
The Purpose of the Suprasystem	
Dysfunction	
Equilibrium	
Interfacing	
Keeping Pace With Change	
Internal Environment	
External Environment	
Objectives of the Outreach Referral Program	
Knowledge Base	
Process	
Common Reasons Clients Are Referred for Service	
Learning Tasks	
Types of Referral by Outreach Workers	
How to Contact Other Subsystems	
How to Act as an Advocate for Your Client	
How to Identify Gaps in Services	
Conclusion	
VIII. HIGHER EDUCATION IN THE OUTREACH PROGRAM—"THE IVORY TOWER HAS ITS ROLE"	
James F. Murphy	169
Intervention Strategies	
Leisure Service Delivery System	
Etiology of the Urban Poor	

Chapter	Page
Community Action on the Streets	
Implications for Recreation and Parks Education	

Appendices

A. THE ROVING RECREATION LEADER'S TRAINING GUIDE	185
B. ROVING RECREATION LEADER'S RATING SCALE	187
C. THE ROVING RECREATION LEADER'S SITUATION-PROBLEM EXERCISE	191
D. ROVING RECREATION LEADER PROJECT GENERAL INFORMATION TEST	207
E. ROVING RECREATION LEADER PROJECT SELF-ASSESSMENT INVENTORY	213
Index	215

OUTREACH

CHAPTER I

THE EVOLUTION OF THE OUTREACH PROGRAM

"How It All Began"

SIDNEY G. LUTZIN

THE HARD YEARS of the Great Depression in America during the 1930's gave visibility to many social issues which they did not necessarily spawn. And out of this era came responses to social problems which have laid the foundation for attempts to deal with some of the pressing problems of a society which was hard beset.

In perspective, it might be said that the era of the 1930's in many ways was a Golden Age for human services. This was the period when new and innovative programs were initiated to deal with social problems which had always been with us, but whose increased intensity and widespread population involvement made possible the development of public and legislative support for appropriate action.

In an era of our history when the economy of our nation was least able to support critical human services, some of its most effective programs were launched.

One of the issues which loomed into public focus during this era was juvenile delinquency. Although the causes of juvenile crime provide an insight into the complexities of human and environmental weaknesses, the Depression created conditions which substantially added to the problem. Widespread unemployment, which reached nearly universal proportions in the poorer neighborhoods of the cities and cast its shadows over impoverished rural slums as well, created many of the conditions which nourished youthful crime. Parental control over young offspring weakened as parents foraged for the means to keep ends together for simple survival in city hovels, and children took to the streets in pursuit of street trades which included shoe-shining, "junking," and street-corner sales of newspapers, shoelaces, and other assorted merchandise.

The street trades brought quick education to young entrepreneurs who found that there was excitement, financial reward, and personal gratification for those who knew the shortcuts and could merchandise stolen articles on the streets or through "fences"; who could strip a car or a vacant house; snatch a purse or roll a drunk.

The excitement of these activities helped to fill drab lives, and the affluence from petty theft helped fill empty stomachs–with folding money to spare. So dependence on the home was no longer critical and was transformed into independence on the street, creating a street society which more and more increased the incidence of juvenile delinquency.

With lessening family controls and faltering supervision, school was no longer a compulsory element in young lives, and as long as the truant officer could be avoided, truancy could be added to the inventory of delinquent behavior–and truancy created a "kindergarten of crime."

But even a street society needs structure and organization, and man (and boy) being gregarious animals, a variety of structures developed to bring young street people together–and to keep them apart as well. Some of these were not new to the immigrant neighborhoods of the big cities and to their slums. They had developed in these areas with the maturing of earlier generations of young people on the city streets. But now, with a substantial increase in youth crime, the street society found that there were viable structures which suited their purposes and their needs.

Some banded together out of common interest in activities which included "stickball," an adaptation of baseball to the limitations of New York City street play; softball as played on debris-strewn sandlots and whatever other open space could be found in cluttered neighborhoods; basketball on courts defined by space available in alleys, backyards of tenements and on the streets; and similar adaptations of "pastimes" which to this kind of city youngster passed as sports.

These young people comprised but a very small portion of the juvenile street population, who for the most part had little interest in this type of recreation and even much less skill in any of the recreational sports. A study of inmates in correctional institutions in that era indicated that fewer than 25 per cent of them had any recreational skills.

Furthermore, while there were school playgrounds, some parks, settlement houses and assorted youth organizations, their resources were rarely used by the street society, other than for occasional fast, disruptive incursions which on the one hand provided a form of recreation and on the other established the sharp demarcation existing between the "organized" institutional programs and that of the "unorganized" street groups.

For some teenagers the need for social interaction led to the evolution of the store-front social club. Since this type of youth neither wanted nor was acceptable in the social activities of the organized programs of the churches, settlement houses, schools and other institutionalized agencies, he created his own resource.

Small stores along the street had been vacated by shopkeepers who had succumbed to the economic blight of the Depression. Landlords were hungry for any income which could be derived from their empty properties. Young people wanted "their own club" where they could be at home away from home, close to the streets they knew so well, and with other young people who like themselves wanted the feeling of "belonging"; the excitement of the parties and other activities they could pursue without parental or societal supervision, and all on their own terms.

So for some on the streets, the store-front social club provided the answer to their needs. Neighborhoods became speckled with "clubs" where in a minimal number of instances this product of its time served the legitimate needs of an adolescent society without substantial ill effect upon either the individual or his neighborhood. But for most, it was another element for spawning increased crime as unbridled youths utilized their "club" as headquarters for unsavory activity, and a place from which they unleashed a variety of atrocities upon the surrounding neighborhoods . . . , all in the pursuit of "fun" and the money it took to satisfy their wants and sustain their "club."

Probably the most widespread form of youth culture which manifested itself in this period was the street gang. Like the other forms of youth society it was not new to the streets of the big cities. The various structures which predominated in this period grew out of those which had previously existed on a much smaller and less obtrusive basis as generations of young slum-bred children grew up through the socially hazardous corridor of the teenage years.

But now the pressures were greater. Society was in the initial stages of a vast transitional period whose changes were only slightly deferred as each new plateau was reached and succeeding after-shocks set in–and the mores and taboos which form the pegs of a stable society were inevitably being plucked out by the effects of the transition itself.

Street gangs began to proliferate throughout the poorer neighborhoods of cities, building on the form and tradition of those which had existed before.

They provided a type of nourishment against the blandness of slum living by supplying elements otherwise missing in the lives of the poor in the crowded tenement districts. A youngster in a gang was no longer "just another kid on the street." He was a "Chaplain," an "Ace," a "Devil" or whatever other name identified his gang. He wore the flamboyant dress of his particular gang. His gang adopted trademarks of dress which made him readily recognizable to the residents of the neighborhood. He belonged . . . and he lived under a set of taboos as real as any which established the life styles of other primitive cultures in lands about which he had never even heard.

Most of his waking hours were spent with his gang, giving him the interaction with others his age; providing him with the activities which were his "recreation" regardless of whether this was a socially desirable or undesirable outlet. He had identity; and as the exploits of the gang attracted the attention of the neighborhood, the public press, and the police, he gained a form of status which he valued very highly. And he was ready to fight for any real or imagined slur or deprecation against his gang, its individual members, or himself. In all, the street gang was in essence a counterpart in the life of the street society, of the structured and organized clubs and fraternal orders upon which established society in higher economic neighborhoods based its recreational and community life.

Some of the gangs had their primary interest in the sports activities, building stickball teams, softball and basketball teams and for the most part created no great problems for the police. Yet even these required the profits from petty thievery to underwrite their activities and to supply them with the equipment they needed.

Other gangs evolved from the store-front clubs, using the stores as headquarters. Some of these, and others as well, began acquiring girl gang auxiliaries providing regular girl friends for the gang members as well as handy weapon carriers when zip guns, knives, and other weapons became the mark of the tough gang. Girls were not as readily subject to the frequent body searches for weapons that police began making on the streets when assaults and homicides by gangs started to increase. Street-wise gangs soon learned this and their girl auxiliaries could safely conceal weapons which the police would have found on the boys.

As the number of gangs increased so did their activities, much of which aimed at establishing a status for themselves. One widely sought image was that of the "tough guys" who could command "respect" from the inhabitants of the neighborhood because of their known exploits. This required physical abuse and bullying of people in the area; thefts with threats of reprisal if victims complained; and related activities contrived to spread fear of the gang wherever and whenever they showed themselves.

Another was the gangster prototype. Using the successful adult "operators" of various criminal activities in the area as models, the young gangs aped them. They loitered about their hangouts, copied their talk, their mode of dress, and even their mode of walking, presenting themselves to the neighborhood as so many carbon copies of the thieves, pimps, and gamblers who were among the few who could display a semblance of affluence and influence in the slums. And like those they mimicked, they "pulled the jobs" and planned and carried out the same types of crimes, taking care only to avoid stepping in on the areas their mentors had taken over for themselves. So the "protection" rackets the street gangs perfected were carried out against young people in the schools, small corner candy store operators, and the other merchants and individuals whose payoff was below the standards of their adult models. Nevertheless, it provided both fun and profit and an image the gang valued.

As the number of street gangs increased, and the efforts to establish themselves intensified, conflicts began to develop not only with the people in the neighborhoods but between the gangs themselves. This was an inevitable outcome of the gang society, because of the critical need of the gang members to be important, to have neighborhood recognition, and to be "number one" in the areas where they were known.

This led to an intensification of criminality by the gangs in order to establish their superiority and eventually resulted in either armed conflict between rival gangs, or as in the more civilized and higher layers of organization and government, into alliances and "turfs." The latter were geographic areas bounded by certain streets which were acknowledged as being exclusively the home and operating bases of specific gangs and their allies.

The effects of increased youth crime were becoming all too well known in the less fortunate neighborhoods of cities, and legislators at local, state, and national levels were more and more vociferously acknowledging its existence and decrying its implications. Workers in the various social fields, too, were struggling to develop responses which would deflect the sharply increased incidence of youth crime. However, all told, the sum of their combined efforts was having little if any effect.

In the first place, delinquency and youth crime were not new phenomena. They had been with us since time immemorial. The principal change was in the scope of the problem; the increased number of young people involved; and its wider and more visible effect on the neighborhoods to which it was indigenous.

Second, in general the problem was being confined to a large extent mainly to the slums where both the young criminals and their victims lived. Aside from an occasional foray for fun and headlines by young scions from the more affluent neighborhoods, the people who held the power to take definitive action were not very often the direct victims of the crimes. The so-called "good neighborhoods" were still good.

Third, as ever, treatment of young criminals reflected the age-old approach to the problem. The principal efforts were limited to treating the symptom rather than the cause; to the application of "justice," uneven and for the most part reflective of the primitive attitude of the public, rather than the rehabilitation intent reflected only in the names of the "correctional" institutions into which they were remanded.

As a matter of fact, the American attitude has never been one conducive to the establishment of sound and effective preventative and treatment services for young delinquents. Although there have been periods of more realistic and more promising experimentation, with few exceptions this has been a short-term effort with innovation being quickly overwhelmed by budgetary reaction. To the average taxpayer and the majority of the voters, the young criminal is a public enemy. He steals, assaults, rapes, and vandalizes, and the taxpayer may one day be victimized by him. Therefore, "he is our enemy; let's put him away where he can't harm us." It has always been difficult for conscientious, concerned officials and workers to secure the appropriation of public funds needed to undertake new and promising programs either in the field of prevention or treatment.

So while there was a general recognition of the problem, and public bodies were demonstrating their concern through special study commissions, very little specific action was being taken to either eliminate causative conditions or to provide better treatment and rehabilitative services.

Nor was there much in the literature to help the aspiring young student, the worker in the field, or even the legislative commissions with the problems of youth crime or its treatment. The symptoms of youthful misbehavior and antisocial activity have been referred to from Biblical times; were well documented by the novelists and writers such as Shakespeare, Dickens, *et al.* However, those looking for current research reflecting the causative and corrective issues were hard-pressed indeed.

There was the 1915 work of William Healy, *The Individual Delinquent,* the product of study done in the Boston area, which provided one of the first of a number of insights into the characteristics of the delinquent. This publication was based upon study of a thousand juvenile recidivists. Contemporary with this was the surprisingly forward-looking (for its time) *Delinquency and Spare Time* by Thurston which was the result of the Cleveland Recreational Survey in 1918. It concluded that delinquent acts were little different from habitual spare-time activity other than that they were a little more unacceptable socially; or because the practitioner was accidentally caught at it; or that the need for money to finance his recreation motivated the delinquent behavior. This was one of the first times that a publication tied the lack of needed recreation facilities to the conditions creating delinquency.

Nothing of note was published in the field again until 1925 when Ciril Burt wrote *The Young Delinquent,* which was a classic of the British mold, denoting some of the specific characteristics of the individual delinquent. Healy and his associate Augusta Bronner, hard at work at the Judge Baker Child Guidance Center in Boston, were studying the delinquents coming through Boston's Juvenile Court and in 1926 authored *Delinquents and Criminals, Their Making and Unmaking.* This work dealt with attitudes as well as physical characteristics which led to criminal behavior.

Then in 1927 came the landmark opus which launched what later became known as the "Chicago School" of delinquency study and started a "bonanza" period of publishing in the field of juvenile delinquency. This was Frederic M. Thrasher's keystone study of 500 youth gangs in Chicago, titled simply *The Gang* and published by the University of Chicago Press.

At about this time legislatures in both New York State and in Illinois were motivated sufficiently by what in terms of that era was a "high incidence of delinquency" and crime, to create commissions to study the problem and recommended legislation. The Crime Commission of New York State produced a series of publications, the first of which was a 1927 study of truants in the New York City schools and then *From Truancy to Crime* treating with the relationship between truancy and delinquent behavior. In 1928 the Crime Commission produced *A Study of Environmental Factors in Juvenile Delinquency*. As the title indicates, this study focuses upon the environmental element of poverty, slums, existing criminal activity and the detrimental elements in the neighborhoods which helped to propel young people into lives of crime. Another one of this series, published in 1930, was called *Crime and the Community* and explored the failures of community institutions to meet the needs of youths growing up in the cities of the state.

In 1929 Healy and Bronner brought out another book, *Reconstructing Behavior in Youth,* which among other things linked physical defects to children's delinquent behavior and noted that the elimination of such defects greatly reduced the likelihood of delinquency.

The Illinois Crime Survey of the Illinois Crime Commission in 1929 produced the first follow-up to Thrasher's *The Gang,* and initiated the type of research into youthful misbehavior and crime which was to make the era of the "30's and the Chicago School." Titled *The Juvenile Delinquent,* it established that any effort to deal with the delinquent as a separate entity, apart from the social and cultural world in which his behavior trends have arisen, necessarily neglects important aspects of the situation.

Clifford R. Shaw in 1931 published *The Natural History of a Delinquent Career,* which followed the development of the young criminal through the subculture of the poverty neighborhoods of the city, and then added in the same year the publication *Delinquency Areas,* in which he showed the relationship between the incidence of delinquency and the neighborhoods from which delinquents originated and the effect of interstitial areas on the delinquency rate.

Reckless and Smith followed with *Juvenile Delinquency* in 1932, highlighting the causes of delinquency, the failure of the schools and other institutions as contributing to the problem. They identified the work of Thurston in correlating the lack of recreation facilities with the delinquency rate, showing a correlation index of .44 based on relatively sound study which considered density of child population, racial composition, and uniformity of police regulation.

Thurston's premise that socially undesirable activity of young people substituted for a lack of recreation opportunity, which was enunciated in the Cleveland study in 1918, was thus reinforced by Reckless and Smith in 1932. Together they probably helped to contribute to the recommendation which was reported in *The White House Conference on Child Health and Protection* and advocated: "For every child, a community which recognizes and plans for his needs; protects him against physical dangers, moral hazards and disease; provides him with safe and wholesome places for play and recreation; and makes provision for his cultural and social needs." The desirability of recreation opportunity as an antidote to delinquency was building up as a popular concept.

Concurrent with the probings of the Chicago group into the problem of delinquency were those of Healy and Bronner and Sheldon and Eleanor Glueck in Boston. The researchers in Chicago and those in Boston represented nearly the totality of the work being done in the field.

The Gluecks studied individual delinquents and criminal careers, producing in 1930 *Five Hundred Criminal Careers* and in 1934 *One Thousand Juvenile Delinquents* and *Five Hundred Delinquent Women*.

The foregoing listing of publications represents not only an identification of the important research and study being reported in the field of juvenile delinquency, but actually records practically all of the literature which through the first half of the 1930's was available for study by the few students who saw in the field of juvenile delinquency prevention an opportunity to serve society. It was also for all intent and purpose about all the reference literature available to those who were already working through various agencies to prevent and treat delinquent behavior. About the only other material was that which had begun to emerge attacking the school for its failure to serve the needs of delinquency-prone youths and listing the school system as a principal contributor to the delinquency of young people.

Thus, the young graduate student of 1935 studying the field of delinquency could indoctrinate himself only from the works of a very few researchers and writers. He could, nevertheless, study in depth their findings of the characteristics of delinquents, gangs, and the physical and environmental causes of crime. Though there was by no means any plethora of writers in the field, the work which had been done in the preceding eight or nine years was of good enough quality to provide a solid body of knowledge relating to the causes of delinquency and the characteristics of its growing number of perpetrators.

However, there was little by way of detailed experience to provide direction for eliminating the causes or indicating the treatment programs which could assist in preventing young people from becoming delinquent or in helping those who had already come into conflict with the law to find their way back into socially acceptable behavior.

Those working face to face in the area of delinquency prevention at this time were for the most part doing it as a peripheral element of their jobs; as a part-time responsibility; or in many instances as a voluntary effort which grew out of involvement in other aspects of youth or welfare work. There were very few people whose professional responsibility was the prevention of delinquency.

The people who were dealing in a face-to-face setting with delinquent and delinquency-prone youths covered a wide range of jobs. There was no police training in juvenile work and practically nowhere was there a police juvenile bureau specializing in youth crime prevention.

Welfare caseworkers were involved, since in their work with the welfare families they had to alleviate the problems arising out of the delinquency of young members of the family. But their principal concern was to keep the family clothed and fed and kept in reasonable health, and their caseloads were too heavy to do even that with any high degree of efficiency.

Truant officers, attendance teachers and others responsible for enforcing compulsory education laws knew more about the behavior of their young charges, but their approach to the problem in most instances was the simple one of trying to get truants back to school. They were not trained for anything more, and when they were not successful they more often than not resorted to inveighing the law which placed the truant first on probation and then invariably into the "reform school."

Teachers sometimes tried to work with the children whose inability to adjust to society was first symptomized in classroom problems. The schools were coming more and more under criticism for creating many of the problems, but the teacher too had neither time nor inclination or any resources upon which he could call for assistance in dealing with disruptive or withdrawn youngsters. Some of the more advanced school systems were beginning to do some minimum counseling work, were talking about visiting teacher programs and other promising services. Yet in few instances was any effective service being implemented.

Juvenile Courts were coming into vogue. The attempt to deal with delinquents on an informal court basis, exploring the causes and devising helpful court direction was a fine one in concept. But in practice most county juvenile court judges were the regular county judges who, in between holding regular court for adult criminals, attempted to fit in hearings and quick disposition of the juveniles remanded to their jurisdiction. Cases were disposed of frequently on an irregular and inconsistent basis, and very little was achieved through the process which would assure that the young delinquent standing before the judge one day would not be back a week or a month later.

Where probation was utilized, the youngster was turned over to a probation officer whose standard practice was to have him report to him each week for what in many instances was hardly more than a routine check-off. Probation officers were not being widely used, and where they were, the juvenile cases were only a small item of their major responsibility which was with adult criminals and family support cases.

A few child protection agencies existed which sometimes did attempt to work with the more serious cases of youth delinquency; to serve as a resource for the juvenile court; and to try in other ways to be helpful. However, even their work was sporadic and not especially effective.

Settlement houses and other group work agencies, community centers, boys' and girls' clubs, Salvation Army and church-related youth groups provided community resources which offered opportunity for some youths who could be interested in the limited scope of activities they afforded. But those most likely to get into trouble were not attracted to the types of programs provided, were even less interested in conforming to the regulated atmosphere of these agencies, and if they did come to those places their disruptive behavior made them much less than welcome or acceptable.

Public recreation services had begun to spread through the cities–some in after-school and evening programs, others in playgrounds, parks and community centers. They were spurred on during this era by Works Progress Administration and National Youth Authority projects which built community facilities and provided a reservoir of leadership services to develop summer and year-round playground programs, parks, community centers, stadiums and swimming pools.

The private agencies and the public ones as well had been benefiting from the popular image of these services as being delinquency preventative. In their appeals for funds through the Community Chest Drives of that period, the private agencies and youth organizations played up their supposed delinquency prevention capabilities. Fund-raising campaign posters claimed for example that "No Boy Scout is a Delinquent." To which some of those who worked with delinquents in the 1930's replied, "No self-respecting delinquent would be a Boy Scout." The fact of the matter was that few programs were designed or otherwise conceived to serve the needs or to meet the interests of unadjusted young people.

And the public agencies were hardly better; while they encouraged the delinquency preventative image at municipal budget hearings in order to fatten their appropriations, they did little to attempt to make the concept a reality.

The author of this chapter was then (1935-1936) preparing a Master's thesis on the subject *Crime, Delinquency and the School*. In the course of his study he had carefully reviewed all of the pertinent literature in the field; had observed the procedures and processes of juvenile courts, probation officers; had explored the role of the schools, the police, churches; he had read the case records in child guidance clinics and talked with group workers in settlement houses, recorded the programs and activities they offered and made friends with their clientele; and finally paid close attention to what was going on in public playground programs and other facilities administered under several different recreation jurisdictions.

As a result of all of this, certain concepts began to emerge. First, that all of the community institutions had some basic responsibilities in serving the needs of the young people growing up in these communities. Second, that some of these institutions which had the ability to effectively serve as deterrents to delinquency were actually in many instances part of the problem and were contributing to it. Third, that while many youth problems were rooted primarily in the family, this was too complex a situation. The possibility of effectively eliminating family problems was so remote that it would be necessary to find resources outside the family to provide children with strength and support to overcome the deleterious effects of their family life. Fourth, that it would be extremely difficult to reach young people with problems through most of the community institutions, or to utilize the beneficial elements of their resources in solving youth problems because in most instances they were too "official." By and large they implied compulsory or mandatory characteristics. Fifth, that to reach young people it would be necessary to present situations which would be attractive and enjoyable to them—and that they would have to be reached *where they were,* both figuratively and literally. Sixth, that recreation provided the most promising approach since it offered an enjoyable situation and opportunities for the young people involved to do the things they liked to do. Seventh, that while recreation held a promising potential, the organized programs of settlement houses, youth organizations, schools and recreational agencies did not attract this type of youth, who were repelled by the structure and by the activities which did not provide a reasonable frame of reference for these street-wise youngsters.

Although several extensive studies were subsequently undertaken to determine whether the availability of recreation or group work services in a neighborhood resulted in diminished delinquent behavior, for the most part they were either inconclusive or indicated that the recreation program had little effect on the delinquency rate. One such study of a major boys' club in New York City undertaken in the 1930's by Frederic M. Thrasher, who had moved from Chicago to New York University, determined that the presence of the boys' club might actually be considered to have caused an increase in delinquency in that area.

The principal weakness of these studies was that there was no way to determine what *other* forces at work in the community or in the family at the time that recreation services were being studied had measurable effect on the delinquent acts recorded. Even more pertinent, however, was the fact that research was being done on recreation programs, which were being studied for their effect on delinquency, when in no instance was the program of recreation agencies being designed for delinquency prevention; nor was the goal of the recreation agency or its services being geared to affect the incidence of delinquency.

Therefore, if recreation were to be used as a tool in delinquency prevention, it would first have to be designed to serve that purpose, and techniques would have to be developed to reach out to bring its benefits to trouble-prone youths. As conceived at that time, it meant that those in the community who were delinquent, or those whose behavior patterns marked them as vulnerable to delinquency, would need to be identified; that individual gross diagnosis of elements contributing to their antisocial behavior would have to be made; then a suitable recreation setting would have to be designated where the adolescent youth could be induced, by the attractiveness of the situation and of an activity designed and prescribed to meet his need, to participate in the recreation activity, preferably in a group situation. Furthermore, it was hoped that other community agencies and institutions which could provide supportive services would be enlisted to collaborate in the efforts undertaken.

To explore the total premise more effectively, the author secured employment in a small upstate city in New York State which operated eight summer playgrounds. The city of about 30,000 population had experienced a sharp increase in the number of juveniles remanded to children's court during the preceding year, and his responsibility was to reverse this trend.

The problem which was laid out provided that first the delinquent and potentially delinquent youth in the community would be identified. This was done in two ways:

1. Through personal contact with the police, probation officer, welfare department workers, school principals and teachers, truant officer, private voluntary agency personnel, and recreation leaders, the names and addresses of known delinquents and those who were considered as potential delinquents were listed. Also included were the types of youngsters who in every neighborhood are pointed out by corner grocers, candy store operators and others by observation: "Some day that boy is going to get into serious trouble!" but who rarely becomes an official concern until the prophesy comes true.

2. A playground registration card was designed to be completed by all children coming to the playgrounds. The blanks to be filled in on casual scrutiny appeared little different from an ordinary registration form, but because it indicated birthdate, number and names of siblings, occupation of each parent, address, school attended and grade achieved, as well as clubs and organizations of which the child was a member, it provided information from which could be deduced such elements as family income; whether or not both parents were employed; if the home was in an area where delinquency was high; whether he was part of an unusually large family; if he was retarded in his school work; and whether he belonged to recognized organizations which indicated that he could already be benefiting from organized programs.

3. Registration cards were cleared through the social service exchange, which noted whether the family was receiving welfare from the public welfare agency or from private voluntary agencies, and also indicated if members of the family had been arrested.

4. All of this information was matched against a "delinquency index," which was a list of criteria for delinquency vulnerability designed to identify youths most likely to get into trouble.

Actually this delinquency index was a forerunner of delinquency prediction tables devised in several places in later years. Work in this field was done by Kvaraceus in *The Community and the Delinquent,* Hathaway and Monachesi in *Analyzing and Predicting Juvenile Delinquency with the MMPS,* and particularly by Sheldon and Eleanor Glueck in their extensive study with the New York City Youth Board.

While there have been many criticisms of prediction scales, nevertheless the delinquency index referred to here helped to develop a list of youngsters who needed help; who certainly could not be harmed by exposure to organized services; and who might well benefit from them. Furthermore, from this list could be determined which of the children identified by responsible agencies and individuals in the community were voluntarily coming to playgrounds for recreation activities and which were finding their recreation in the streets, junk yards, and the other questionable resources for youthful misbehavior present in every community.

5. An intensive training program was provided for the playground leaders so that:

    a. they would understand the basic elements of delinquency causation and the symptoms of delinquency behavior;

    b. they would be enthused about the opportunity to have a positive effect on delinquent and potentially delinquent youngsters and motivated to attract them to their playgrounds and to hold their interest there through innovative, prescriptive programming;

    c. they would understand how the "special lists" developed from the delinquency index were compiled and recognize the fact that these were gross determinations;

d. they would be familiar with techniques and resources for developing activities to serve needs of specified young people and for integrating these activities into the total program of the playground;

e. they would know the role of the worker who would be making the contacts and getting the "specials" to the playgrounds;

f. they would know some of the problems which could be foreseen when unadjusted youngsters came to the playgrounds and be able to work toward overcoming these problems.

This was a big challenge for playground leaders anticipating a "normal" type of summer on the playgrounds. But their interest in the whole concept and the personal challenge and subsequent gratification it promised created a great enthusiasm and dedication to the project.

With the playgrounds established as the resource to which the unaffiliated young people could be brought, and with the playleaders given the basic training which would make them effective in working with them, the author was now ready to become the first of what later was known as a "Detached Worker," and subsequently as "Street Club Worker" or "Roving Leader."

Without going into great detail concerning the step-by-step methodology used, it can be reported that a number of unaffiliated youth groups were contacted on the streets in their neighborhoods; rapport was established with them; they were induced by various guises to come as a group to the playground in their area; the playleader was advised in advance of their coming and the worker proposed activities and devised settings for these activities which would be attractive to the group and would also involve the "regular" playground participants.

The groups which seemed to be most ready for this approach were involved at first, and as both worker and playleaders became more experienced, more difficult groups or gangs were contacted. As the work progressed, one of the playleaders who showed unusual aptitude for this work was added as a second detached worker, and then specific, known delinquents were contacted; frequently they were "loners" who were not involved in gang activity.

There was excellent reception of this new approach, because first of all a number of troublesome groups were moved from the streets to the playgrounds. Here they received "planned" acceptance from the leaders and by many of the playground children who recognized and followed the example of the leaders. The gangs brought in found new and exciting activities which were designed for them and other children. The playground eventually became an attractive place for the group members.

Second, the playground program became enriched by innovative activities which had to be designed and carried out if the gangs were to be motivated to come back after their first encounter. This made the program more exciting for all children and was undoubtedly responsible for increased playground attendance.

For example, three brothers, the oldest of whom was thirteen and had a background of multiple juvenile court appearances, were first seen by the detached worker locked in their yard by their parents and playing with a golf club and small rubber ball. Contacts with the parents to spell out the possibility of having the boys participate in a supervised program, and then exciting the boys with the prospect of designing and building a miniature golf course on the playground, resulted in attracting them to the playground. They were given responsibility there by the playleader who had been assigned to plan a course in one area of the playground. Other children were asked to help them by bringing the coffee cans which would be the cups; others made flags for the holes as part of the crafts program; clubs and balls were secured and miniature golf became a popular activity for all.

The youngsters for whom this ploy was designed received both acceptance and recognition which previously had been denied them by children in the neighborhood, and the playground had an effective new and popular activity. The three brothers were then helped by the playleader to move into other playground activities, and by the end of the summer were among the most regular attenders.

This type of experience was multiplied many times that first summer and the one which followed. And while this approach and the description given could be categorized as "overly simplified," it nevertheless did indicate that, particularly for a substantial group of young people for whom their delinquent behavior was a mode of recreation, organized recreation programs of a socially desirable character could be substituted–*if* they were specifically designed for this purpose; if the program leadership was sympathetic and trained for it; and if the "outreach" to bridge the gap between the organized service and the antisocial behavior was provided through the use of detached workers.

There were many other elements involved in the strategies utilized as the program was continued from a summer playground base into indoor centers and other facilities and resources during other times of the year. However, one of the more noticeable factors was that as the police, school personnel, clergymen, and others in the community started to become aware of the success of this approach, they began to volunteer assistance, information, and referrals to the detached workers. There were certainly set-backs as well when disruptive groups were sometimes brought too soon into the YMCA or other indoor recreation centers, creating havoc with ongoing programs. In time these experiences led to other techniques, such as using these facilities first at special times by individual gangs and then eventually working them into regular programs by twos and threes, and by helping the leadership in these institutions to understand the value of adjusting their own attitudes and programs–which contributed to improvement of their own programs, increased participation in their activities and, as the results became known, provided better community acceptance of their agencies. The increased income which was supplied to the agencies for their support of these special services, through local service clubs who were sold on the concept and by the summer demonstrations, also helped to make the additional effort required of the agencies more palatable to them.

The involvement of overseas nations in war during the late 1930's and of the United States during most of the first half of the 1940's diverted attention from the problems of young people in the cities during this period. However, delinquency increased substantially, making itself very much felt in the communities as attention shifted after 1945 from the problems of war to those of the peace that followed.

Officials discovered that new populations moving into the cities to man the machines that supplied the war had brought more congestion, different cultural attitudes, continued poverty, and families with two working parents, into already distressed and disturbed neighborhoods. Children ran uncontrolled in streets that had already overflowed with crime, and the traditional gang activity had increased as young people sought status and identity in the "asphalt jungles."

State governments moved to respond legislatively to these issues–some by merely passing more laws based on little understanding of the problems and contributing even less to their solution. Others made more sincere and better founded efforts–but only a very few put money in the hopper to back up their drive against youth crime.

In New York State, a joint legislative study commission recommended the establishment of a state agency whose primary responsibility would be the prevention of juvenile delinquency. Governor Dewey not only accepted the recommendations, but in 1945 supported legislation which promoted an even broader approach through the provision of a strong and substantial grants-in-aid program for the municipalities of the state under a New York State Youth Commission. The funding available from the Youth Commission was substantial enough to motivate municipalities to undertake new services for youth in both the field of delinquency prevention and in recreation services. In a number of the state's larger cities, including New York City, establishment of prototypes of the new state agency was encouraged by supplementary grants available to them for the creation of what were known as Youth

Bureaus. These were municipal bureaus of government serving as the principal municipal agency for dealing with delinquency prevention and the coordination of the public and private voluntary youth services in the community.

The author joined the staff of the Youth Commission shortly after its establishment and assisted in the organization of the youth bureaus created in 1946 and 1947 and of the New York City Youth Board when it was adopted in 1948.

One of the first critical problems that the new Youth Board faced was the challenge created by the increased intensity of crime and other antisocial behavior of fast proliferating youth gangs. In comparison with the street gangs of the '30's, these gangs had become much greater in number; were responsible for much more serious types of criminal activity, as their organization and structure had become more sophisticated; they had developed new arsenals of weapons of great variety and ingenuity; had expanded on the concept of "turf"; and were waging warfare between gangs and alliances of gangs on a grand scale.

In the late 1940's and throughout the 1950's the gang in New York City was a solidly entrenched element in the life of the city–capable of creating turmoil, striking terror, and in certain instances, committing murder. It was a highly structured social phenomenon, representing an evolution from the gangs of the 1930's into both horizontal and vertical organizational forms.

For the most part, this type of gang society was made up of a great number of units. Those organized vertically had intertwined ties based on age; gangs membered by older teenagers nurtured related gangs in the lower teenages and other gangs of preteeners. All of these gangs had affinity to one another, and the younger gangs fed into the older ones as the members progressed in age. By the time the junior gang member moved up to the top gang, he was experienced in the ways and taboos of the gang, trained by the older gang members and frequently was already hardened by inter-gang "rumbles," the gang warfare of that era.

Many gangs organized themselves into a horizontal structure of alliances between a number of gangs, which like the nations at war, brought together the combined strength of many gangs, friendly to each other or responding for other self-serving purposes. Thus enlarged by their allies, conflicting gangs could and did stage massive rumbles where gang members on occasions numbering into the thousands employed every type of weapon to wound, scar, and sometimes kill their enemies–but in the end settled nothing.

The gang wars were only one element of a many-faceted attack by gangs on the peace, tranquility, and safety of the neighborhoods and their inhabitants. No aspect of life in these areas was immune from fear and victimization caused by gang activity. A whole recreation center could be emptied of participants and sometimes even of the security guards by the word that "The Chaplains are coming!"

Discussions between the State Youth Commission staff and the staff of the New York City Youth Board concerning program planning by the Board led to exploration of the problem of gang activity and the difficulty of designing methods to combat it in 1949. The experience of the detached worker demonstration in upstate New York was described at that time. It was pointed out that this same approach might work in specified neighborhoods of New York City where neighborhood populations were not much greater than that of the city where it was tried.

By the following year a Gang Worker program had been established by the New York City Youth Board. A group of about 10 workers had been set up with its own headquarters. This first contingent of men became a closely knit, thoroughly dedicated group who in a way made history in pioneering a new approach to the severe youth crime problems in the large metropolises.

The technique for gang contact first tried in this program was infiltration. The premise assumed was that gangs would not accept an outsider from a city agency to work with them. So the Gang Workers went to the hangout areas of the gang they had targeted in on, hung around until they were familiar with sights in the area, and eventually worked their way in as a member of the gang. Once infiltration had been accomplished, their goal was to attempt to move the gang interest away from rumbles and criminal action and into some of the sports activities, organized recreation programs and in general to hold the gang in check.

This approach was short-lived. In the first place it took too long to infiltrate; it was often dangerous; and when successful, frequently resulted in arrest of the worker along with the rest of his gang when they came into conflict with the police. The undercover technique, while ineffective did bring new insights into gang attitudes which led the Board to believe that some gangs would accept the attachment of a worker to their group.

This undercover technique also created the first of a long series of disagreements between the police and the Gang Workers and the Street Club Workers who succeeded them. The disagreement was based on the police belief that criminal behavior was the jurisdiction of the police and the courts– and the intervention of the gang workers frequently spawned illegal activity, interfered with police work, and covered overt criminal acts by gangs. The police approach to the gang problem in that period was constant harassment; frequent street searches of gang members for weapons; and "official" declarations of war against the gangs every time a particularly heinous crime hit the newspapers. The *New York Herald Tribune,* in an 18-month period, reported four such war declarations by one police commissioner . . . but no decrease in gang activity resulted.

In changing from the Gang Worker approach to the Streetclub Worker, the Youth Board classified hundreds of New York City gangs and identified those most likely to commit the most dangerous acts. Street Club Workers then made contacts with selected gangs, identifying themselves as Streetclub Workers and offering to assist gang members with special problems–appearing with them in court; visiting with them when they were held in jail; helping to get them employment; arranging medical attention when this was necessary; and taking them on excursions to amusement parks, camping trips, and other places.

The workers were accepted in most instances, although they were frequently put through a sort of probationary experience until the members felt secure with them. The gangs liked the idea of a worker because they found that the things he could do for them were helpful; he didn't moralize; got them to places they could not have gone to on their own, often buffered their contacts with police; and, very importantly, could be a resource for prevention of gang rumbles without loss of gang "face." Another element in acceptance of the Streetclub Worker was the status that the assignment of the worker to the gang brought with it. This was public and official recognition that this was a "tough" gang!

Within a short period of time nearly 90 gangs had workers attached to them, assigned on a 24-hour call basis, on duty whenever the gang was active.

One of the first efforts by the workers was to attempt to reduce gang wars. Many of these conflicts were simple face-saving responses to real or imagined insults. Often the cause of conflict could be identified by the admonition to "cherchez la femme," because rejected girl friends, spurned or thrown over by a gang member, would spread rumors with competing gangs designed to cause trouble. Sometimes a casual brush with members of other gangs at amusement parks, beaches, or similar places away from home neighborhoods set up rumbles. And invasion of gang turf was a steady source of trouble.

Streetclub Workers found that with workers attached to gangs most likely to rumble, those attached to gangs in conflict, having foreknowledge of trouble could work together to keep gangs apart. Then "conciliation" sessions could be set up where gangs seeking to save face without risking limb could be helped to ameliorate their differences.

Ordinarily conciliation sessions were held in a place agreed upon by the war ministers of the gangs involved. The war ministers and sometimes the gang leaders, the Streetclub Workers attached to the gangs, and a neutral individual who was looked up to by the gangs and who often was a well-known athlete, made up the personnel of the conciliation sessions. They sat around a table, aired the grievances of the gangs, and attempted to come up with solutions acceptable to the gangs.

Many times it was a matter of spelling out turf. In Brooklyn, areas of Prospect Park were the basis for constant turf conflict between gangs. Turf was also a big issue in congested neighborhoods where competing gangs sought recognition. Solutions were not always simple, but they were possible. Certain streets where shops, restaurants, theaters were clustered were basic to the life of the neighborhood youths. These kinds of streets were usually agreed upon as neutral territory where any gang member could go. Other streets and sections off this main thoroughfare would be agreed upon as the exclusive turf of one or another gang, with equal and acceptable sections of the neighborhood marked off as the turf of the other gang.

Very much in the manner of nations making peace treaties and negotiating national boundaries, the conciliation sessions laid out turf boundaries for gangs in order to offset rumbles. This technique, one example of a variety of conciliation settlements, was reasonably successful although it was frequently a precarious undertaking. On one occasion a disgruntled war minister pulled a zip gun, disrupting the session, and left workers, neutral members, and others crouched for self-preservation under table and behind chairs.

Police were not pleased with the sessions because they believed that turf agreements provided sanctions for illegal actions, since no citizen, under the law, could be deprived of the right to walk on any street of the city. They were also concerned that the sessions would cover over other illicit activity.

Eventually an agreement was made between the Youth Board and the Police Department which provided that the Streetclub Workers would report to the police any crimes of gangs or gang members about which they knew, and that no agreements would be made which were contrary to law. By this time rapport between gangs and their workers was strong enough for the gangs to accept the worker under these terms and the effect of their efforts with the gang were not appreciably diminished.

The success of the Streetclub Worker program was established, and the ability of these workers to redirect gang activity soon became an accepted fact. Yet the difficulty of providing even those services demonstrated as being effective where they were needed in a big city was well documented by an incident in New York City.

Continuing studies by the Youth Board had identified several gangs in the Washington Heights area which had turned from relatively innocuous activity into dangerous assaultive behavior. The Board requested 80,000 dollars from the city fathers to permit attaching Streetclub Workers to these gangs to prevent the dangerous actions the gangs were believed capable of at that time. The money was not appropriated and workers could not be assigned.

Shortly after their rejection of the request, a young boy, who was a cerebral palsy victim and the son of a New York City fireman, was brutally murdered by one of the gangs which had been identified as dangerous and for which a Streetclub Worker had been requested. The press of New York and throughout the country raised a great cry over this terrible, senseless crime. The crime which could probably have been avoided by an 80,000-dollar appropriation for which money "could not be found," spawned a trial which in all cost nearly half a million dollars for which there was no trouble in "finding" the money–to say nothing of the cost of maintaining seven boys for the duration of long prison terms . . . and to say even less about the lives blighted by prison and the life already wiped out by their crime.

As far back as 1847 Horace Mann in *Life and Works of Horace Mann* noted: "Governments do not see the future criminal in the neglected child, and therefore they sit calmly by, until aroused from their stupor by the spectacle of crime. They erect the prison and the gibbet to arrest or mitigate the evils which timely caution might have prevented." He further observed, "If any percentage of all children can be rescued from vice and crime and can be so educated and trained as to become valuable citizens but the state declines or refuses to do this work–then the state itself becomes the culprit."

These sentiments can be accepted by most individuals as being as pertinent today as they were then. However, the translation of these concepts into official action and the provision of adequate funds for preventative programs have rarely been achieved in American society. Nevertheless, the programs for Streetclub Workers, Detached Workers, Roving Leaders–or whatever else the services they represent might be called in different places–have had more popular appeal and therefore have been more successful in receiving funding than many other preventative approaches. Perhaps because the service is a direct one, the results of which are more readily observable, and because the predatory character of the gangs it serves is disruptive of the neighborhood in which it exists, there is greater inclination to provide the funds needed.

The apparent success of the New York City experience with Street Club Workers led to the establishment of the program in other cities of the state, notably in Rochester and Buffalo. However, in both of these cities the programs were not directly administered by the Youth Bureau of each city. Funds for the service were allocated jointly by the State Youth Commission and the Youth Bureau. But the Youth Bureaus contracted with local agencies to employ and direct the efforts of the Detached Workers.

In Rochester, the Detached Worker program was first begun by the YMCA with funds supplied by a private foundation. When this source dried up, the Youth Bureau contracted with the YMCA to provide the service, with 50 per cent of the cost being reimbursed to the city bureau by the State Youth Commission.

The Buffalo Youth Bureau contracted with several agencies in the city to furnish Detached Workers to work in the neighborhoods, and the State Youth Commission, as in Rochester, reimbursed the city 50 per cent of the cost of these programs. An additional element in the Buffalo program was the understanding among the public and private voluntary agencies, with facility resources in the areas served by the Detached Workers, that in the process of their work with the gangs they served, the Detached Workers could utilize any facility in the area as it was needed to carry out their function with their gangs. This was true regardless of which of the agencies employed the worker. Thus, if a Detached Worker was employed by the YMCA and found himself in the neighborhood of one of the settlement houses with his gang, and it suited his purposes to bring his gang into the settlement house, they would be welcome there. Preplanning of activities using all of the resources, and not only those of the agency employing the worker, broadened the opportunities of the Detached Worker to be effective with his gang.

Knowledge of the Streetclub Program of the New York City Youth Board, and of those upstate which were spread through reports, pamphlets and other publications of the local youth agencies, as well as of the State Youth Commission and the State Division of Youth (which succeeded the Youth Commission), created interest in this approach on the part of agencies in other cities throughout the country. Presentations by workers and other staff members at national and regional conferences stimulated further interest. Soon these programs were being visited by representatives of agencies and organizations planning to undertake similar services in their own communities, and eventually under what was coming to be called Roving Leader Programs, the concept of *outreach through street workers* was a widely implemented service.

Cities like Chicago and Washington, Oakland, Los Angeles and Columbus are typical of the many centers where this type of program has been duplicated. The techniques and methodology differ from place to place but not in any material way. The basic concept is the propellant which carries the services and provides a common element for all of them.

There have been some important evolutionary elements as this type of outreach program developed from the first detached worker in that small upstate city in New York State in 1936. In the initial efforts of outreach, the personnel employed as workers were college trained in the field of delinquency, sociology, social work, recreation, or a related field. In addition, the men employed had the cultural background of the distressed neighborhoods, having grown up understanding the taboos and mores of these areas.

Both of these qualifications were helpful. But as the need for greater numbers of workers developed, compromise had to be made, since there were relatively few college trained people coming out of slum neighborhoods in those days, and even fewer who wanted to pursue a career in the field of gang work. Therefore, recruitment for Street Club Workers, Roving Leaders, had to be limited to what was found to be a basic qualification–knowledge and experience in slum living and of the street society in depressed neighborhoods.

By this time it was recognized that the girl auxiliaries of the gangs were a critical element in the total program. If a worker was attached to a gang, he could not be effective if the girl auxiliary to this gang was unattended. Therefore the female Streetclub Worker evolved, with basically the same problems to deal with as those working with the boy gangs–and requiring the same background knowledge and experience.

Recognizing that the preparation of people for outreach work with gangs and other unaffiliated youth would have to be primarily an on-the-job training effort if the ranks were to be filled, the Department of Health, Education, and Welfare contracted with the National Recreation and Park Association in 1968 to develop a guide for the training of Roving Leaders.

The Association subcontracted this project to the University of Illinois, which appointed Dr. Joseph Bannon as the project director. The manual was completed and provided the first definitive guidelines for the experience requirements in this specialized work. The input and expertise of a number of individuals who had worked in this field for long periods of time provided authenticity to the training guide.

This project was further implemented by a series of regional workshops designed to test its effectiveness and to assure its value as a resource in training promising young people, indigenous to the neighborhoods most deeply afflicted by gang activity, to become successful Roving Leaders.

From the period of the thirties when the outreach techniques were first developed and demonstrated, and through the fifties and sixties when it grew into a strong and effective service, there has been considerable evolution in the gang and youthful criminal as well as in the approaches to work with them. The sixties spawned a new element of drug involvement, movement of gangs and criminals into the school buildings and classrooms, among other things. The Roving Leader has apparently adjusted well to these changing situations, and the dependence upon his services has grown stronger.

In Washington, D. C., for example, the popularity of the Roving Leaders propelled the director of its program into such prominence that he was appointed by the President of the United States to the first City Council established to serve the residents of the nation's capital. When the school system was experiencing particularly violent crime in the District's schools, including murder of students and faculty, the recommendation of the administration was not for more police, but for well over a million dollars which was appropriated by Congress, the District, and governmental agencies to add workers to the Roving Leader program.

While the Roving Leader programs are being so well received, there appears to be one hazard which should be avoided if their effectiveness is to be maintained and increased. Emphasis on the techniques and methodology of the worker frequently overlooks the primacy of program and activity design in supportive public and private agencies to meet the needs of the youth with whom the Roving Leader works.

Let us therefore emphasize, in closing, that the outreach concept was developed and evolved successfully, not as an end in itself, but as a means for relating unaffiliated young people to organized services which can give them support. Otherwise, the situation becomes one similar to that of bringing the horse to water but finding the trough dry.

CHAPTER REFERENCES AND SELECTED READINGS

Ackerson, Luton: *Children's Behavior Problems*. Chicago, Child Behavior Research Fund Monographs, 1931.

Bagley, W. C.: *Education, Crime, and Social Progress*. New York, Macmillan Co., 1931.

Beldon, E.: *Children's Bureau Publication 195*. Washington, United State Department of Labor, 1930.

Betman: *Report Number IV*. Washington, Wickersham Crime Commission, 1928.

Bigelow, Maurice A.: *Sex Education*. New York, Macmillan Co., 1916.

Burt, Ciril: *The Young Delinquent*. New York, D. Appleton and Co., 1925.

Butcher, W.; Hoey, J. M.; McGinnis, J. A.: *A Study of Problem Boys and Their Brothers*. Albany, Crime Commission of New York State, 1929.

Crime and the Community. Albany, Crime Commission of New York State, 1930.

From Truancy to Crime: A Study of 251 Adolescents. Albany, Crime Commission of New York State, 1928.

Gleim, Sophie C.: *The Visiting Teacher*. Washington, Department of Interior, Bureau of Education, 1921.

Glueck, S. and Glueck, E.: *One Thousand Juvenile Delinquents*. Cambridge, Harvard University Press, 1934.

———: *Five Hundred Criminal Careers*. New York, Alfred Knopf, 1930.

———: *Five Hundred Delinquent Women*. New York, Alfred Knopf, 1934.

Grigg, H. H., and Haynes, G. E.: *Junk Dealing and Juvenile Delinquency*. Chicago, Juvenile Protective Association, 1918.

Groves, Ernest: *Social Problems and Education*. New York, Longmans Green Company, 1925.

Healy and Bronner: *Judge Baker Foundation Case Studies*. Boston, Unpublished.

———: *Reconstructing Behavior in Youth*. New York, Alfred Knopf, Inc., 1929.

———: *Delinquents: Their Making and Unmaking*. New York, Macmillan Co., 1926.

Healy, William: *The Individual Delinquent*. Boston, Little, Brown, and Co., 1915.

Irwin, Elizabeth: *Truancy*. New York, Public Education Association of the City of New York, 1915.

The Juvenile Delinquent. Chicago, Illinois Crime Commission, 1929.

Lutzin, Sidney: *Casework in Recreation, The Community Courier* (Community Programmes Branch, Province of Ontario, 1951).

MacIver, Robert: *Juvenile Delinquency, The Nation's Children: Problems and Prospects,* Volume 3, ed. by Eli Ginzberg, 1960 White House Conference on Children and Youth. New York, Columbia University Press, 1960.

Mann, Horace: *Life and Works of Horace Mann.* Boston, Lee and Shepard Publishers, 1891.

Mower, Harriet R.: *Personality Adjustment and Domestic Discord.* Chicago, American Book Co., 1935.

Miller, Randolph A.: *Psychiatric Child Guidance Service in the Public School System.* Tufts College Masters Thesis, 1934.

Nudd, Howard: *The Problem Child in School.* New York, Joint Committee on Methods of Preventing Delinquency, 1925.

Oppenheimer, J. J.: *The Visiting Teacher Movement.* Joint Committee on Methods of Preventing Delinquency, 1925.

Parsons, P. H.: *Crime and the Criminal.* New York, Alfred Knopf Inc., 1926.

Reckless, W. C. and Smith, M.: *Juvenile Delinquency.* New York, McGraw-Hill Book Co., 1932.

Robinson, E. (Editor): *Vocational Education.* New York, H. W. Wilson Co., 1921.

Scudder, Kenyon J.: *Who Is Delinquent?* Los Angeles, Los Angeles Rotary Club, 1934.

Shaw, Clifford R., and Associates: *Delinquency Areas.* Chicago, University of Chicago Press, 1931.

Shaw, Clifford R.: *The Jack Roller.* Chicago, University of Chicago Press, 1930.

———: *The Natural History of a Delinquent Career.* Chicago, University of Chicago Press, 1931.

Shaw, Clifford R., and McKary, H. D.: *Social Factors in Juvenile Delinquency.* Washington, National Commission on Law Enforcement, Report on the Causes of Crime, Vol. II, No. 13.

A Study of Environmental Factors in Juvenile Delinquency. Albany, Crime Commission of New York State, 1928.

A Study of 201 Truants in the New York City Schools. Albany, Crime Commission of New York State, 1927.

Teenage Gangs. New York City Youth Board, 1957.

Thomas, W. I.: *The Unadjusted Girl.* New York, Alfred Knopf, Inc., 1923.

Thomas and Thomas: *The Child in America.* New York, Alfred Knopf, Inc., 1928.

Thrasher, Frederic: The Boys' Club and Juvenile Delinquency, *American Journal of Sociology,* XLII (July 1936), pp. 66-80.

———: *The Gang.* Chicago, University of Chicago Press, 1927.

Three Problem Children. New York, Community Fund, Division of Publications, 1928.

Thurston, *Delinquency and Spare Time.* Cleveland, The Cleveland Recreational Survey, 1918.

Treadway, W. L.: *Psychiatric Studies of Delinquency.* Washington, United States Public Health Reprint No. 598, 1920.

Troth, Dennis C. (Editor): *Selected Readings in Character Education.* Boston, Beacon Press, Inc., 1935.

Wickman, E. W.: *Children's Behavior and Teachers' Attitudes.* Boston, The Commonwealth Fund Publications, 1929.

CHAPTER II

COMMUNITY OUTREACH IN RECREATION

"We're Coming After You"

JOSEPH J. BANNON

Introduction

MOST SOCIAL WORK has not directly attacked social problems. In many instances, professionals have been solely concerned with handling individual manifestations of larger problems. Social workers have attempted to help "maladjusted" people *adapt* themselves to society, rather than trying *to change* those aspects of society which hurt people.[1] This is the crux of the revolt in social services today. The task of adapting society to individuals is not meant to be apocalyptic, but is intended to expand the concept of social work from its narrow preoccupation of the past few decades:

> Social workers, in particular, have made Freud their God when they should have been worshipping at the shrine of the sociologist Emile Durkheim. For the problems of the slum stem less from individual neuroses (though certainly there are plenty of those) than from an objective lack of opportunity, from a social system that denies that individual dignity and status.[2]

This chapter presents the outreach concept in its broadest sense, not confining the discussion to recreation alone. Many outreach recreation workers are not solely employed by departments of parks and recreation in the inner city, but by other public and private agencies, from YMCA's to police community relations departments. Thus, we try to avoid a too limited focus on the experience of the recreation profession. In addition, this chapter touches on several topics which are covered in more depth in subsequent chapters,

---

[1] This same controversy has developed in psychotherapy: Jerome Angel: *The Radical Therapist* (New York, Ballantine Books, 1971), who argues that therapy means change not adjustment. A more encompassing argument is given in R. D. Laing's *The Politics of Experience* (New York, Ballantine Books, 1967), which attacks our most prevalent assumptions about normality and maladjustment. Both of these books are relevant to the issue of social welfare "therapy."

[2] Charles E. Silberman: *Crisis in Black and White* (New York, Vintage Books, Random House, 1964), p. 312. See also, Richard A. Cloward and Lloyd Ohlin: *Delinquency and Opportunity: A Theory of Delinquent Gangs* (New York, The Free Press, 1960), which was the main theoretical impetus for the now-defunct Mobilization for Youth, Inc.; and Oscar Lewis, *La Vida* (New York, Random House, 1965) for a discussion of "The Culture of Poverty."

especially on various aspects of working with inner-city youth. Therefore, what is stated here is not intended to be inclusive, nor to reflect the opinion of the other contributors. Rather, it is an overview of community action programs as I perceive them.

Outreach work in recreation and parks attempts to learn from the multitude of previous attempts by other social services to help the urban poor. Our preoccupation throughout most of this book is with urban youth, especially those of the inner city, for this is the one area of social work which has caused the greatest controversy and difficulty. This is not to ignore the problems of working with suburban and rural youth, since many problems previously confined to America's ghettos have sprung up in other locations as well.[3]

Perhaps the strongest quality of recreation today is its relative lack of stigma among ghetto youth. This lack of stigma is not only achieved because of the more potent criticisms directed toward welfare and other social service agencies, but by the comparatively low profile of recreation services in the inner city to begin with. Low profile here does not mean low in number but rather in impact. As noted in an extensive survey of city recreation needs and services in 1954, it was shown that the *availability* of recreation facilities in a community did not necessarily determine the quality and extent of their use.[4]

Parks dominated by swings and slides or gyms stressing basketball or swimming are clearly not enough. A belief in the positive effects of "wholesome" recreation on delinquency has been seriously challenged for over thirty years, and yet most of us hopefully cling to its fading validity. For this reason, recreation officials must expand their notion of service beyond that of fun and games as a sure-fire antidote to crime:

> A score of years ago, and to some extent even today, it was felt that the provision of wholesome recreation activities would solve much of the problem of juvenile delinquency. Since the studies of Thraser, Shanas and Dunning, Reed, and the excellent review by Witmer and Tufts, however, the impact of recreation upon delinquency must be questioned. For most communities, the provision of wholesome leisure-time pursuits is a viable role for social agencies. But, given the pathology [of the inner city] . . . , questions can be raised concerning this restrictive role of these social agencies. . . .[5]

---

[3] For an early discussion of problems with suburban youth, see Harrison Salisbury: *The Shook-Up Generation* (New York, Harper & Row, 1958).

[4] Helen Witmer and Edith Tufts: *The Effectiveness of Delinquency Prevention Programs*, U. S. Department of Health, Education, and Welfare, Children's Bureau, Publication No. 350 (Washington, D. C., Government Printing Office, 1954).

[5] *Youth in the Ghetto: A Study of the Consequences of Powerlessness and a Blueprint for Change* (New York, Harlem Youth Opportunities Unlimited, Inc., HARYOU, 1964), p. 298. References in this quote are to Frederic M. Thrasher: The Boys' Club and Juvenile Delinquency, *American Journal of Sociology*, Vol. 42 (1936), 66-80; Ethel Shanas and Cath-

Outreach: A New Strategy

Not surprisingly, most of the above research is largely ignored as recreation and social workers perpetuate traditional platitudes about the positive effect of recreation on inner-city youth. Recreation has a potential to affect the wellbeing and life experiences of most people to some extent, of that there is not much question. However, unless recreation as presently conceived is expanded and made sensitive to the crucial issues of the inner city, it will continue to have limited impact. Its lack of stigma as a social service will diminish if we simply appropriate radical platitudes in lieu of substantive changes in perspective and policy. If changes are *not* forthcoming, we will surely earn the response youth have given to most of the other social services: "You can't trust the emissaries of that larger society. Because they're liars. They may want to 'help' you but they sure as hell don't want you to help yourself through getting some of what they have–power."[6]

The increase in the importance of city recreation has brought with it a host of organizational and social problems. Youth are more leisure oriented, either because of increased free time from work, or more likely, because of involuntary leisure due to unemployment and lack of real opportunity in the community. Thus, recreation services for inner-city youth must be designed with a concept which exceeds the traditional use of parks, centers, or playgrounds. As recreation personnel, we must expand our image and abilities as leaders of broad and complex leisure-oriented programs, programs which reach out into the community and aggressively and competently engage the interest and involvement of youth and their families. Passively waiting for young people to come to our centers and parks is unrealistic, for we can never adequately perceive our potential with such passivity. We must be aware of the crises and pressures urban residents endure and how these relate to an expanded concept of recreation.

Initially, two significant changes come to mind which have broadened the objectives of recreation in response to social and economic forces. First,

---

erine Dunning: *Recreation and Delinquency* (Chicago, Chicago Recreation Commission, 1942); and Ellery Reed: How effective are group work agencies in preventing delinquency? *Social Service Review,* Vol. 22 (1948), 340-48. The reference to Witmer and Tufts is noted in the preceding footnote. For further discussion of this issue, see also Milton L. Barron: *The Juvenile in Delinquent Society* (New York, Knopf, 1954); Helen L. Witmer (ed.): Prevention of Juvenile Delinquency, in *The Annals of the American Academy of Political and Social Science,* 1959; and more recently, Bruce G. Ogilvie and Thomas A. Tutko, in the October 1971 issue of *Psychology Today* (reporting on research with 15,000 athletes who conclude there was little to support the traditional idea that sports build character): If you want to build character, try something else, pp. 60-63.

[6] Nat Hentoff: Whose Existential Crisis? In Eli E. Cohen and Louise Kapp (eds.): *Manpower Policies for Youth* (New York, Columbia University Press, 1966), p. 22.

and perhaps more important, it is now generally accepted that providing recreation for the nation's urban dwellers is basically a local responsibility. That is, recreation must be considered as essential a municipal service as sanitation, fire, and police protection. Second, cities have found that simply providing services is not enough; it is imperative to have programs which provide youth with an opportunity to exercise *leadership* and *control* over their own lives. Offering games and physical outlets, as noted already, is not a solution for preventing youth from engaging in so-called "antisocial" or "maladjustive" acts.

Of course, when we equate recreation with local municipal services, we immediately cringe at the distressing state of these services in most inner cities. It is not intended that recreation as a local service resemble the crisis in delivering many municipal services in the inner city. Rather, it is hoped that recreation would be timely, and of quality and relevance to the residents of such communities.

Through outreach service, even with recreation used in its narrowest sense, opportunities are provided for physical development and formation of neighborhood-based athletic groups–for example, the sponsoring of athletic teams by organizations outside the recreation department. Activities are organized and promoted, with supervision and leadership offered and developed in the youth. In addition, city officials in coordination with other services must devise new, imaginative and creative approaches to health, employment, training, education, and recreation which will aid in the maximum use of existing resources with community participation.

Trying to solve the problems of recreation, without perceiving the relationship of it to the larger social structure, only produces repeated failure in attempts to relate to youth. What benefit is physical fitness if youth have no realistic outlet for such development? Must all inner-city youth strive to excel in sports simply because that has been an "approved" and highly successful channel for their upward mobility? How many want to in the first place? We must avoid romanticizing about the athletes who have overcome the difficulty of the inner city, but rather seek to furnish services and outlets which will broaden the base and concept of recreation services to encourage youth to express themselves and succeed in a *variety* of ways.

We are primarily interested in offering recreation services to inner-city youth (and adults) which will enhance and expand their lives and opportunities. We do not set larger social objectives for ourselves, because frankly these are outside the purview and power of recreation. It would be somewhat herculean for the recreation profession to attempt to achieve what other more encompassing social services have been unable to do. What we do want, however, is to recognize the errors of the past and avoid the simple belief that any one effort in the inner city will make a difference, especially if this effort is paternalistic or short-sighted to start with. What we also want to avoid is a collection of fine but meaningless sentiments about services we can never hope to offer and power we never intend to relinquish.

However, the inability to achieve larger social objectives in no way diminishes the necessity to perceive recreation in relation to these. We want to eliminate a piecemeal approach to recreation services as much as possible, with an awareness of the social problems and concerns of the powerless in our nation's cities. Without such a framework, we would be fruitlessly offering services in a milieu calculated to diminish their value.

Stated simply, outreach work occurs when a social service agency reaches out and assists through personal contacts those previously excluded from, unaware of, or unreceptive to its services. Detached work is a partial synonym for outreach work, but outreach encompasses an added dimension: that of advocacy. Advocacy is seen as essential to outreach work, rather than the more benign forms of community help, because it appears as an inevitable development for the social services. Advocacy is both fashionable and relevant, and that is both its strength and weakness. Outreach work has enormous potential; coupled with advocacy it can be relevant or explosive. Yet it must be faced and understood before recreation personnel make judgments about its efficacy or risk.

Recreation and other professional social services have decided to use the outreach concept to reach the youth of inner cities and other marginal groups. To do so effectively, and to avoid the outreach concept going the way of so many other "solutions" to urban ills, we must be critically aware of its shortcomings and the overall environment in which it is used.

Some Trends

At first it might seem as if outreach as a social service strategy is contradictory: on the one hand, it desires to get away from the narrow casework approach of social welfare (with its attention on individual pathology) and, on the other hand, it encourages face-to-face individual encounters with urban dwellers. However, this concept stresses both personal *attention* to individual needs and *advocacy* toward eliminating institutional and social maladies which cause these needs. What developed in social work and sociology beginning with the Depression was, in essence, a retreat from a reformist philosophy of social work to an adaptive one.

More recently, we have witnessed a radical switch in the adaptive attitude of many social work professionals and aides, followed by the other human services. This change in its broadest sense is known as *advocacy for the poor,* which originated in law, and which puts the social worker in the position of agitator or representative for the poor with the social agency or agencies–including city hall–who are to perform a distinct service. Advocacy for the poor is growing in most social services, but has been most active in the legal profession.[7]

The restrictive regulations and practices of social agencies toward the poor are being tested in courts, and direct legal services are offered by the Office of Economic Opportunity's Legal Services in many inner-city areas, though these have been sorely threatened by the Nixon Administration.[8] These outreach professionals and paraprofessionals who work with inner-city residents on their problems are hired by and responsive to public and private agencies which many times represent other motives and interests.[9] However, this is not to deny that the poor have benefited from such advocacy and from attempts to integrate them in local and national politics through participation in community development.

The advocacy role was preceded by what is called the *enabler* or *broker* role in social welfare. The enabler role is the more traditional function of social services and is based generally on two assumptions: first, that a community can describe its own social needs and, second, that these needs can then be met by the enabler representative of the welfare agency; needless to say, the second assumption has proved invalid.[10] The first assumption has grown in importance and validity.

Criticism of the enabler role, with its frustrating insistence of focus on the individual, is prodigiously documented; it is not the purpose of this discussion to overly reiterate this criticism, but to show why the role has not worked.[11] In fact, most social welfare or community development discussions of the past five to ten years invariably cover this controversy with great success and fervor, though not necessarily with certitude. There is little need for us to throw our coal on the fire, except in a supportive sense. We will try to avoid what Nat Hentoff calls "the dulling litany of what needs to be done," though some repetition is necessary for our work in recreation and parks.

We want to avoid repeating the obvious, the known, and offer some sug-

---

[7] See, for instance, Bruce Wasserstein and Mark J. Green, eds.: *With Justice for Some: An Indictment of the Law by Young Advocates* (Boston, Beacon Press, 1971).

[8] The New Legal Services, *The New Republic,* May 26, 1973, pp. 10-11.

[9] Frances Fox Piven: Whom does the advocate planner serve? *Social Policy* (May-June 1970), pp. 32-37.

[10] *See* Mobilization for Youth, Inc.: *Notes from the Ghetto: Papers from the MFY Experience* (New York, MFY, July 1966), for definitions of the enabler and broker roles.

[11] A good discussion of the prelude to current developments in social work is discussed in Charles E. Silberman: *Crisis in Black and White,* esp. Ch. x: The revolt against "welfare capitalism," pp. 308-358. Also, Henry Miller: Social work in the Black Ghetto: The new colonialism. In *Social Work,* Vol. 14 (July 1969), pp. 65-76. See also, Kenneth B. Clark and Jeanette Hopkins: *A Relevant War Against Poverty. A Study of Community Action Programs and Observable Social Change* (New York, Harper and Row, 1969).

gestions on how parks and recreation can grasp the elements of the problem, learn from the mistakes of the other social services, and seek realistic, workable solutions and remedies in their area. Anything less would be a waste of everyone's time.

A large part of the crisis in welfare and the revolt of many social workers and welfare recipients are tied to the dysfunction of social workers as enablers. In many instances, they are well-intentioned enablers, but this is not enough. We should add that the crisis in welfare against the impotency of the enabler function is far from over—in some cities it is incipient, and in others it has coalesced into welfare rights and welfare-workers-for-change organizations.

That these organizations are clear about the scope of their struggle (and it is broad) is evidenced by an announcement by Rep. Shirley Chisholm (N. Y.) at the fifth annual National Welfare Rights Organization Conference in 1971 on her candidacy for the U. S. presidency.[12] It is not by chance the announcement occurred there, for Ms. Chisholm is Black and was well aware of the potential impact of such groups. Indeed, in such instances, concern with social service has led directly to concern with power structures and politics.

A growing number of social scientists, social and community workers, as well as welfare recipients, have become increasingly disenchanted with the entire welfare and social services system. These are not reactionaries out to reduce or increase welfare rolls, or encourage enforced labor of those on welfare, but thoughtful and angry people—observers of and participants in the prevalent malaise inherent in our "social" philosophy as manifested through the social services.

Welfare colonialism is found where "wave after wave of welfare workers are sent into the jungle of the poor," ignoring the loud and clear advice of those whom they wish to serve and those who have preceded them in their highly motivated tasks. "The middle-class social scientist . . . however well-intentioned, is not radical enough to deal existentially with the problems. . . ."[13] The criticism is that welfare as presently constituted perpetuates rather than eliminates the social problems it was designed to alleviate. "Welfare assistance in its present form tends to encourage dependence, withdrawal, diffused hostility, indifference, ennui."[14]

Another serious manifestation of the dysfunction of most social services is a myopic concentration on *symptoms,* rather than on *causes* of problems, which merely leads to substituting a new set of symptoms for the old. Per-

---

[12] Howard Romaine: Why a Black man [sic] should run, *The Nation,* Sept. 27, 1971, pp. 264-268.
[13] Nat Hentoff: *Op. cit.,* p. 26.
[14] S. M. Miller as quoted in Silberman: *Crisis in Black and White,* p. 309.

haps the best known, most notorious example of this is the elimination of gang wars and the subsequent proliferation of drug traffic in the inner city:

> Herculean efforts by the [New York] city's Youth Board, the police, the courts, and a host of voluntary agencies, succeeded in taming the fighting gangs that had erupted in the early 1950's. But if ever there was a Phyrric victory, this was it; 'bopping' has now been replaced by alcoholism and drug addiction, which are much harder to combat, and far more crippling in their long-run effects. And so it goes.[15]

This is an especially crucial insight for recreation center personnel, who often encounter the dual symptoms of gangs and drugs in their facilities and programs, and seek somewhat desperately to eliminate them while discarding the root causes of these "symptoms." One story is told of a recreation center director who was pleased to have youth groups use his pool regularly for "wholesome recreation." It came out later that these dips served as conferences for gang decisions on their drug trade:

> There is a large 'youth center' in Harlem, for example, where administrators drew great satisfaction from the fact that the center's professional staff provides counseling to some five thousand youngsters a year. But the staff did not know that the center also served as a major contact point for the sale of narcotics, or that the heads of the local narcotic ring met every Sunday morning in the center's swimming pool. . . .[16]

The concentration on casework and individual problems has led to an emphasis on serving "multi-problem families," those with the highest profile in urban ghettos, and ignoring those who may be struggling to avoid these problems, who may be the neighbors of these same people. This has caused an enormous focus of resources on the grossest signs of ghetto pathology and a miniscule amount on prevention and analysis of social disorders.[17] Social work and most human services thrive on detection and treatment of disorder and negligence, with little or no direct attention given to prevention and elimination of these disorders.

We concentrate on the welfare system's problems and failings because they in many ways are indicative of the frustrations and issues that are encountered in recreation and parks, or that certainly will be. Most human services in this country reflect the failing philosophy of social work and foster its dubious perceptions under a variety of guises. Only by beginning to

---

[15] Silberman: *Op. cit.*, p. 311.
[16] *Ibid.*
[17] We should be sensitive to such terms as *pathology*. Such terms for defining ghetto problems can lead to a shift of the burden for these difficulties to those who are experiencing them and an avoidance of their causes. Pathology flourishes in the ghetto, it does not originate there. The problems of the inner city invariably stem from the outer city.

recognize the entrenched "enabler" philosophy in recreation can we hope to gain wisdom from the welfare fiasco and circumvent its many "great-white-father" entanglements. Otherwise–needless to say–we are doomed to walk its path, if we have not already begun. Thus, the dull litany offered here is one of historical foresight, if that makes sense–combining the hard lessons of social welfare with a prognosis of what can and should be done within the sphere of our profession.

The break from a focus on symptoms emerged with the development of a "broker" role, with an emphasis on collective rather than individual action. In this role, the community worker brings collective action to his work through collective brokerage activity; that is, "administrative and policy changes are undertaken to affect whole classes of persons rather than a single individual such as in rent strikes, tenants' unions, class suits, etc."[18] This role was first instituted in the Mobilization for Youth Project.

Symptoms recognized and treated separately from broader social and political analyses have proved ineffective, even in the broker's role. Collective action to be successful must also be *encompassing* action–a comprehension of and pressure on the forces which debilitate and frustrate most attempts at forceful social remedies. It has been the experience of community workers that the broker role is too often insufficiently impowered to affect substantive change. Such a recognition has led to the push for advocacy as a key role in the social services.

Advocacy

Advocacy is chosen because too often the institutions which urban residents must deal with are not neutral, but paternalistic or even hostile toward those community groups who most need their help. Often they seek to distort information about their procedures, rules, and office hours in an attempt to subvert or dilute the efforts of citizens to obtain access to resources intended exclusively for them. For the community outreach worker to offer such resources to urban residents, he or she must facilitate *productive* interaction between these residents and the various agencies and institutions, and this facilitation is primarily achieved by the outreach worker as an advocate for the poor, eliciting correct information, giving referrals that lead somewhere, defending a "client's" position, and challenging the policies of the institution when at fault.[19]

Advocacy can provide a means for legitimizing the interests and values

---

[18] Mobilization for Youth, Inc., *ibid.*, p. 24.
[19] The term "client" is most appropriate in the context of advocacy as it develops out of law; however, it is offensive to many welfare and social service recipients because it puts community workers in a paternalistic or superior position to those they serve.

of community residents by providing decentralization and pluralism in decision-making. Advocacy can provide a unique way for new interest groups to enter and influence public policy-making and planning.[20] While in an advocate's position (which any effective outreach worker is from time to time), the worker shifts from that of enabler and broker, to partner in a social conflict, with his professional expertise available to the people he seeks to help. This position, no matter how infrequently the outreach worker holds it, nor how it is glossed or rationalized, raises a clear dilemma for the worker, his agency, and the community residents.

The dilemma for an outreach worker and for the agency he represents is: "Should we try to change people, or should we try to change conditions?"[21] Of course, most of us respond "both," taking the easy way out by avoiding the true dilemma which exists, especially for the community outreach worker. Ira Goldberg calls those who take this position "cautious crusaders," who do not wish to offend either viewpoint and hope this paradox will resolve itself while they voice sentiments of social justice. Yet as an advocate, the outreach worker must drop the impotency of the enabler and the liaison function of the broker roles and enter into conflict. His conflict may often be with other enabler or broker community workers whose aims for the recipient remain somewhat narrower or different. However, it is not uncommon to find social service workers in dispute; that is not the main problem. The issue is this: Can community workers, regardless of ideology or political views, be effective in outreach work and still serve the agency which employs them?[22]

---

[20] Earl M. Blecher: *Advocacy Planning for Urban Development* (New York, Praeger, 1971); Office of Economic Opportunity: *Participation of the Poor in the Community Decision-Making Process* (Washington, D. C., Government Publication Office, 1969); Milton Kotler: *Neighborhood Government: The Local Foundations of Political Life* (Indianapolis, Bobbs-Merrill, 1969); and Alan A. Altshuler: *Community Control: The Black Demand for Participation in Large American Cities* (New York, Pegasus, 1970).

[21] Ira Goldberg: *Build Me A Mountain: Youth, Poverty, and the Creation of New Settings* (Cambridge, MIT Press, 1971), p. 116. The dedication of this book is also timely: "To those (particularly in the university community) who have yet to learn that the questioning of traditions, far from symbolizing a rejection of the past, constitutes its very affirmation in the service of the future." We accept this criticism, but add that it often occurs with practitioners as well, who view all inscrutable behavior as antisocial.

[22] A comprehensive discussion of this dilemma is given in Peter Marris and Martin Rein: *Dilemmas of Social Reform: Poverty and Community Action in the United States* (New York, Atherton Press, 1967). This book is concerned with discussing strategies of reform within the confines of community action and the conflicts which often undermine or detract from such action. See also Alvin N. Taylor: The Oakland Recreation Department: A study in institutional transition. Unpublished Master's thesis, University of California, 1962; Charles E. Lindblom: *The Intelligence of Democracy: Decision Making Through Mutual Adjustment* (New York, The Free Press, 1965); William L. Taylor: Strategies for change: Together and autonomous, in *Hanging Together* (New York, Simon and Schuster, 1971); and Kenneth P. Clark: *Dark Ghetto-Dilemmas of Social Power* (New York, Harper & Row, 1965), a discussion of Clark's HARYOU experience.

Outside the courtroom, attorneys for defendants and plaintiffs (as well as judges) often mingle in an atmosphere of friendliness and goodwill, so why can't outreach workers and agencies behave in a comparable manner? Advocacy does not require a worker to become an adversary of an agency, except when the agency is reluctant to change or resists questions about its premises or traditions, and *forces* the worker to become its adversary–employee.

Yet there is hostility and ambivalence by all involved in advocacy because something more is at stake than agency policies or viewpoints, and the name of the game is and remains *power*. Any time we decide to use an outreach worker in a community, a decision must be how much power we will yield through this worker to the community. It's as simple as that, at least theoretically: "This is the major issue confronting those involved in the War on Poverty, and until this issue is dealt with directly and honestly, we will be no more successful than our now-maligned predecessors in effecting any meaningful change either in the conditions of poverty or in the poor themselves."[23]

The thesis advanced by Goldberg and others to solve this dilemma is that we will not produce any real or lasting results in community work until the focus of our work shifts from the objects of change (the poor) to the agents of change, and the settings in which change can occur. An excellent case study on agents and objects of change, with clear implications for recreation and other social services, was the experience of the Mobilization for Youth Project in New York City with its revolutionary conception of Maximum Feasible Participation by the poor.

Mobilization for Youth

The concept of Maximum Feasible Participation (MFP) had its initial roots in community development programs of underdeveloped countries. It was transferred into domestic community work in the mid-sixties as the connection between efforts to reduce paternalism abroad and "welfare colonialism" at home became more related. These projects were promoted and largely financed by the Ford Foundation and the Juvenile Delinquency and Youth Offenses Control Act of 1961, absorbed into the War on Poverty which followed, and then expanded as a national strategy later known as Community Action Projects (CAP's) through the 1964 Economic Opportunity Act, The Demonstration Cities and Metropolitan Development Act, and The Neighborhood Service Pilot Program.[24]

There was a growing dissatisfaction with existing welfare policies and pat-

---

[23] Goldberg: *Op. cit.,* p. 117.
[24] Stanley J. Brody: Maximum participation of the poor—Another Holy Grail? *Social Work,* Vol. 15, no. 1 (Jan. 1970), pp. 68-75.

terns of paternalism which debilitated rather than rehabilitated recipients. This dissatisfaction resulted in the conception of federal CAP's which burgeoned in most inner-city areas. These are demonstration projects emphasizing the need for neighborhood involvement intended as a substitute or supplement to the present welfare system. Mobilization for Youth was the first domestic prototype of these projects.

The Mobilization for Youth Program, launched in 1962, was one of the earliest demonstration projects using a form of maximum feasible participation and was designed to help inner-city residents deal with poverty, deprivation, and discrimination.[25] This nontraditional approach to community problems focused on the *social conditions* which shaped the "deviant" behavior of inner-city residents, rather than solely on their behavior. An underlying assumption of the MFY project, and of advocacy in general, was that existing community resources were either unavailable or noncongenial to poor people. In fact, most private social agencies did not (and still do not) serve poor people in proportion to their community representation:[26]

> One of the obvious anomalies in the organization of social services in American cities is that the many organizations possessing resources for the supportive solution of personal problems have very limited access to the population(s) with the problems, while organizations having access to these populations have very limited resources for the solution of the problems encountered.[27]

The public agencies, of course, attempt to serve these people, but not very successfully, usually because of restrictive legislation and rules, limited budgets, and a paucity of properly trained personnel. The public agencies have often been forced by these circumstances to tread their way carefully through a "political jungle along the paths of caution and conservatism." Thus, those who do seek to serve the poor are most times unable to serve them well.[28]

Mobilization's service programs were undertaken to train lower-income residents in "clientsmanship," to ensure their awareness of their rights and

---

[25] For a discussion of Mobilization's theoretical perspectives, see *A Proposal for the Prevention and Control of Juvenile Delinquency by Expanding Opportunities* (New York, MFY, 1961), Chapter 2; and Richard A. Cloward and Lloyd E. Ohlin: *Op. cit.,* the theoretical basis for much of MFY's work.

[26] Richard A. Cloward and Irwin Epstein: Private social welfare's disengagement from the poor: The case of family adjustment agencies. In Arthur Pearl and Frank Riessman: *Poverty and Lower Income Culture: Ten Views* (Washington, D. C., National Institutes of Health, 1971).

[27] David J. Bordua: Comments on Police-Community Relations in *Law Enforcement Science and Technology II,* S. I. Cohn, ed. (Chicago, Illinois Institute of Technology Research Center, 1968), p. 124.

[28] Mobilization for Youth, Inc.: *Action on the Lower East Side: Progress Report and Proposal* (MFY, 1964), p. 2.

privileges, to enable them to articulate to agencies and to demand the proper service and treatment. This objective encompassed not only the services given to individuals, but helped to redress the imbalance of power between client and agency, so the client could influence agency policies and practices to some extent.

There were four objectives of change which Mobilization concentrated on: institutional change, program change, new social service techniques, and community impact. A major goal of *institutional change* was to increase the responsiveness of conventional persons and institutions to the needs and culture of lower-income people. Of course, the success of any attempt to influence institutional change depends, in general, on the substances of the proposed change, the resources available to the "change-agent," and the strategies used.[29]

The development of *program changes* and innovations in content, structure, or auspices was another aspect of the MFY project. For example, Mobilization was encouraged by New York City officials to contract a part of its grant to the N. Y. Health Department to offer dental services for youths. No such program had existed in New York prior to this. Although this program was not pertinent to Mobilization's objectives, nor especially relevant to the project's goal to advance social knowledge, it was promoted as a concrete example of a health need of lower-income teenagers. In this case, the program represented a demonstration of what can or ought to be done, rather than simply offering theoretical suggestions emanating from remote social scientists.

Improvement of the social service *techniques* of educators, social workers, vocational counselors, and other human relations personnel was the third aspect of Mobilization's task. The professions, largely middle class in orientation, had developed methodologies which failed to acknowledge and use the differing style and needs of lower-income cultures. The demonstration of new methods, particularly geared to lower-income people, as well as experimentation with generic practices, was seen as especially important.

Finally, the expansion of *community impact* and opportunity involved many resources ordinarily unavailable or insufficiently available in inner-city communities. Since the community itself was the target of the MFY effort, services had to reach and affect the community residents primarily through outreach work. Community demand, however, far exceeded even Mobilization's considerable resources. Many agencies responded by seeking the easiest way to serve. In Mobilization's case, however, policy established that priority be given to persons in the lowest twenty per cent economic bracket.

The central preoccupation of the community action programs, as evi-

---

[29] Martin Rein and S. W. Miller: The demonstration as a strategy of change. Paper presented at the Columbia University Mobilization for Youth Training Institutes, April 1964.

denced in the Economic Opportunity Act of 1964, was the planning and development of relevant social activities and services, an effective and efficient allocation of resources, as well as maximum feasible participation of area residents to be served. While the Economic Opportunity Act does not use Mobilization For Youth language, it does reflect the atmosphere created by this project:

> The first OEO Community Action Guide, in its suggested procedures and program measures, clearly shows the influence of MFY. Pre-school education [largely suggested by HARYOU], legal aid for the poor (not just to defend them, but to serve them as plaintiffs) . . . , a theory of community organization, an emphasis on research and evaluation, and most especially the insistence on the involvement of the poor, all these were the legacy of Mobilization for Youth. It was no small achievement.[30]

The mandatory requirement of enlisting the active participation of indigenous people in forming decisions affecting their own welfare distinguishes CAP from earlier attempts to involve local groups. CAP can be viewed as a contemporary blend of social *action* and community *development*.

Four basic rationales were given to defend the need for resident participation: (1) an attempt to gain a realistic perspective on the effectiveness of social services; (2) the creation of a power base for the poor so they could direct their own lives; (3) the administrative and psychological potential of resident involvement; and (4) the general value of participatory democracy.[31]

Under CAP, poverty is defined as the inability of certain groups to obtain and exercise the power which is vital to effective political participation. This powerlessness results in the disenfranchisement of the poor and perpetuates the poverty cycle. Intervention should, therefore, concentrate on aiding the poor to obtain power, or pressuring institutions to become more responsive to their needs; it is usually the latter concern that involves the outreach community worker.

Community control and participation usually take the form of neighbor-

---

[30] Daniel P. Moynihan: *Maximum Feasible Misunderstanding: Community Action in the War on Poverty* (New York, The Free Press, 1969), p. 123.

[31] James J. Vanecko: Community mobilization and institutional change: The influence of the Community Action Program in large cities, *Social Science Quarterly,* 50, 3 (Dec. 1969), pp. 609-630; James Vanecko: *National Evaluation of Urban Community Action Programs* (Chicago, National Opinion Research Corporation, June 1969); James Vanecko: *Community Organization Efforts, Political and Institutional Change, and the Diffusion of Change Produced by Community Action Programs* (Chicago, National Opinion Research Corporation, April 1970); and all by Harold H. Weissman, as follows: *Individual and Group Services in the Mobilization for Youth Experience; Employment and Educational Services in the Mobilization for Youth Experience;* and *Justice and the Law in the Mobilization for Youth Experience* (New York, Association Press, 1969).

hood corporations. These are private, non-profit organizations governed by resident-selected boards who control their own funds. The first generation of community corporations appeared in 1966 as part of the CAP's. The advisory committee has long been used by government agencies, but not until CAP was it broadened to include the poor, as well as middle- and upper-class city leaders and community workers.

In CAP, the usual community action agency is governed by a tripartite board of public officials, representatives of the poor, and representatives of the private agencies.[32] The central board contracts with community corporations to run specific programs. In the Model Cities Program, for instance, the resident-controlled body participated as an equal partner with another body controlled by city hall, each group having an equal share of the funds. As we know, the Model Cities Program, enacted in 1966, tried to avoid the controversial citizen control precedents established by CAP with a clear statement that the program must be run locally by a public agency designated by a city or county governing body. However, ghetto residents would not be ignored and the Model Cities program became the focus of an intense struggle for community control.

Neighborhood control has been a success in terms of resident reception. In efficiency and program effectiveness, community corporations seem to be doing no worse than similar decentralized operations lacking resident control. Leadership, unity, and technical expertise are the major factors in achieving success. Direct selection by ballot and selection of representatives in neighborhood organizations are used to obtain a representative board.

A literature review on maximum feasible participation indicates the *functions* of advisory boards to be vague and confusing. The term *advisory* should be abandoned in favor of "community policy board." If "advisory board" is maintained, it should be understood to imply more than the giving of advice. The board should have clear policy-making power on those issues which affect the community residents. As advice is ignored, less will be given, or antagonisms and anomie will develop. The board needs to involve specialized groups, including recipients of service and youth between 16 and 21, as well as the more visible leaders. "Community residents are expected to be effective partners with those who operate community programs; they must help assure representativeness and responsiveness."[33]

A recent study discusses the difference between the effect of this participation on the board and on the poor who are representatives. The commu-

---

[32] Howard W. Hallman: *Community Corporations and Neighborhood Control* (Washington, D. C., Center for Governmental Studies, 1970); and Harold H. Weissman: *Community Councils and Community Control; The Workings of Democratic Mythology* (Pittsburgh, University Press, 1970).

[33] Donald Brieland: Community Advisory Boards and maximum feasible participation, *Journal of Public Health,* 61, 2 (February 1971), pp. 292-296.

nity representatives were radicalized by their board experiences, raising their level of participation in the political system, increasing their personal and political efficacy, and developing images of themselves as leaders. These community representatives continued to be distinguished from other board members "by their greater dissatisfaction with established patterns of dealing with poverty and their interest in faster change. Leaders for social change are being created where they did not exist before."[34]

However, the "representatives of the poor" who became board members often were middle-class neighborhood politicians or their carefully selected followers, most of whose identifications were with personal success. The poor who did join were often outmaneuvered or condescended to. Staff jobs provided to poor were often dead-end. Workers entered at minimum wages and could move neither vertically nor laterally. With no structured way to advance within the agency and no credentials to move to another agency, the worker is vocationally immobilized and is dependent on the refunding of that agency or the retention of its supervisors and boards.[35]

In any event, this idea of Maximum Feasible Participation through the CAP's had a profound impact on the society in general, especially on poor urban communities and the agency personnel who served them. This impact still reverberates through most of the human services. Even though there is much concern that future politicians and policy-makers may try to emasculate this concept, as the federal government is attempting to do in the 1970's, the seed of the idea has taken root as evidenced in "New Careers" and other community-based programs, and in a wider self-awareness and political acuity among the so-called disadvantaged.[36]

Outreach is intimately related to new careers because many outreach workers are new career paraprofessionals recruited from inner-city communities, whose greatest assets are their compatibility and understanding of those with whom they work, as well as their knowledge of and background in the community. The New Careers movement has taken advantage of these assets. A program of the U. S. Department of Labor, New Careers involves the development of jobs, training, employment, and careers in human ser-

---

[34] Dale Rogers Marshall: *The Politics of Participation in Poverty* (Berkeley, University of California Press, 1971); Dale Rogers Marshall: Public participation and the politics of poverty. In Peter Orleans and William Russell Ellis, Jr., eds.: *Race, Change, and Urban Society* (Beverly Hills, Calif., Sage Publications, 1971), pp. 450-482.

[35] Irving Lazar: Which citizens to participate in what? In Edgar S. Cahn and Barry A. Passett, eds.: *Citizen Participation: Effecting Community Change* (New York, Praeger, 1971), pp. 92-109.

[36] For details on New Careers, see Frank Riessman and Hermine I. Popper, eds.: *Up From Poverty; New Career Ladders for Non-professionals* (New York, Harper & Row, 1968); Arthur Pearl: *New Careers for the Poor: The Nonprofessional in Human Service* (New York, The Free Press, 1965); and Frank Riessman: *New Careers—A Basic Strategy Against Poverty* (New York, A. Philip Randolph Educational Fund, 1968).

vices at the nonprofessional or associate levels. While primarily aimed at assisting disadvantaged groups to help themselves, New Careers is also concerned with meeting manpower needs for trained personnel and improving the human services field, especially in urban areas. It has proved one of the more promising manpower human service programs, with the potential to affect public policy, agencies, their professional and nonprofessional staffs, as well as educational and training institutions. Even more important, New Careers focuses directly on the potential of the individual to be trained and educated in the context of work within and on behalf of the community.

The expansion of recreation and parks programs around the country, of course, is largely contingent on the ability to recruit trained and competent staff in a field which has a current and projected shortage of trained professionals.[37] One solution to this problem is providing new career-type opportunities with jobs and training for disadvantaged youth (and adults) by employing them in positions as recreation outreach workers. The idea is to provide jobs and training with built-in and definite career ladders designating opportunities for advancement.

The semi-professional outreach worker in recreation has the potential of increasing the quality and scope of services offered to the poor community, as well as reducing the manpower pressures for additional field staff. In essence, the basic philosophy of the Mobilization for Youth and of Maximum Feasible Participation–and certainly that of New Careers–is "disaffiliation ends when active commitment to the possibility of change in one's life begins."[38]

The philosophy of MFP and of advocacy generally is to increase the involvement of agency clientele in the actual workings of an agency, to solicit their views, and consider their suggestions and recommendations. The forefront for such community participation is the outreach worker. It is crucial that he or she be truly representative of the community, and that the agency support this person as much as possible in confronting the inevitable dilemmas and paradoxes of such a position. Outreach, then, is two things: *to extend the arm of the social agency into the community,* and *to extend the arm of the community into the agency;* and of course this means giving some *power* and *control* to community residents.

During the same period as the Mobilization for Youth project on the lower east side in New York, Kenneth Clark and his associates were designing the large study from which the community action agency of Harlem, HARYOU-ACT, was shaped. Where Mobilization for Youth was somewhat

---

[37] Donald E. Hawkins and Peter J. Verhoven: Recreation and Park manpower needs: A quantitative analysis In *Educating Tomorrow's Leaders in Parks, Recreation and Conservation* (Washington, D. C., National Recreation and Park Association, 1968).

[38] Hentoff: *Op. cit.,* p. 21.

theory-oriented, Clark's study rested largely on field research: What did the youth of Harlem feel? What did they need? Both projects came to almost the same conclusion–powerlessness.

The core of the HARYOU program, and the basis on which it was judged, was in the persistent emphasis on social action rather than dependence on social services: local community leaders, many without formal education and the style and polish of professional social workers, were stimulated to develop the competence required to be able to use the skills of the professions in implementing social action, education and social welfare programs, conducting systematic community research, and informing local residents about available resources. HARYOU was and continues to be on reflection "a creature of controversy." This project ended pretty much as it had begun with a firm sense of powerlessness and frustration.

> The tremendous amount of time, energy, and risk which were involved in the development of this plan for the youth of Harlem will be more than justified if our society is able to mobilize the commitment and the resources which are essential for its implementation. This program is designed to see that the youth of Central Harlem receive the respect, the preparation, and the living conditions which are essential for creative lives. Democracy demands no less; past denial requires even more.[39]

There is no other way to achieve a successful outreach program without relinquishing some power and control; otherwise, it is simply rhetoric, and the young have had enough of that. If we desire authenticity as recreation workers, we must mean what we say, and do what we intend as much as is possible within the limitations of the power we possess. After all, we have problems with city hall too, so there will be times we'll be advocates for issues we wish to gain support for as an agency as well! But it is a waste of resources to recruit quality and forceful indigenous workers, only to have to back off when they most need the support and encouragement of the employing agency. Outreach work, bringing new people into an agency's activities, inevitably brings new tensions and conflicts to an already existing agency arrangement. Some wish to avoid this conflict by avoiding outreach work lest it cause serious internal dissension. Others are fatigued at the thought that they must immerse themselves daily into the obvious ambivalences of outreach work in dynamic, changing communities.[40]

The Impact of Community Participation

Though the HARYOU project failed, as did Mobilization for Youth, both have been the influencers of many later community action programs. They

---

[39] *Youth in the Ghetto, op. cit.,* p. xii.

[40] Getting together. In *Live It! Communalism* (Canyon, Calif., Canyon Collective, 1971), pp. 3-4, with a discussion of problems of political outreach work, which is certainly analogous to agency-community efforts.

bit off too much in moving from alienation and delinquency in the inner city to an attack on the power structure via advocacy for the poor. The blunt substance of their failure was that sponsors of community action programs expected to use the conflict strategy of Saul D. Alinsky and at the same time be recipients of large sums of public money.[41] It didn't work.

An important consideration in the recruitment of indigenous outreach workers is the question of loyalty and community pressure. If the worker is to be truly effective, he or she will have to maintain effective connections with the community and its young people. Therefore, when considering an outreach assignment, this person may be jeopardizing the respect he currently has with youth by joining forces with the "establishment." We have to recognize and cope with the dilemma faced by paraprofessionals, and professionals as well, when they work for social agencies in their own or comparable communities.

Are these workers to be advocates for their people, or representatives of an agency with its implied value system and objectives, or both? If a Black or other minority person is respected by his community, he may not be interested in joining the "majority" and working in his community. If the majority (outside middle-class professionals) respect him, he may be downgraded in his own community *simply* for earning this respect, for being too compliant with the white man by earning respect while you are supposedly agitating against him for change. Thus, the outreach worker is expected by the community group with whom he works to take clear and supportive positions on issues which arise. If he defers to directives from his supervisors, or to the dictates of so-called "professional" neutrality, he may lose the confidence of the community.

Other conflicts seem to reside in the strategies for selecting and cultivating indigenous leadership. When these individuals are paid, in an effort to compensate for the absence of other incentives for leadership in the low-income community, they tend to orient themselves predominantly to the organization which pays them. Volunteers, when they can be cultivated, also come to expect similar compensation, though they may form no agency attachment.

These are real problems that have caused agencies to lose many excellent community outreach workers as they confront the dilemma of an advocacy role in the community and lose agency or community support. There is no simple answer, except to push for and support the outreach worker as a true advocate in his or her community–an advocate who represents the community while avoiding an adversary position with the employing agency.

Outreach workers, in developing means of community organization, have to go beyond their roles as enabler or advocate when necessary, to a new

---

[41] Moynihan: *Op. cit.*

role in strengthening client self-determination and developing self-reliance within the community. The outreach worker could assume three roles: (1) as organizer-advocate, stimulating change through system confrontation; (2) as organizer-educator, with the youth gradually assuming the role of self-advocacy; and (3) as organizer-technical assistant, remaining invisible as an advisor.[42]

Implicit in the advocate's role is that the poor can influence neighborhood planning decisions. Examples can be cited of the overwhelming disillusionment to the poor which can result from such involvement. Involving local groups in elaborate planning procedures guides them into a narrowly circumscribed form of political action for which they are ill equipped. Not only are low-income groups severely handicapped in planning activities, they are diverted from the political action that may most increase their political power.[43] In addition, the preconditions for developing community power are generally lacking in the Black ghetto, for social change itself requires organization, power, and wealth. It will be necessary to recognize these factors as well as to devise models of community control and strategies to achieve it.[44]

From the literature on community participation and leadership two types of activity emerge: programs of action directed toward the accomplishment of specific goals, and acts by individuals directed toward relating a given program to others. These are referred to, respectively, as "task accomplishment" and "structure development." Certain problems arise on both levels which are bases for classification of action roles: (1) awareness–initiating and spreading interest in a community need; (2) organization–of a community–also contributing to efficiency in resource use.

Failures in city planning and development frequently can be traced to a failure to develop citizen participation at crucial stages. The outcome of any community issue depends on the distribution of political power among the residents. However, unless the objectives are carefully defined, there is the danger of unintentionally promoting more political inequality through increased participation: the result may simply be more participation by those who already hold the balance of political and economic power within a community.

The benefits of participation for the individual vary with his or her role, status, objectives, and beliefs. They can be psychological, economic, or social. If some persons are not participating as much as desirable, it might

---

[42] Paul A. Kurzman and Jeffrey R. Solomon: *Beyond Advocacy: A New Model for Community Organization, Social Work Practice* (New York, Columbia University Press, 1970).

[43] Frances Fox Piven: *Op. cit.,* pp. 32-37.

[44] Marvin Surkin: The myth of community control: Rhetorical and political aspects of the Ocean Hill-Brownsville controversy. In Peter Orleans and William Russell Ellis, Jr., eds.: *Race, Change, and Urban Society, op. cit.*

mean that the costs to them of such participation outweigh the gains. Efforts in the past have been concentrated on the removal of barriers to political participation. The next step is the attainment of equal opportunity to participate in the decision-making process as well.

Two patterns of participation now emerging are the following: (1) a small degree of resident involvement as policymakers; and (2) a greater amount of involvement as nonprofessional community workers. There was, however, some confusion concerning OEO's expectations of participation by the poor. It was generally understood that one-third of local poverty boards were to be drawn from the poor, but that was never clearly stated. The right of the poor to sanction a policy must also be clarified. The final issue involves the decision of *which* people to involve: spokesmen for the poor, residents of poverty areas who may not be poor, or the poor themselves? These issues directly affect the workings of the community action programs to a large extent and are far from resolved.

It should be noted that participation of the poor in poverty-program jobs and as paraprofessionals is generally the least controversial form of participation. Another participation involves the poor as advisors to poverty programs. The third type is shared power, in which the poor sit at equal members on policy-making boards. A fourth form of participation is *social action* and is, of course, the most controversial. The success of participation, in whatever form it takes, will depend on the implementation of reforms in employment, housing, welfare, and health care. "The issue of participation by the poor in the political system has been raised in a most compelling manner, and this major strategy for reform is having an important influence on racial and urban problems in the United States."[45]

A case history might highlight some of the difficulties involved in community action programs. The Topeka, Kansas, Office of Economic Opportunity (TOEO) introduced two distinct sets of goals for which it sought community consensus: the program content as expressed in OEO community-action proposals and the maximum feasible participation experience for the poor.[46] Both goals were alien to established patterns of community action and produced dissonance between staff and program participants, as might be expected. For the TOEO to function adequately, it was necessary to balance its efforts to innovate and to effect beneficial social change for the poor against the need to establish and maintain good relationships with other segments of the community and the government.

TOEO staff found themselves in the middle of conflicts among agency of-

---
[45] Dale Rogers Marshall: Public participation and the politics of poverty, *op. cit.*
[46] Louis A. Zurcher, Jr.: Dilemmas and staff stresses. In *Poverty Warriors: The Human Experience of Planned Social Intervention* (Austin, University of Texas Press, 1970), pp. 32-53.

ficials. They were also involved in the development of the Target Neighborhood Committees and were under the scrutiny of the community at large, the local press, the regional and national OEO, and researchers. Often attempts to involve the poor, particularly in meaningful program control, produced critical comments from agency officials about going too fast and not using proper channels.

As the poor increasingly exercised their prerogative to participate in decision-making, some of the agency representatives accustomed to doing "for" the poor were forced to shift their preceptions from treating them as clients to treating them as colleagues. This shift in expectations often disrupted the TOEO's efforts to implement the local program. As the national War on Poverty grew, specific requirements, regulations, and procedures deluged poverty organizations. When operating as planned, the TOEO had to be at the center of community controversy and to be able to resist pressure to identify exclusively *either* with the poor or with the power structure.

Conclusion

Some early experiences with these sorts of programs reveal persistent problems in overcoming barriers to low-income participation and influence in community affairs. When concrete services are the motive for initial participation, they tend to remain the focus for later activity. The real need for concrete services seems to override any less pressing activities and takes up both the staff's and recipients' time and energy.

Many existing low-income organizations are weak and often seem to be mere emblems of power for leaders whose personal ambition is tied, not to a low-income following but to the service organization. These organizations may use facilities or funds they receive to acquire the furnishings of respectability. However, the role of professionals in community organizations remains dubious. Local people tend to regard them with uneasiness–and justifiably so. The professionals themselves must deal with the dilemma of their role in low-income organizations, the foundations and methodology of their professional training, and the organizational requirements of any antipoverty project.

Citizens' participation, in all its varied aspects and dimensions, has shown that they can make major and unique contributions to the problems of the inner city. Attempts to implement the concept of MFP have given the poor a chance to confront teachers, social workers, government officials, and community leaders. "If the poor are given a voice in the management and design of programs operated for their benefit, they are likely to begin operating as a quasi-political force in their own communities. Citizen participation must mean participation in every dimension of our culture, our political system, our decision-making process."[47]

There is a risk, however. Social protest actions, because they offer simple and dramatic definitions of problems, may penetrate apathy and override the puzzled disengagement bred from lack of information. These actions also require less personal and economic stability than sustained organizational participation. It should be noted that urban renewal programs elicited protest action from local groups in response to the threats posed by renewal. However, social protest is likely to incur hostile and repressive reactions from other groups in the community and from public authorities. Low-income groups may in consequence be even further cut off from channels to influence and also from the services that can become a basis for more stable organization. Experience with antipoverty programs dramatically articulates this risk.

SELECTED READINGS

Bannon, Joseph J.: The Roving Leader: A new look, *Parks and Recreation,* Vol. VII, no. 2, Feb. 1972.

Black and White—A major survey of U. S. racial attitudes today, *Newsweek,* Aug. 22, 1966.

Davis, John P. (Ed.): *The American Negro Reference Book,* New York, Prentice-Hall, Inc., 1966.

Gardner, John W.: Our commitment to people, *Public Welfare,* Vol. 4, Jan. 1966.

Harrington, Michael: If you're Black, stay back, *The Other America,* Baltimore, Penguin Books, 1963.

Madison, James A.: Urban recreation problems, *Parks and Recreation,* Vol. 3, Dec. 1968.

Myrdal, Gunnar. *An American Dilemma,* Vol. II. New York, McGraw-Hill Book Co., 1964.

Questions about community and alienation. In *Toward a Social Report,* Washington, D. C., Department of Health, Education and Welfare, 1969.

Recreation in the Nation's Cities: Problems and Approaches, Washington, D. C., National League of Cities, 1968.

Riessman, F. and Popper, H. L.: *Up From Poverty,* New York, Harper & Row, 1968.

Youth in the Ghetto: A Study of the Consequences of Powerlessness and a Blueprint for Change. New York, Harlem Youth Opportunities Unlimited, Inc., HARYOU, 1964.

---

[47] Edgar S. and Jean Camper Cahn: Maximum feasible participation: A general overview. In Cahn and Passett: *Op. cit.,* pp. 9-66.

CHAPTER III

ROLE AND FUNCTION OF THE OUTREACH PROGRAM

"The Street Is My Turf"

EDWIN GREENIDGE
MILTON C. DOUGLAS, JR.

IN EVERY SUCCESSFUL outreach program with youth, a major reason for success was that the outreach worker *expected* the youths to do well, involved them in the planning and implementation of the program, learned as much about the youths as possible, and held himself responsible if the program failed. This chapter discusses one outreach program which has proved successful in work with inner-city youth, The Roving Leader Program, as well as several aspects of inner-city life which must be understood and appreciated before any outreach worker attempts to communicate with the young men and women in our nation's slums.

Social Aspects

Outreach is designed to meet youth in their own neighborhood, initially on their terms, and then show them a way out of their dilemma if they desire one. Outreach workers must desist from assuming that their aspirations for ghetto youth are better than what the youth themselves perceive as valuable. But we must offer alternatives which are operable and not illusory—like elaborate training programs with no jobs or with jobs that are short-lived.

In New York City, for instance, street academies are putting the outreach concept to work in education. Street academies are small store-front schools manned by one or two teachers in addition to an outreach worker, who recruits the students from the streets and act as motivator, counselor, friend, father, disciplinarian, and companion:

> Why do these schools succeed where the public schools fail? . . . The difference is that Harlem Prep and CAM Academy . . . start where the student is and take him someplace else. The big mistake most schools have made . . . is in showing reluctance to meet the child in his own territory and then to take him for the

ride. Until now we have been asking the child to meet us in *our* territory and then to begin the ride from there.[1]

Although these academies are primarily educational, their conceptions are of value to work in recreation outreach. The essence of their experiences and success has been to work with youth in their own territory, to take them at their own evaluation, and then to expose them to other viewpoints, other perspectives and aspirations, where applicable and of value to their lives. Thus, it might appear as if street academies try to co-opt youth and lead them into eventually conforming to middle-class values and morals. Not so; the method of the street academies is to expose the young people to a variety of options and let them decide what *they* care to learn and use in their lives. In outreach work, this same philosophy can be quite effective if we resist arming ourselves with predetermined concepts and values, entering a community with the attitude that *we-know-best*. Such an attitude is bound to fail.

Most street academies have links with job training and placement, but not every one has had full success. CAM Academy (Christian Action Ministry) has had its failures–not every student can be enticed to leave the street culture, and others are hopelessly hooked on drugs, or have little trust that social service programs might substantively affect their lives for the better.

This lack of trust is well founded. Social agencies and projects permeate ghettos, yet youth still face utter powerlessness in most areas of their lives. The HARYOU project stressed that social action programs be evaluated by how much they alleviate the problems of individuals and reduce the pathology of the community.[2] Any other yardstick, especially a citation of how much money and resources have been devoted to community programs, will not suffice.

Social agencies tend to view themselves as organizations which step in and put the pieces together when other institutions (e.g., home and school) fail, or they seek to supplement the efforts of these institutions, as is primarily the case with recreation. Statistics clearly show there has been a massive failure in these other institutions; and the social agencies–as presently organized, staffed, and financed–are simply not equal to the task of massive rehabilitation of youth, not to mention adults.

For instance, although there were more than 90 social service organizations in the Harlem community at the time of the HARYOU project

---

[1] Mario D. Fantini and Gerald Weinstein: *Toward a Contact Curriculum* (New York, Anti-Defamation League of B'nai B'rith). Reported in Charles E. Silberman: *Crisis in the Classroom* (New York, Random House, 1970), pp. 48-49. See also Mario D. Fantini and Gerald Weinstein: *The Disadvantaged: Challenge to Education* (New York, Harper & Row, 1968).

[2] *Youth in the Ghetto: A Study of the Consequences of Powerlessness and A Blueprint for Change* (New York, Harlem Youth Opportunities Unlimited, Inc., HARYOU, 1964), p. 299; see also, Waverly Poston: *The Gang and The Establishment* (New York, Harper & Row, 1971).

(1964), it was the opinion of social services personnel that the area was in need of more adequate social services. A 1963 city-wide study of recreation services and needs indicated Central Harlem had 27 playgrounds and playing fields, 20 part-time afternoon and evening centers, and 18 public and voluntary full-time centers. When the number of these facilities was compared with the city as a whole, Central Harlem was above the norm. From these data it was shown that Harlem was about average for playground facilities and public part-time centers, and considerably above average for full-time operations. In fact, Central Harlem ranked sixth out of the 74 neighborhoods in the survey. In addition to these data, it is known that social work is one of New York's major injustries.[3] Thus, the failure of social agencies is not simply from lack of facilities. Contributing to the failure of social services are the high rates of personal and social pathology, poor or nonexistent referral services, and inadequate central services for social welfare information on an ongoing basis.

The residents of Central Harlem at the time of the survey generally believed the social agencies were trying to do a good job. Their function was perceived as providing recreation for youth to keep them off the streets. For many communities, this is a viable service in which the agencies provide stability and direction for youth. However, whether such simple programs can be fruitful in inner-city areas, such as Central Harlem, was seriously questioned:

> It is clear that the basic community problems such as housing, education, drug addiction, and economic marginality cannot be affected by providing a nice place to play or attempting merely to ameliorate the persistent personal and social consequences of ghetto living. These problems demand a consistent and systematic approach of planned social change. If the agencies of the community are to develop programs that deal more directly with these problems, they must sharply re-examine and redirect their programs and determine whether they are keeping pace with the rapid changes occurring in the community, city, and nation. . . . Program inadequacies can no longer be excused in terms of inadequate budget, staff, and facilities. The essential inadequacies may be in the areas of imagination, vision, and flexibility which block meaningful involvement with the real problems of the community and people.[4]

All this is applicable to youth, and has been reiterated so often in the past decade, that it is frustrating to hear it again. The present social service system is clearly not working, is in fact a travesty of what it was intended to be, and inner-city youth are becoming increasingly alienated and angry at attempts to work with them. We are fast approaching the time, if we have

---

[3] In Harlem as of 1963, there were 156 separate agencies serving an estimated 240,000, about 40 per cent of the population. Cf. Charles E. Silberman's *Crisis in Black and White* (New York, Random House, 1964), p. 310.

[4] *Ibid.,* pp. 310-311.

not done so already, where any service regardless of how potentially useful to a community, will be considered by youth and others as irrelevant and as the "same old song," none of which encounters the basic problem of powerlessness in the ghetto:

> Until those who are concerned with this crisis, moreover, can actually engage in role reversal, can project themselves to some extent into the young of the underclass, nothing durable or basic is going to happen. Quite aside . . . from the impossibility of finding meaningful work . . . how are you going to bring these youngsters into the 'larger society' and into a commitment to 'middle-class values' without also telling them that you know the larger society is in many ways sicker than they are and that so large a proportion of those middle-class values are false?[5]

Many gang members, delinquents, dropouts, and older slum dwellers are justified in their cynicism of social programs: "Americans have used welfare programs and social work agencies the way the Romans used bread and circuses—to keep the poor happy and non-threatening."[6] This attitude, known as welfare colonialism, finds social and human service workers faced with a growing communication and credibility gap between themselves and those they seek to help. Social workers remain alien in a world they can never comprehend and frequently do not even see. Their only desire is to change that world, which is impossible before one comprehends the milieu of inner-city life.

What all this means is simple: Black youth, like any other minority group, be they Chicano, Chinese, Puerto Rican, Indian or whatever, can be helped by giving them the means to help themselves. And, in the final analysis, youth will succeed only if adults make it first, setting an example for them. The general powerlessness of the inner-city resident is not simply the effects of slum living, but explains why certain minority groups are confined to ghettos in the first place. Any social program has to recognize the systematic prejudice that perpetuates ghetto life for nonwhite minority groups.

The pervasive racism in our society has really not diminished in the past twenty-five years, regardless of the much heralded reforms for Blacks. To read Gunnar Myrdal's 1944 treatise on "the Negro problem" is to understand clearly the intransigence of our racial dilemma:

> The American Negro problem is a problem in the heart of the American. It is there that the interracial tension has its focus. It is there that the decisive struggle goes on. This is the central viewpoint of this treatise. Though our study in-

---

[5] Nat Hentoff: Whose Existential Crisis? In Eli E. Cohen and Louise Kapp, eds.: *Manpower Policies for Youth* (New York, Columbia University Press, 1966), p. 19; see also Paul Goodman: *Like A Conquered Province; The Moral Ambiguity of America* (New York, Random House, 1966).

[6] Silberman: *Crisis in Black and White,* p. 312.

cludes economics, social and political race relations, at bottom our problem is the moral dilemma of the American—the conflict between his moral valuations on various levels of consciousness and generality. The 'American Dilemma' . . . is the ever-raging conflict between, on the one hand, the valuations preserved on the general plane which we shall call the 'American Creed,' where the American thinks, talks, and acts under the influence of high national and Christian precepts, and, on the other hand, the valuations on specific planes of individual and group living, where personal and local interests; economic, social, and sexual jealousies; considerations of community prestige and conformity; group prejudice against particular persons or types of people; and all sorts of miscellaneous wants, impulses, and habits dominate his outlook.[7]

The essence of our moral dilemma as exposed by Myrdal is how to create and maintain a sense of community in this nation, when that community is composed of groups as well as individuals, and when specific factions of that nation will not yield power it has systematically denied other groups for centuries.

"Some observers feel many black views have become so desperate that they are thinking now not of how to use their lives but of how to use their deaths in violent, valiant attacks on white society."[8] This quote clearly brings to mind the massacre at Attica. A willingness to die on the part of young Black men does not mean a disrespect for life; quite the contrary. Because of their deep respect for life, these men comprehend the full value of its sacrifice. This is to offset recent media and other speculation that Black militants and extremists do not value their own lives, that it is easy for them to die and thus easier for us to kill them. It is because they have seen the futility of both prison and ghetto life, that they have revolted. For most of them to leave the prison is to enter a larger prison–a society that purposefully denies them opportunities and realistic options.

Too many programs and foundation grants often ignore the really hard and controversial issues which lie at the heart of the Black and other minority group problems–issues which involve the most fundamental conflict of interest between nonwhites who want jobs and whites reluctant to surrender job monopolies, between Black tenants and white landlords, between Black homeowners and white universities seeking land for expansion, between Black students and white-controlled universities.[9] The crux of the problem is not simply the pathology of the ghetto, but the outer forces which create *and* maintain this pathology at such an enormous human cost. Outreach

---

[7] Gunnar Myrdal: *An American Dilemma: The Negro Problem and Modern Democracy* (New York, Harper and Bros., 1944), p. xlvii.

[8] John Lombardi: *Student Activism in the Junior Colleges: An Administrator's Views* (Washington, D. C., American Association of Junior Colleges, n.d.), pp. 65-66.

[9] *Ibid.;* and Paul Jacobs: *Prelude to Riot: A View of Urban America From the Bottom* (New York, Vintage Books, 1966).

"I drew life . . . how about you?"

Copyright, Los Angeles Times; reprinted with permission; editorial cartoon by Paul Conrad.

FIGURE III-1.

workers, at the least, should comprehend this framework and undertake their assignments in view of it.

Many recreation centers have improved their service to youth because they have learned that inner-city youth have to be reached where they are– on the streets, in poolhalls, etc.–and be encouraged to use recreation and parks facilities. Needless to say, these youth are so suspicious of "do-gooders" that they do not respond to formal publicity lures from established agencies.[10] In an article discussing plans for a communal housing development for the inner-city poor, Black Panther leader Bobby Seale recognized the importance and draw of poolhalls for young Blacks: "We have even figured out places where we could locate pool rooms (in the housing development), because in the black community a lot of young kids hang out at the pool hall."[11]

The Outreach Worker's Task

Working with young people from poverty areas requires someone who is flexible in outlook and able to cope with unexpected daily crises–a good re-

---

[10] Helaine S. Dawson: *On the Outskirts of Hope: Educating Youth from Poverty Areas* (New York, McGraw-Hill, 1968), p. 7.

[11] Seale on Communalism, *Ramparts,* August 1971, pp. 45-48.

quirement for the outreach worker in recreation or any social service. Before you work with youth in recreational activities, it is important to find out what you can do about referrals to help them with vocational, employment, family, health and other problems outside the sphere of recreation. Extensive knowledge of various agency functions, and the overlap among social services, are invaluable in work with such youth.

Such referral expertise is especially effective if the outreach worker is indigenous to the area. He or she can then combine a knowledge of inner-city life and culture with practical knowledge of agencies and resources to aid inner-city youth. The most effective outreach worker is one who has established a liaison with other social agencies *prior to* the inception of street work. This way he or she can be assured of concrete support for young clients and can ensure these young people they won't get a run-around from one agency to another.

Outreach workers introduce their young clients to these agencies and then encourage them to work directly with the agencies themselves, once they are *convinced* the agency will adequately and consistently help these youth. The outreach worker should resist being a middleman for the youth once the original contact and referral to a social agency is made, but should not assume any agency will properly handle the matter without careful follow-up; at the least, the worker should check periodically with the youth and agency to evaluate the services given. In this way, the worker can serve as a resource person while avoiding the paternalism of so many social services.[12] This detachment also encourages the young person to act independent of social workers, and to relate to his friends and families the kind of experiences and success he has had with outreach workers as liaisons to social services.

It cannot be stressed enough that the *most* valuable service any outreach worker can offer is to alleviate, to whatever degree possible, the social and human needs of inner-city youth. These needs are real and pressing–a job, food stamps, drug relief programs, welfare for those with families or disabilities, information on educational and vocational opportunities, as well as places they can go to relax and have a good time (e.g., a recreation center where they won't be harrassed by police or others trying to interfere in their lives).

Before an outreach worker begins relating to inner-city youth, a critical objective is to understand and comprehend as much as possible about their world, ethos, values and diversity, and to genuinely relate to this environment nonjudgmentally, and free of paternalism. The worker has to learn how youth behave, how they think, how they communicate with their peers, what

---

[12] See Harry Edwards: *Black Students* (New York, The Free Press, 1970), Chapter on "The Re-entry of Whites: From Intruding Samaritans to Allies," for analogies to the re-entry of white social workers as advocates for the poor.

values they respect or disrespect, how they view their family, the police, drugs, and most importantly, how they spend their leisure or would like to spend their free time. The latter is most important since the bulk of ghetto youth are rich in time from the enforced leisure they endure because of massive unemployment, especially for young Black males.

Unemployment for Blacks is aggravated by any serious national unemployment, but is nonetheless a reality of ghetto life, regardless of the national employment situation. If the employment possibilities loosen up for whites, there is a trickle down to the Black world of jobs previously desperate whites no longer need. Most of these jobs are menial or low-paying white or blue collar positions. As of this writing, the national unemployment rate, released by the U. S. Department of Labor, hovers around 5 per cent. For nonwhites, there is a perpetual recession, which is magnified when jobs are tight for whites, but the job problem exists untempered by the national climate.[13]

One has only to read *Ebony, Jet,* or *Essence* magazines to see which Blacks have received increased job opportunities–the middle-class Black who has acquired, no matter how arduously, the educational and social credentials of this society. The white response to the Black liberation movement has been largely to reward those Blacks who most resemble whites in social attributes and aspirations. Ghetto youth have only received sporadic attention, even with such full-scale attempts as the Mobilization For Youth and HARYOU projects. When the job market expands, and the guilty conscience of whites tingles, educated and "qualified" Blacks are once more in demand. Ghetto youth are avoided as an annoyingly persistent dilemma most would like to see vanish in the "Advancement" of integrated television ads and other token accommodations made to Blacks.

Reaching the Young Black

We can be certain, however, that the most volatile force in America is or at least was Black youth. It was the young of the ghetto who participated in the urban riots that stimulated the upsurge in social programs for Blacks. The high incidence and availability of drugs in the inner city, which are supplied by the outer city, may have passified the riot-prone youth, but it has not diminished the anger and *full* knowledge of the persistent degradation of Blacks in this country. We may look upon riots as relatively benign expressions of outrage if we continue to *ignore* or sugarcoat the problems daily faced and endured in the ghettos of this nation.

---

[13] There have been estimates that unemployment among young Black males in the slums has been as high as 32 per cent. In Chinatown (San Francisco), unemployment rates as high as 14 per cent have been reported. *Cf.* Min S. Yee: Crack in the Great Wall of Chinatown, *Ramparts,* Oct. 1972, p. 34 *ff.*

If the outreach worker understands and is sensitive to this reality, and has a respect for youth and not simply phoney jibes to infiltrate or co-opt their activities, it should be somewhat easier to offer the resources he or she has and to have them accepted by these youth. At the same time, the worker must clearly understand what his function is, why he is there, and what are the objectives a recreation organization can realistically achieve in the inner city.

Regardless of the sub-objectives an outreach worker sets, a comprehension of inner-city and racial problems must go beyond mere rhetoric. Nothing is more tiresome (and insulting) to an oppressed people than verbal commiseration with their oppression. Blacks do not need sympathy; they need immediate relief from their basic social and psychological needs, and power to control their lives and design their destiny. Anything less as an ultimate objective for an outreach worker or advocate is perpetuating the status quo, and the status quo maligns inner-city Blacks, young and old. There is no way to avoid this fact.

One temptation for an outreach worker to overcome when first comprehending the toughness of ghetto life is to glamorize inner-city youth as they endure the enormous difficulties and pressures encountered in their environment. While we recognize "there are qualities in the slum life which the middle class could well emulate,"[14] we need to perceive the full picture, to include the many negative aspects. We can still respect the strength and tenacity needed for survival in an environment which would cripple most middle-class people. However, this respect should not diminish our desire as outreach workers to relieve the many injustices inner-city folks endure.

Black Language

After establishing liaison with various social agencies, the outreach worker must then learn the *language* of inner-city youth to be sincerely interested in understanding their style of communication, and not in simply appropriating their language to appear hip or cool. One only knows "what's happenin" by living it, not by intellectually taking on the problems of ghetto youth. The outreach worker must not be another "honkey liberal." Nothing is dated more quickly than slang, especially that used by inner-city youth and other minority groups, so if the worker does not want to look foolish, his interest in language must be constant and sincere, and not a quicky course on current fad words and no more. Too soon he will sound like an

---

[14] Hentoff: *Op. cit.,* p. 24. "I am not romanticizing here, and would refer you to the work of Frank Reissman and Edgar Friedenberg, among others, for elaboration." A contrary view to Hentoff's is offered in Henry Etzkowitz and Gerald M. Schaflander: *Ghetto Crisis: Riots or Reconciliation?* (Boston, Little, Brown and Co., 1969), esp. Chapter 3: The Negro Ghetto Nonfamily, pp. 14-18, which leaves no room for positive aspects in ghetto life.

oldtimer, and will most assuredly lose any authenticity he may have earned with a group of youngsters.

Language is important to oppressed groups, for it is a way of maintaining anonymity and privacy in the larger white society, a society which pervades their world with such tenacity that there is little personal or cultural development not readily assimilable by the outer society. A private language also *protects* Blacks and enables them to exchange extra-legal, illegal, or personal information under the nose of their oppressor. (Telephone exchanges of such information might diminish now as more operators are Black women, who clearly pick up the message.) To overhear an intense conversation among Blacks is to hear another language, full of implications, humor, and suggestion, and rich with the reality of daily survival.

The appropriation of Black language by white is notorious; most of the "in-words" of white youth and liberal hipsters are taken directly from the idiom of Blacks. *Black World* magazine (formerly *Negro Digest*) printed a joke which showed two Black men on a street corner being audited by a sociologist with a tape-recorder. One Black youth said to the other something like, "Quick, think up some *new* words so he can record them!" In fact, most texts and discussion on community work offer "current" glossaries of ghetto slang so no one will be caught short. These are embarrassingly outdated before they are off the press. Simply review any Black slang glossary a year or more old and see how quickly outsiders lose contact with *insiders*' language. The point is not to publish up-to-date glossaries, a clearly Sisyphan task and somewhat suspect, but to inculcate an admiration and interest in Black language; the rest will follow naturally.

Now that Tony the Tiger, Dagwood, and Nixon say, "Right on" and conservative politicians mouth "Power to the People" and "Black Power," we realize why Black idioms have to be created more quickly as whites extend deeper into the ghetto and are exposed to its daily language, or as ghetto youth refuse to give up their language for the "refined" language of the upward-bound.[15] Outreach workers have to be sincere in their interest in Black language and not simply memorize in-words. Any expediency or crassness will be detected by the youth, and the worker will be left behind in a false quest for understanding. Memorization of words can never mask lack of interest or motivation in learning a language.

The sincerest approach, and undoubtedly the most operable for learning and understanding the inner-city youth language, is to ask kids when they talk what various expressions mean, if there is any difficulty in understand-

---

[15] That Blacks are capable of innovative language should never be doubted. Cf. Addison Gayle, Jr., ed.: *The Black Aesthetic* (New York, Doubleday, 1971); and Arthur L. Smith: *Language, Communication, and Rehtoric for Black Americans* (New York, Holt, Rinehart and Winston, 1972).

ing, or if previously learned slang is obviously dated. Black language is very evocative, and the contextual tones colorful and sharp, so that many non-indigenous outreach workers will have little difficulty in absorbing the *intention* of the message. In fact, much of the objection to the Black liberation movement is toward its harsh rhetoric. Blacks demanding change leave little doubt as to the intent of their message. Outreach workers could never claim they do not understand what Blacks want–the message is too clear. They can only claim that whites refuse to hear that message or to relinquish power to Blacks. As the rhetoric becomes harsher too many of us appear to concentrate on the poor manners of Blacks and astutely ignore their message. The change in rhetoric attracts the penetrating attention of the white society (and of some well-off Blacks as well), while interest in the goals of Black liberation seems to have become less intense.

It is important that the worker speak his own language and not take on the tough dialect in a short-cut attempt to gain recognition and authenticity. We should respect the separate and distinct language of Black youth and other minority groups, and not cheapen it by a hasty appropriation and assimilation for *our own ends*. Any person can respect you if you use your own language well (and not for snobbish or intellectual intimidation), listen and comprehend when they speak, and perhaps eventually develop a natural blending of both languages.

Social workers, as well as linguists and educators, often assume Black language is inferior to formal English. They fail to see the richness of the Black language, even though this is well documented and evident if one truly listens to Black people.[16] Instead of listening, we set standard English as the norm and label any deviation as substandard, or the speaker is considered "language deficient." This is arrogant. Despite evidence in the publications cited, which indicates there is a high level of linguistic sophistication among speakers of Black language, social workers and educators continue to stick to their assumptions about language superiority of standard English speakers over nonstandard speakers.

Unfortunately, many academic researchers who hold such negative views about nonstandard English, or who more subtly and unthinkingly overevaluate and push the illiteracies of Black language as being viable, are involved in preschool training programs for Black children. "Any training program that assumes the inferiority of the child's native language is one that denies

---

[16] F. Williams, ed.: *Language and Poverty* (Chicago, Markham, 1970); W. Stewart, ed.: *Non-standard Speech and the Teaching of English* (Washington, D. C., Center for Applied Linguistics, 1964); A. Frazier: *New Directions in Elementary English* (Champaign, Illinois, National Council of Teachers of English, 1967); and R. Schuy, *Social Dialects and Language Learning* (Champaign, Illinois, National Council of Teachers of English, 1965). See also footnote 15 above.

that child an important part of his cultural integrity. Further, indications are that . . . assumptions of middle-class superiority (from which . . . derive the language inferiority hypothesis) will be detected and believed by the children. The inferiority hypothesis then becomes self-fulfilling–children who are made to feel inferior in a middle-class school setting end up becoming inferior performers in that setting."[17] The implications of these attitudes in working with youths are clear.

It is refreshing to see that some ghetto schools have begun to teach formal English as a *second* language and not as the mother tongue. This recognition places the language of the Black culture where it belongs–in the center–and teaches English as a specific, limited tool for dealing with the larger white society, as a vehicle to help Black youth confront social agencies and institutions, while at the same time refusing to denigrate the complex, variative, and traditional language of their race.

Outreach workers should desist from pushing their own language norms in preference to any inner-city dialect. Too many otherwise sensitive discussions about working with inner-city youth are marred by a tendency to consider formal English as the ultimate and to persistently correct or ridicule Black expressions. On the other hand, a more subtle attack is to give overriding importance to informal illiteracies in the Black language and pretend there is no need for formalizing the language to any extent. To teach illiteracies as equal to a formal language is as insulting as denigrating that language in the first place.

It is not the function of the outreach worker to correct or tolerate the language of inner-city youth, but to appreciate its extensive connotations and creativeness, recognize their skill in using it, and attempt to combine the two languages in a shared communication between two "cultures," a communication which enables youth to equally interact with representatives of the white culture. Too many social and community workers attempt to correct or eliminate street language in their youthful clients and see this as a sign of achievement. All they may accomplish, in reality, is no longer being exposed to the in-language of youth. The kids talk the "dead-ass" white language to placate oversensitive ears.[18]

The Black Family

Since we strongly value a *nuclear family* in white society, there has been a preponderance of social science research and pontification about the destruction of the nuclear Black family and the loss of male influence within

---

[17] White words, *The Boneyard Examiner* (Champaign-Urbana, Ill.), Vol. 1, no. 6, Oct. 18, 1971.

[18] A contrary view to this is offered in Dawson: *Op. cit.*

the family. While most of the material on the Black family deals with the real difficulties of ghetto living, and its attendant pathologies, there is still too great a tendency to judge ghetto Blacks on *our* terms. We must remember that most of this analysis has come from white researchers and not from the Blacks themselves. While the castigation of the Black has led to the destruction of even the most rudimentary amenities of life for many Black families, their sense of community and racial identity is strong, especially so in the last decade. Their sense of identity and community is different than ours, and for that reason we too often miss its presence.

As Joyce Ladner, a Black sociologist, stresses in *Tomorrow's Tomorrow* (a book which challenged established theories about Black family life in the USA), the dominant American society should be examined to find pathological behavior it attributes to minority groups. In her mind, the Black community has a separate social system which regulates much of its own behavior and establishes its own familial values.[19]

This discussion is not to ignore the tremendous brutalization of the Black, both historically and currently, in terms of family structure and personal lives. But the absence of male influence in the home is always cited as an example of the prime problem of the Black family, again primarily by white researchers and psychologists.[20]

We should be cautious about readily assuming that the extended family without a male head, which is quite prominent in lower-income Black communities, is somehow less desirable than our more self-contained, one-family unit with one dad per house. It is simpler to speak of family structures, with a mother, father, and children, and more difficult to analyze the Black family and to see the dynamic situation which does exist:

> It is certainly not likely that Black people in America have adapted to circumstances as boxed-in individuals or couples. With a structurally segregated and rather uniformally depressed group as this, it seems more likely that there has been a hothouse atmosphere for new collective adaptations. This means that

---

[19] Joyce Ladner: *Tomorrow's Tomorrow: The Black Woman* (Garden City, New York, Doubleday, 1971).
[20] See Etzkowitz and Schaflander: *Op. cit.;* Robert Coles: *Children of Crisis* (Boston, 1964); Frank Riessman: *The Culturally Deprived Child* (New York, 1962); and Reynolds Farley: "Family Types and Family Headship" for a fuller discussion of this issue. See also work of Daniel P. Moynihan, who touted the scourge of the Black Matriarch; the discussion of matriarchy in William H. Grier and Price M. Cobbs: *Black Rage* (New York, Bantam Books, 1968), two Black psychiatrists who rely quite heavily on traditional schools of psychoanalysis and whose views are also related to this issue. Their book, in many ways, shows that Blacks have the same psychological hang-ups as whites. In fact a reaction from reading this book is that it seems one sure sign of integration and status is the catching of white diseases by Blacks.

there is good reason to look out for internal cultural developments in the ghetto community. . . .[21]

While it is not our intention to pass a final judgment on the controversy of the Black family, it *is* our intention to warn of too readily accepting popular social-science notions of what is wrong with the ghetto family. Nor should we use arguments on the positive aspects of Black family life as an excuse for perpetuating ghetto existence for the millions who now endure it. Too often when youth get in trouble we hear the rationalization that they have "no father figure" to protect them from such problems. This assumes that the Black father figure would be any better able to offset the preponderous problems of inner-city living than a mother-figure, and is naive in its suggestion.

It was once said by a Black man, and not heeded, that we should stop studying the inner city and concentrate on the outer city which is the *source* of ghetto problems, and more importantly we should stop blaming these problems on the elusive Black matriarchy or inadequate family structure. It is a cheap trick to blame oppressed people for their own oppression, to make them turn on themselves for personal and familial inadequacies, and to play down their resourcefulness in creating alternatives to forces calculated to mess them over:

> the picture of what a [Black] man can do seems to list only components with negative valences; it says little about what men are really like. Its variables are those defined as important in the mainstream model, and in this way it is potentially biased . . . it largely leaves out the creative responses the black community has made to its circumstances. . . .[22]

While there may be an absence of a father in the lives of many Black children, there is not an absence of males. In tightly constructed communities, these children have access to many males—both good and bad. This is not a community of women, but a community of people. The values young men emulate, for better or worse, are male values and not female ones.[23] The fact that Black women have been granted more economic "stability" relative to their men does not mean this has brought an overemphasis on female attitudes in the Black community. Quite the opposite is speculated by those who believe the young Black thrives on his maleness because of innumerable attempts to destroy it, by his equating masculinity with superiority, and by the conspicuous absence of a Black father. Young males very early become

---

[21] Alf Hannerz: *Soulside: Inquiries into Ghetto Culture and Community* (New York, Columbia University Press, 1969), p. 77.
[22] Etzkowitz and Schaflender: *Op. cit.,* pp. 78-79.
[23] Cellestine Ware: Black Feminism. In *Woman Power: Transitions in American Feminism* (New York, Tower Publications, 1970).

surrogate fathers in the home and bring "masculine" qualities to bear on their lives.

The seeming lack of adult male influence in the home is greatly lamented by white researchers, while the female influence is ignored or underrated, and yet this lament is rarely voiced by Blacks. Their complaints are more pragmatic and do not involve luxurious psychological games of whether a home lacks or has too much of one sex or another. Young people need love, care, nurturing, and sustenance. Whether these come in pants or a dress is not relevant; what is relevant is their absence in most ghetto lives, and their absence has little to do with any imbalance in stereotypic sexual roles:

> The simplistic view of the black family as a matriarchy is an unfortunate theme repeated too often by scholars who should know better. If a man is stripped of his authority in the home by forces outside that home, the woman naturally must assume the status of head of household. This is the safety factor inherent in a household which includes two adults and it by no means suggests that the woman prefers it that way. If a woman is widowed she may assume many masculine functions, but the household may be a patriarchy without a patriarch.[24]

The community problems of drinking, gambling, crime and wife and child beatings do not develop because a wife has a job, but because the man is too often unable to obtain one also. He is not put out of work by his wife; the woman is more able to obtain domestic and other low-paying jobs because she is considered more palatable and safer to white employers. An interesting short story by Richard Wright is of a Black man forced to dress as a woman to get a job; now who is oppressing him, his wife or someone else?

Why should a patriarchy be any better than a matriarchy even if such did exist in the Black community? Isn't one of our goals to eliminate or reappraise sexual roles, and have children raised in an environment where their parents and community residents can lead lives of integrity and fulfillment? Stressing a strong male influence is not the need of the ghetto, for that influence was never lost, whatever the mental set of social scientists. It is most often the arrogance of whites which assumes Black males did lose their manhood. Such an analysis clearly ignores the male impact behind the Black power and liberation movements, both presently and historically, in addition to the sustained contributions of women. The need is for power and influence over their own lives, not for clearly defined sexual attributes in terms of white norms. It is time we stopped playing the nuclear-family game and left Blacks to determine their own familial and communal preferences.

The regret that females dominate Black life is not coming from Black communities, but from outsiders who analyze the community in terms of

---

[24] Grier and Cobbs: *Op. cit.,* p. 51.

their own values: This is not to deny the presence of male dominance in such organizations as the Black Panthers and other community groups who insist their women should wait until men are liberated, much to the chagrin of their women.[25]

We have no real justification, other than a desire for theoretical tidiness, to suppose that any "scientific" theories of Black family life emanating from white researchers and popularizers are in accordance with the realities of Black life. Indeed, considering our limited outlook and the often patchy character of our insights into other cultures, the troublesome contradictions that keep rising in such theories are more *likely* to approach objective reality than any neat conceptualizing on our part.

It is imperative, if we are to work successfully with inner-city youth, that we understand *their* view of family life, *their* aspirations for community, and desist from imposing our values on them. Outreach work will quickly deteriorate to "no-reach" if we do not seriously reconsider unquestioned assumptions about social values. Unless we work to alleviate the real and crushing forces which have destroyed Black life, the Black *individual* life, a stress on sociological and familial symptoms is short-sighted, cruel, and destined to fail. If the Black community desires and values the nuclear family, then we should do what we can to enable them to maintain this; if they do not, we should respect this decision equally.

Needs of Inner City Youth

We need to begin to ask, *and listen,* to what Black people want for themselves, their children, their communities, their employment, and so forth. Outreach can only be effective if we meet inner-city minority groups on their own terms, with a willingness to listen to their solutions to their problems–solutions they have been clearly articulating for years–while we deafly enter with yet another set of programs and policies to ease their difficulties as we perceive them.

White Man Listen! by Richard Wright[26] needs to be heeded by outreach workers, to make any outreach viable and meaningful for the worker and youth. Those who are oppressed, while often losing sight of the cause of their oppression, are usually the best able to offer remedies, and very succinct ones, for its resolution. The quagmire in the inner city is not how to solve the problems, but how to get the power and control to do so. We know what needs to be done. Why we are not doing it is a clue to our personal impotence and our racialist intransigency.

---

[25] Black Panther Sisters talk about Women's Liberation, *The Movement,* September, 1969; and somewhat peripheral but bearing on this discussion, Why Black women support the abortion struggle, *The Militant,* Oct. 29, 1971, p. 10; Dick Gregory: My answer to Genocide, *Ebony,* Dec. 1971; and Cellestine Ware: *Op. cit.*

[26] Richard Wright: *White Man Listen!* (New York, Doubleday, 1957).

We are too keenly concerned with how life in a Black community differs from ours–their entertainment, eating habits, family structure, etc.–and spend too little time on the outer forces which have caused their lives to be constricted and distorted. While it is certainly important to understand that most young persons, especially in the inner city, do not eat regularly or well, we should also realize that the informality of eating whenever one wishes is not an antisocial act which needs correcting, but that the absence of money for nutritional food, the inflated prices of most items in ghetto areas, and the poor cooking facilities in ghetto apartments are the issue. The problem is lack of nutritional, reasonably priced food, not how or when this food is ingested. We must move beyond such myopic examinations of the world of Black youth.

Another issue replete with misunderstandings and ignorance is *drugs*. There are no simple answers to drug abuse, and we should avoid an either/or approach to evaluating its pervasive influence in both the inner-city and middle-class urban communities:

> We must stop seeing the narcotics problem as one big issue, whose only alternatives are to give up and resign ourselves to absolute debauchery or to continue on the sterile road of blindly stiffening narcotics law penalties and increasing police budgets. . . . We must separate the questions of moral judgment from the questions of social control.[27]

We should seek as much information from disparate viewpoints on the drug problem so that we can make some judicious evaluations about its presence in the inner city. There is a great deal of controversy on drugs presently, and we should avail ourselves of this material to reach some decision about how recreation and outreach workers can relate to its use by inner-city youth.[28]

Drugs are a symptom, not the problem, and if we put all our energies into combating drug use and ignore the cause of their profusion, we will repeat the mistake of earlier campaigns against gang wars, where the reduction in gang rumbles seems to have led to urban riots, then drugs. It is not the function of the outreach worker to blindly attack drugs, but to understand why a youth is on them and to work to offer realistic outlets and alternatives to drugs. Interest in and dependency on drugs have a chance of diminishing if youth have more forceful and engaging outlets; we will not alleviate the symptoms which cause drug abuse by a repressive crackdown to rid the ghetto of them.

Drugs serve a twofold purpose, and that is why they are so embedded in ghetto life: they serve to passify an entire generation, the riot-prone youth,

---

[27] William P. Brown: Narcotics Squad: The Golden Arm of the Law, *The Nation*, Oct. 25, 1971, p. 395.

[28] See Frank Gannon: *Drugs: What they are, What they do* (New York, Warner Books, 1972) for a fairly straightforward introduction to the world of drugs.

and they give an ecstatic high (especially heroin) to youth living in urban ugliness and frustration. Even if we rooted out the need for pacifying Black youth, drugs would undoubtedly proliferate in the inner city. As we know, drugs are a major problem in the white society as well, most notably among Vietnam veterans.[29]

> American troops in Vietnam . . . have been infected in epidemic proportion; the generation gap seems widest over the issue of drug restrictions and there are estimates that up to 20 million of our youths have used at least marijuana, an activity which is labeled as criminal and vigorously prosecuted as such.[30]

Nationwide drug addiction is said to account for 50 to 80 per cent of all crime. "Many black militants say police and politicians are confused and that the real culprit is poverty."[31] Most slum kids attribute the narcotics problem to a genocidal conspiracy against Blacks by the white power structure, a desire to passify their political vivacity and aspirations. Conspiracy or not, the drug problem, as long as it was confined to the ghetto, was tolerated by white society. Now that it is endemic to the larger society as well, much attention and hysteria are directed toward it, causing many youth who could benefit from drug therapy or relief to be jailed for drug use or sale.

We cannot afford to make criminals of ten per cent of our population, the youth who use drugs. We might further ask whether drug addiction arrests are ever justified, especially in municipalities without effective drug therapy programs. "Obviously, if drug usage were made noncriminal, more addicts would be willing to accept guidance and enter such programs as methadone maintenance, which could reduce their need to commit crime."[32] This, of course, is speculative, but at least avoids the narrow-minded approach to drug abuse.

For these reasons, it is crucial that the outreach worker avoid moral judgments on drug use, based on scanty knowledge of the world of drugs, or romantic notions of underworld characters "making it" in opposition to the moral prescriptions of the larger society. The truth is probably in between these extremes and, in any event, reveals that there is no sound social or moral policy yet in existence for drugs and their potential abuse. The best approach for the outreach agency is to obtain material on drugs, especially the insights and experiences of former and present addicts, in an attempt to

---

[29] Samuel A. Simon: G. I. addicts: The catch in amnesty, *The Nation,* Oct. 4, 1971, pp. 308-309.

[30] William P. Brown: *Op. cit.,* p. 393.

[31] K. Scott Christianson: Albany's fix: The cops can't find the pusher, *The Nation,* Nov. 29, 1971, p. 563.

[32] Brown: *Op. cit.,* p. 396. Illegal methadone is now a problem as well. It is available on the streets at prices less than heroin. Some users feel a methadone high is better than heroin, but that it is actually more addictive! Others claim it leads to crimes of violence, rather than property thefts. *See* Police State politics, *The Nation,* Jan. 22, 1973, p. 98.

comprehend the notoriously controversial subject of drugs and inner-city youth.

When we offer *jobs and training* to inner-city youth, through agency or personal referrals, we have to be sure these jobs are not dead-end or in settings replete with subtle or overt racism. Outreach workers must create follow-up methods for the referrals they make. We must be interested in the youth we place, in jobs or training programs, encourage them in their goals, and check on the surroundings in which they work and how they feel treated. Too many social workers interview the boss and neglect to ask the youths what they feel about the job. Since many youth can make good money "hustling" on the streets, to offer them less money at jobs taking more of their time and in nongenial surroundings, is illusory. The alternatives have to be more alluring, and not merely options to what we view as "bad." If we believe their life as presently lived is not a good one, then we must lure them away by creating more meaningful and lucrative forms of survival and existence. Anything less is pussyfooting and incredibly short-sighted.

Many have questioned the significance of *protracted education* for Blacks and other minority groups. They argue that academic achievement is a less important source of social and economic mobility than currently believed, especially for Blacks. Until now, Blacks have received a substantially lower return on their educational investment than whites. "Negro and white men in the same line of work, with the same amount of formal schooling, with equal ability, from families of the same size and same socio-economic level, simply do not draw the same wages and salaries."[33]

Duncan has raised a major point: dropping out of school may be more rational for Black youth than we have been willing to accept. For instance, a recent survey indicated that Illinois in the past year trained enough teachers to fill all openings in the entire nation! This lack of foresight by educators was termed "immoral" by one legislator. If young middle-class whites are beginning to feel the pinch of employment and its seemingly dubious relation to education, the Black youth are simply ahead of them on that score. However, we should not use such reasoning as a rationale, from our point of view, to discourage Blacks from getting more education.

For college-educated Blacks this phenomenon seems to be diminishing, with Black graduates earning equal or more than white counterparts, but these are usually confined to Blacks with advanced degrees. The paucity of Blacks in higher-level positions, and the pressure on most organizations and institutions to implement affirmation action programs, have caused the demand for Black professionals to increase. The scarcity of Blacks with higher

---

[33] Otis Dudley Duncan: Inheritance of poverty or inheritance of race. In Daniel P. Moynihan, ed.: *On Understanding Poverty* (New York, Basic Books, 1969), as cited in Silberman: *Crisis in the Classroom, op. cit.,* p. 65.

degrees has made the salaries offered to them quite lucrative, at least for the time being. But for high school educated Blacks, and the dropout, the outlook is none too encouraging. There are too many of those kind of Blacks!

Another issue, not directly related to education, but critical in the hiring of young Blacks is their attitudes about reliability and punctuality on the job:

> Despite much popular rhetoric, there is little evidence that academic competence is critically important. . . . If you ask employers why they won't hire dropouts, for example, or why they promote certain kinds of people and not others, they seldom complain that dropouts can't read. Instead, they complain that dropouts don't get to work on time, can't be counted on to do a careful job, don't get along with others in the plant or office, can't be trusted to keep their hands out of the till, and so on.[34]

However, even when these middle-class attitudes are taken on by Blacks in an attempt to gain acceptance in the job market, employers fall back on the lack-of-education complaint. In too many instances, especially in recruiting for indigenous outreach workers, even where youth have "acceptable" attitudes toward work, the bogus of lack of sufficient education is raised. We cannot simply accept employers' vacillating evaluations of education as a healthy sign. As soon as middle-class attitudes are appropriated or simulated by Black youth seeking jobs, the need for more education will be raised once more, and so on. . . . It is interesting to see the effect of Blacks' attitudes about punctuality and productiveness being considered by white workers, who have begun to question the value of efficiency and production as previously immutable laws of their work world.[35]

The United States is becoming more and more of a credential-oriented society. When youth indigenous to a community are suggested for outreach or social work, too often and with the most ludicrous logic possible, social agencies have turned them down based on their lack of educational achievement. "These tendencies have been aggravated by the various campaigns to

---

[34] Christopher Jenks: A reappraisal of the most controversial educational document of our time, *New York Times Magazine,* August 10, 1969. The report Jenks is reviewing is James S. Coleman, *et al.: Equality of Educational Opportunity* (Washington, D. C., Government Printing Office, 1966). Jenks sums up in this reappraisal: "The net effect of the [Coleman] report's various errors was to *under-* estimate the importance of family background and *over-* estimate the importance of school in determining achievement." Cf. Equal Educational Opportunity, *Harvard Educational Review* (Boston, Harvard University Press, 1969); U. S. Civil Rights Commission: *Racial Isolation in the Public Schools* (Washington, D. C., Government Printing Office, 1967). See also, Arthur Pearl: *The Atrocity of Education* (St. Louis, New Critics Press, 1972).

[35] Bill Watson: Counter-planning on the shop floor, in *Radical America* (1971); describes a workers' struggle which focuses on making the working day more palatable and not simply negotiating a higher wage while maintaining strict loyalty to the cult of production. See also Wayne Oates: *Confessions of a Workaholic* (New York, World, 1971).

persuade youngsters to finish high school."[36] Such propaganda has persuaded both youth and employers that dropouts are indeed unemployable. "The fact that there seems to be little correlation between people's performance on the job and either the amount of education they have had or the marks they have received does not help the young man [or woman] who has been turned down, on the grounds of insufficient education, before he can demonstrate his competence or before he can develop that competence on the job itself."[37]

One of the prime difficulties an outreach worker faces is that many of the recreational facilities close early in the evening, about 9 or 10 p.m., when most youth are still on the streets looking for activities. If these facilities are not open, these youth will seek outlets in other less desirable forms. If pressure exists for community mental health, food, and drug facilities to be open on a 24-hour basis, then we can certainly argue for recreational facilities to be open for longer periods, especially into the late evening and even early morning hours. We have got to design our policies and program with the needs of youth in mind, not the reverse.

There are many voluntary agencies in the recreation field in most cities, agencies such as the Boy Scouts, Girl Scouts, YMCA, YWCA and other religious organizations which provide a relatively small proportion of their services to inner-city youth. Other organizations, like the Boys' Clubs, provide a greater proportion of their services to lower socioeconomic groups. However, these agencies are all limited in size and despite their fine efforts, the total impact is still negligible as far as the needs of the poor go. Also, few of these agencies are involved in outreach work, but confine their attempts to more narrowly defined recreational needs.

Some efforts have been made to expand the conception of recreation to include personal and vocational counseling to youth, adult literacy classes, health education for ADC mothers, leadership for predelinquent street groups, classes in job-related skills (such as reading, spelling, clerical skills, etc.), leadership to street gangs and groups, tutorial and cultural enrichment for children with school problems, casefinding and treatment, information and referral services for housing project residents, consumer education and credit union programs, group counseling with ADC mothers, day care, counseling of school dropouts, summer youth employment service, work with block clubs, health counseling, rehabilitative services for first offenders, and so forth.

Departments of parks and recreation should, in conjunction with boards of education, design a formal policy regarding the use of public schools and

---

[36] Silberman: *Crisis in the Classroom, op. cit.*, p. 68.

[37] Ivar Berg: *Education and Jobs: The Great Training Robbery* (New York, Frederick A. Praeger, 1970).

universities for recreation activities to enhance and expand both the use of such facilities as well as the concept of recreation. The department should have major responsibility for the provision of additional physical recreational facilities in low-income neighborhoods, including acquisition of more outdoor space for recreation. This is an especially acute problem in urban areas.

These additional physical recreation facilities should be close to low-income people, be oriented to the lifestyle, interest, needs and abilities of the poor, make use of staff who understand and can communicate with low-income people, aggressively reach out to the poor with face-to-face contacts to encourage participation, and eliminate restrictions regarding fees or religion which have previously limited recreation opportunities for the poor.

We must remember in our work that while the negative conditions of ghetto living far outweigh the positive, the ability to survive in this environment indicates incredibly positive strengths in the youth. This is an aspect that has received too little respect. "The fact that they have developed a culture that helps them survive, even though it is a culture alien to the middle class, shows strength. . . . We should stop trying to make the black a carbon copy of the middle-class white."[38] And we should start asking them what their recreation needs are, instead of telling them.

The Roving Leader Program

One program that attempts to determine what youth want in the way of recreation and other services is the Roving Leader Program. When talking about working with youth, the Roving Leader considers housing, drugs, health, education, and the other aspects of young people's lives we have discussed. Unless youth in the ghetto, both in family and community life, are able to reach their potential, then we as outreach specialists are not even touching the needs of these youngsters.

The Roving Leader is known by a variety of names: Streetclub Worker, Gang Leader, Detached Worker, Extension Worker, Outreach Worker, or Recreation Leader. There are probably other names, but for our purposes the Roving Leader is an outreach worker who goes out and works with young people and with adults in the community where they live. The Roving Leader is the individual (male and female) who walks the streets and alleys in urban, suburban, and rural communities, seeks out idle youth, and engages them in constructive activity. Initial contact and rapport are usually established through a game, sports, or an informal recreational activity.

Once the Roving Leader has gained the confidence of youth, he tries to motivate them to return to school–i.e., to a Manpower Development and Training Act (MDTA) occupational training program, or other vocational-technical or college program–or to get a job. In general the Roving Leader

---

[38] Dawson: *Op. cit.,* pp. 155-156.

seeks to channel the energies of youth into constructive community activities as a means of keeping them from getting into trouble with the law and helping them to develop into responsible citizens. The use of Roving Leaders is another proven way of combating and curbing delinquency in rural as well as urban areas.

The Roving Leader Program represents a somewhat new dimension in providing leadership for hard-to-reach, delinquency-prone youth that has proved highly successful. The Roving Leader usually spends weeks, sometimes months, establishing rapport with individuals and groups. He must start at the level of the group. This is not a short-term undertaking; he works with the youth for a long time–sometimes several years. The final test of the Roving Leader's success is when he is no longer needed. However, as Bordua warns:

> I have seen so-called detached workers glowing with gratification because they were able to gain rapport with 'tough' gangs when all they did was constantly warn the boys that if they did not straighten out they would get 'busted.' The rapport of the worker is purchased by increasing hostility toward the police.[39]

The Roving Leader is employed as a field representative to work with hard-to-reach groups and individuals who are known or anticipated as problems in the community. Hours are odd, in that the Leader continuously maintains contact by frequenting the youths' places of interest and observing their activities. The Leader stimulates these youth to participate in ongoing agency programs, such as making court appearances, school or employment referrals, family and individual counseling, and referrals to other supportive services. The Leader's role and function vis-a-vis the client is that of counselor, enabler, reinforcer, advisor, intermediator, and friend. The major emphasis is on friendship and flexibility.

There is no structured program the Roving Leader can follow in his work. He has no office in which to carry out a program, but seeks to make use of community facilities as the need arises. He must develop the creative ability to use whatever is available at any time. The Leader does not receive on-the-spot supervision as such; therefore, he must take the responsibility for making decisions and acting when necessary.

The Roving Leader Program, a problem-oriented service (as contrasted to an agency-oriented or professional, discipline-oriented service), can be viewed as a fundamentalist orientation to social organization for helping people. The basic idea is to reach out to youth in need by providing face-to-face leadership and at the same time attempting to overcome narrow specialization. The Roving Leader uses the simplest and most direct means possible to provide services of unlimited scope and high personal identity. Through

---

[39] Bordua: *Op. cit.*, p. 121.

the program, the Roving Leader is able to mobilize the community's faith in the potential for positive change in its most aggressive, deviant youth. It is necessary for a Roving Leader to have the ability to show kindness under trying circumstances. He must also have emotional stability and be a good listener.[40]

In other words, a Roving Leader doesn't sit and wait for youth to come to him, he goes where the action is. It might be a poolroom, a playground, a school, a movie theater, almost any place, on the streets; anywhere young people hang out, that is where the Roving Leader is. Stated simply, the street is his place of business, his "turf," which is the prime distinction between outreach work and other tasks in the social and human services.

Too often the function of the Roving Leader is considered an *ad hoc* profession. There are those who feel one has to be a natural leader to work effectively with youth. Although one should be people-oriented, sympathetic, sensitive, and aware, working with youth can also be straightforward as one goes about relating to people and dealing with problems in neglected areas. These communities are neglected because they are the areas where the wheels aren't squeaking, which haven't gotten oil for a long time, and now, as Malcolm X predicted: "The chickens are coming home to roost," and society has to pay its dues for ignoring such communities for so long.

There is great concern with inner-city communities by the outer city; yet, we hear criticism about the Roving Leader's function of keeping the lid on the inner city; this is simply not true. We are not for keeping the lid on the city. Keeping things cool is not what the Roving Leader Program should be about. The Leader must be concerned with the failures of all other social institutions which affect ghetto youth. If these institutions were providing effective services, there would be no real need for a Roving Leader Program. Education, recreation, employment, health, all have clearly failed to meet the needs of many inner-city youth. If a Roving Leader is to be effective in a community, his or her prime aim is ultimately to make himself or herself superfluous. That is, Roving Leaders should not encourage dependency if youth continue to look to them for leadership or guidance. That most decidedly is not their function; the goal is to have youngsters become self-sufficient.

The role of advocacy for youth is an extremely important part of the Roving Leader concept. The aim is also to encourage youth to become advocates for themselves. Unfortunately, there are many Roving Leaders who have held onto kids–they do not seem to want to let go. If leaders are doing that, they are not really helping these kids. Not that Roving Leaders should

---

[40] U. S. Department of Health, Education, and Welfare: *The Roving Recreation Leader Training Guide: An Inservice Training Source for Inner-City Youth Services Personnel* (Washington, D. C., Government Printing Office, 1971).

avoid youngsters if they need to talk, or seek guidance, but if there is a dependency for a long time, something is wrong. The Roving Leader must be able to wean youngsters, to have them stand alone and become their own advocates.

It is extremely important if you are going to be a proponent of advocacy, that the employing agency clearly understand your position. If they do not really grasp this, there will probably be a lot of static. For example, one youth worker worked in a community which had a serious sanitation problem. This worker, along with many community residents, piled garbage in the middle of the street to emphasize the lack of adequate sanitation service. There was a great commotion, but the sanitation department came and picked up the garbage.

This worker could successfully function in any agency with administrative support of the advocacy concept. Yet even with administrative support, the Roving Leader has to use a great deal of discretion to know when to move. For example, you don't take a frontal position–you are not the one who carries the flag and says "Charge!" But for organizing, helping residents understand the issues, and for identifying issues they might support, the Roving Leader is a key participant. The Roving Leader has to be clearly identified as part of the community.

Of course, we all know Roving Leaders work for an agency, that they are paid employees. We also know that anyone associated with the "establishment" is basically suspect. So what does a Roving Leader depend on? As an individual, he has to really emphasize face-to-face relationships. As a Roving Leader, he is not apocalyptic, but attempts to meet youth and to talk with them about their needs and interests. No high pressure–a Roving Leader is not selling anything. His or her success will not come from sympathetic statements about the hardship of ghetto life; that's too shallow. It is going to come from a demonstration of a sincere interest and concern about the needs of ghetto residents *and* an ability to help.

Very often we hear residents in the inner city complain about social services: they want a "piece of the action," not charity. If you are going to be an effective Roving Leader, you must know what social resources will ensure that those you serve get maximum use of them. It is extremely important for the Roving Leader to have an effective relationship with the social structure. This does not mean that he or she is caught up in the establishment, or that they have sold out. Roving Leaders need to have a relationship, for example, with schools, courts, and police. We mention these three specifically because most youth are seriously alienated from them; there are times when these relationships cause Roving Leaders to have problems with youth. Young people accuse them of betrayal because a Leader was seen at the police station, or in school talking with the principal. The youths do not seem to care that you may be establishing a foothold for them with these institutions. They simply wonder: "What's that cat doing–he's selling out, or spilling what's happenin' on the street involving us. . . ."

In conflicts like these, the relationship the Roving Leader has previously established with youth is crucial. If the relationship is sound, the Roving Leader should be able to handle such objections. Youth must understand that, for a Roving Leader to be effective, he or she must establish and maintain rapport with the above named and other institutions. It is hoped that through advocacy the more onerous aspects of these (establishment) institutions can eventually be eliminated or changed.

Advocacy can be on a city-government level or a local level. For instance, a roving leader may encounter a youngster having a problem with school. He visits the principal and counselor about getting this youngster back in school, and in so doing he is performing an advocacy role in the local school. Another example of advocacy at the community level is when a youngster has a problem with his employer and has been fired: the Roving Leader would visit the employer in an attempt to resolve the problem.

How can one be an advocate at the city-government level? In a city agency there are usually commissioners. The Leader can, for example, meet the commissioner in charge of manpower responsible for youth jobs. They discuss youngsters who need help and try to put them in touch with someone who can offer them what they need–counseling, job placement, etc. It is the same for the Board of Education, meeting with the board president or the superintendent of schools. Perhaps the Roving Leader wants to use certain facilities or get on the board. Such appointments are valuable because Roving Leaders can make a tremendous contribution. The youngsters he works with are in that school system, and most school boards face potentially explosive situations. How can a Leader ensure that the interests and objectives of the youngsters are considered?

This representation of students can be best achieved if the Roving Leader can ease the communications between youth and the school administration in high schools and junior high. The function of the Roving Leader is not to be monitors or guards in the schools; their role is not to pacify the students, but primarily to establish communication with the youngsters, and between administration and students. Therefore, when the Leader talks with the school administration, he or she will relate the students' viewpoint in a way that the administration can understand and presumably accept. The Roving Leader seeks to bring the parties together, to have these students handle their own negotiations once the initial mediation is handled for them.

When a child fails in school either academically or socially, a cycle of failure is often initiated. Schools face a problem in accounting for their students. There are some young people who come in the morning, check into home room, but never attend classes. These might be called the professional hallwalkers. Sometimes the schools believe they have outsiders with so many kids in the halls.

The Roving Leader is in competition with addicts, hustlers, pimps and shoplifters for the admiration and attention of youth. These people are in the community, not only talking about how to make quick money, but have a big car, sharp clothes, money in their pocket, a 50-cent loan for kids that need it; this is a reality. And here comes the Roving Leader on a government salary, who can't give a dime. The hustler offers a system where one doesn't take a civil service exam, doesn't have a supervisor, no high school diploma, and it all leads to money. The hustlers talk about jobs as a numbers runner, no references needed, no interviews, no exams, and the job is available immediately with quick cash. Therefore, if a young person has to choose between the red tape of an establishment job and this, you can easily guess which is chosen. These are real choices young people face, and we need to be aware of them.

Of course, there are problems encountered in Roving Leaders acting as advocates for youth; for some reason advocacy is often narrowly construed as organizing demonstrations and pickets. However, there are many ways to be an advocate for youth. Consider advocacy at the federal level. In Washington, D. C., there are a multitude of youth programs in various agencies, without any one agency overseeing all activities. Although everyone is aware of the tremendous problems and interests of young people, there is no Cabinet position or department which is really designed to deal with the total concerns of youth.

It is also extremely important that Roving Leaders know the community in which they work. He or she should be aware that each community they work in is different, even though the social service resources remain fairly static. Each community has a different power structure–politics with a big as well as small "p." There are various kinds of relationships a Roving Leader has to be aware of, such as the pecking order, the various strata, and the "power brokers."

Another important factor is the age of the youth one works with. In New York City, we are talking about youth up to 23 years of age; they don't cut loose at sixteen, seventeen or eighteen in New York City. Here we are talking about men and women. For example, leaders of clubs or gangs are often 22 or 23. So you are not dealing with a fifteen or sixteen year old, but someone who has some maturity, leadership ability, and time. If a youth can survive in that street corner world, and come out of it and be a leader, he or she must have valuable skills. The issue becomes how can Roving Leaders direct those skills so the youth can help himself and those in his community? Thus, as Roving Leaders, we must involve such youngsters in whatever decision-making and problem-solving we do.

The older concept of a Youth Council, where young people make decisions about *what* they want to do, *how* they want to do it, and *when* they want to do it, is still valuable. Too often we exclude youth from having a say in program planning, about who the staff is going to be, or what activities are to occur during the next year. Yet, the whole direction, focus, and movement of the outreach program must come from those young people, because it is *their* program. And if they really believe it is theirs, they will make a commitment and prove more reliable and dependable than adults. This is because they don't have as many hidden "agendas" as adults. If they disagree, they tell you, and won't falsely agree as many adults do only to ignore the issue later.

It is not enough simply to tell young people what they should do, one has to offer ideas and suggestions for dealing with a variety of situations so they can realize there are other ways of solving problems beyond conflict or confrontation. Many youths an outreach worker meets do not necessarily accept or reject services from established institutions. They do not even in many cases attend school, but simply have a knack for getting into trouble. These young people often lack positive leadership, or adequate attention, and alternatives for them to channel their energies elsewhere are not likely.

The Roving Leader has to devote a great deal of attention and time to young people, to be not only accessible and available emotionally and physically, but to be one who really *listens* when these youths speak; a person who understands what they say, and who doesn't simply have a lot of words bouncing off his head. Realistically, you visualize this person as not restricted to an office; his office is his hip pocket. Traditional youth and social workers file telephone messages on their desk, but the Roving Leader stacks them in his head, or rolls the excess messages up and throws them away, because he knows who he has to see and who is looking for him. Thus, what we are talking about is a professional, not necessarily one with college degrees, but a professional's professional. A real professional is one who gets the job done. Unfortunately, many of us fall into another category–pseudo-professional with a graduate or undergraduate college degree, but who never get beyond the rhetoric for helping people. Roving Leaders must not be pseudo-professionals, but professionals, with or without a college degree. This can't be stressed enough.

It is more important what one *does,* not what credentials one has. The Roving Leader needs to move around the community and be out there and involved. He is often trying to convince individuals or business groups with money to give some of it to provide experiences to enrich the lives of young people. One function of the job is getting people to understand youth.

Too often we confine outreach work to an urban ghetto setting. But there are many problems in suburbs among kids with money, and many suburban areas have Roving Leaders or detached workers and need more. You find them working with youths from families who have substantial incomes and access to many of life's opportunities and amenities.[41] The Roving Leader functions as someone who is available to them, who can talk with them, and who often is able to intercede with parents and other authority figures.

In helping youth, the outreach worker has to deal with other professionals and has to risk not being a nice or well-liked person. Many times our colleagues are sitting behind a desk, representing services, and talking a lot of meaningless rhetoric. Yet a Roving Leader has to call a spade a spade. At the same time, the Roving Leader has to see that services are delivered, not only creating new services which are needed, but also assuring that existing services achieve what they are supposed to.

Outreach services should be viewed not only as individual services but group services as well. The services are more or less group- and individual-centered, rather than activity-centered, with recreation as a lure. A lot of kids like to hang around as spectators even if they are not participating in an activity. A professional can see that sitting around not participating is an activity in itself, which a lot of young people do. There is no need in telling them, as many of our all-American "ideal" professionals do, that nonparticipants should become involved in an activity. The Roving Leader should be intelligent enough to see that they are already involved in an activity which makes sense to them. It might be good for the Roving Leader to sit on the ground with them and start talking about whatever subject may come up. As a professional, the concept of a conversation without an appointment may be a new experience. As a Roving Leader your function might be conversation or observation. It might also mean simply being around, but if you are not sensitive to what you say or do, the young people might be turned off. Keep in mind you are not there for yourself, you are there for them.

Many times while sitting with youth, something might occur which gives the Roving Leader an opening to a relationship: it may simply be the opportunity to say at a game, "Did you see that shot?" The Roving Leader has got to determine what point might be an opener into the group. Regardless what point it may be, the leader should avoid using their slang. Be yourself. On the other hand, there is no need in saying to the youths, "I feel you have a problem." You can imagine the response. What a Roving Leader really needs is to talk about anything to get a conversation started with the youths.

Following are specific situations a Roving Leader may encounter. A young man, who has a young wife or pregnant girl friend, is angry because she is seeing another guy. He confronts the Roving Leader: "Man I'm going

---

[41] See Harrison Salisbury: *The Shook-up Generation* (New York, Harper & Row, 1958).

to kill that girl." At such a point, the Roving Leader can use the unborn child as an "innocent victim," and tell the guy the child doesn't have anything to do with it. "Why do you want to do it? Don't do it." At the same time, the Leader must recognize there is a problem. What he or she has to do is buy some time. It would be foolish to let the issue of adultery or unfaithfulness surface for that is too complicated to resolve; really, it is not an issue of morals.

At this point, the Leader may have to push to get a delayed action to prevent this particular youth from physically harming the girl. A Leader is dealing with blame and must remember that such blame has no scientific basis nor does it resolve problems. So to prevent some kind of scuffle, the Leader might say: "Hey, look, if I have to fight you physically to stop you from doing that and sacrificing my life and our friendship, I might just do that." Physical confrontation is an issue which always concerns humans. To threaten physical confrontation is dangerous, but as an alternative to *real* physical action, it's better. At this point, the youth might respond, "I probably can whip you," and the Leader: "Could be, you probably can, but I will just lay myself out there. You'll just have to whip me."

Such a confrontation has given the youth something else to deal with. The fact is, you are his friend, he knows that. He also knows he's hurt and wrong too. Now he has to deal with the fact that the Roving Leader is sacrificing himself for him, and this may leave him with no one else to turn to if he eliminates the Roving Leader. There is no use in saying "I feel you're upset," or "Let's sit down." That will lead nowhere.

The outreach worker has to understand that some Black staff will sell Black youth down the river. He also knows that some Black staff talk about Black Power but could really care less about it. You also have Black staff who secretly question the presence of whites in ghetto areas. You'll also have white staff who supervise Blacks and because of deep-seated prejudices try to mark this with liberal-white rhetoric. Roving Leaders have got to stay at the thinking level. Everybody's got their game going. What the Leader has to do is understand this. He or she must be able to see what it is worth, to work with all segments, and be emotionally stable. The Leader must not crack, he is not permitted a nervous breakdown! When a youth worker goes to an analyst, it is for the benefit of those he works with, not himself.

Some Concluding Thoughts

Basically, outreach work has three phases: making contact, rendering services, and terminating those services. It is most important for these phases that the Roving Leader help youth use community resources. This does not mean wasting time complaining about what is not available, but to use services which are available. Young people know your main function is to help them stabilize themselves. A significant role a Leader plays is that of a stable adult who remains basically the same over time. As you know, parents play games with their own children. When they don't feel like being bothered with their children, they lie instead of admitting they are busy, they duck issues and leave young people suspended. This phenomenon has nothing to do with economic or social status, but has more to do with American life. We lie at home, at work, to our friends, and in the community. All of this presents a disconcerting lack of trust and continuity in our lives, especially for young people.

In seeking success with inner-city youth, a Roving Leader must comprehend all the problems of these youth, most especially their class values and cultural aspects as discussed earlier. The role and function of an outreach worker is meaningless without an ongoing, dynamic perspective of the needs and reality of youth. This chapter serves as a basis for such a perspective, but outreach workers should also create their own perspective based on personal experience and insights in working with disadvantaged youth.

CHAPTER REFERENCES AND SELECTED READINGS

Ackerley, Ethel G., and Fliegel, Beverly R.: A social work approach to street-corner girls, *Social Work,* Vol. 5, no. 4, 1960.

Bernstein, Saul: *Youth on the Streets.* New York, Association Press, 1964.

Brager, George: The indigenous worker: A new approach to the Social Work technician, *Social Work,* Vol. 5, no. 2, 1965.

Cartwright, Desmond S., and Ronnal, Lee L.: Consulting with detached workers. Boulder, Colo., University of Colorado, undated memo.

Conant, James B.: *Slums and Suburbs,* New York, New American Library, 1961.

Neighborhood Gangs: A Case Book for Youth Workers. New York, National Federation of Settlements and Neighborhood Centers, 1967.

Nesbitt, J. A.; Brown, Paul; and Murphy, James: *Recreation and Leisure Service for the Disadvantaged,* Philadelphia, Lea Febiger, 1970.

Pearl, A.: Youth in lower class settings. *In* Glazer and Creedon (Eds.): *Poverty and Children: Some Sociological and Psychological Perspectives.* Chicago, Rand-McNally and Co., 1968.

Schorr, A. L.: *Poor Kids: A Report on Children in Poverty.* New York, Basic Books, 1966.

CHAPTER IV

PROGRAM PLANNING

"My Bag of Goodies"

JOSEPH J. BANNON

IN CONSIDERING program planning in outreach, one needs to answer two questions: How does the Roving Leader deliver services, and which ones does he deliver? First, rapport must be established between the Roving Leader and any youth he or she seeks to help before services can be successfully offered; second, effective leisure and related services must be carefully and systematically planned for youth. That is, the Leader has to develop a "bag" or mix of services, and what is included must be stimulating, conducive to ongoing relationships, and helpful in opening up meaningful work and leisure activities for youth.

Developing a "bag of goodies" is not easy, but comes from a combination of training and experience, a blending of tried and proven activities, with new, different, and somewhat risky programs. A Roving Leader does not automatically attract inner-city youths eager for services. Quite the contrary; most residents of inner cities are minorities denied the social amenities that most recreation professionals regard as prime needs. In some cases, inner-city dwellers may not even be familiar with the many services available to them.

In working in urban slums, a Leader might expect the following setting:

> In the alley it's mostly dark, even if the sun is out. But if you look around, you can find things. I know how to get into every building, except that it's like night once you're inside them, because they don't have lights. So, I stay here. You're better off. It's no good on the street. You can get hurt all the time, one way or the other. And in buildings, like I told you, it's bad in them, too. But here it's o.k. You can find your own corner, and if someone tries to move in you fight him off. We meet here all the time, and figure out what we'll do next. It might be a game, or over for some pool, or a coke or something. You need to have a place to start out from and that's like it is in the alley; you can always know your buddy will be there, provided it's the right time. So you go there, and you're on your way, man.[1]

---

[1] Robert Coles: Like it is in the alley. In Martin Meyerson, ed.: *The Conscience of a City* (New York, G. Braziller, 1970), pp. 243-58. Reprinted by the U. S. Department of Health, Education, and Welfare, Social and Rehabilitation Service, Children's Bureau, with permission from *Daedalus* (Journal of the American Academy of Arts and Sciences), Fall 1968.

The Roving Leader might well ask, "How am I going to deal with a person in a setting like that?" To deal with it, one has to have the courage to proceed, but must proceed in the proper way. Therefore, before discussing specific programs and services for youth, it is important to have some ideas on how to attract such youth in the first place.

A basic aim in devising programs for youth is to understand the youth we seek to serve, clarify the values and standards we feel they should consider (presumably in lieu of more unsatisfactory values and standards they presently hold), as well as to help them change their own harmful behavior. The aim of such programs is to aid youths become independent of adults as well as to become independent adults themselves. However, the aim is *not* to have youth replicate a middle-class lifestyle, no matter how efficacious we judge such living. If inner-city youth are alienated from middle-class values, we have to respect and comprehend their reasons. We should not patronize them with "revolutionary" jargon on the one hand, and implied suggestions for behavior modification on the other. It is very difficult in outreach, or any social work for that matter, to be clear about what we really expect of youth. Yet some hard thinking has to precede fieldwork. If not, Roving Leaders will become embroiled in the snares of "welfare colonialism," an attitude that has undercut the effectiveness of most human services to the inner city.

Establishing Rapport With Youth

Disadvantaged youth won't run up to a Roving Leader to shake hands at their first meeting. Rapport is something to be *earned* before any service can be delivered. The youths must relate to the Leader as one of their own; they must readily identify with him. Of course, this is easier when a Leader has grown up in the community or has lived there for several years. An outsider may not be aware of the real problems of a neighborhood, especially as perceived by youth. The Leader has to meet youth on their own terms and deal with their perceptions of reality and conflict. He should not impose his perceptions of the "real world" lightly, nor assume without reflection that his perceptions are better or more accurate. His role is not to "cool" youth off in some sociological vacuum, but to understand the world of inner-city youth and the internal and external forces which form that world.

In practical terms, verbal or body-language cues can be useful in initial dealings with young people. Julius Fast discusses many body-language cues he feels are relevant for communication.[2] Analysis of body-language cues has been limited, especially for disadvantaged groups in their own environment. However, communication using verbal and body language are vital to achieving rapport with youth. The Leader has to understand the language of a neighborhood, as this can vary from city to city, and even among neigh-

---

[2] Julius Fast: *Body Language.* (New York, M. Evans and Co., 1970).

borhoods. For example, inner-city Blacks of Detroit may have a different vocabulary than those of New Orleans. The Leader would do well to differentiate the basic terms indigenous to a particular area.

Equally important to skill with slang and body language, is a Leader's ability to remain relaxed and confident in conversations with youth. If a youth feels the Leader is afraid, even if this feeling is sensed only sporadically, rapport can be seriously jeopardized. A Roving Leader who is insecure, insincere, defensive, or who gets angry when confronted with challenging talk or viewpoints, should not be a Roving Leader. Roving Leaders have to "cool it"; they do not cool the kids, nor get upset by youth who are quite different from themselves. They must understand their bag of goodies can't be forced on the youth they confront. If it's forced, it's lost–it's that simple.

Suggested Training Tools

Appendices B, C, D, and E in this book are training instruments used with Roving Leaders in preparing and afterward in measuring the various skills and aptitudes considered vital for successful outreach work. These can be quite useful in predicting and evaluating various skills essential for working with youths and adults in outreach programs. "The Self-Assessment Inventory" (Appendix E), designed to determine whether Roving Leaders perceive themselves as effective, deals with three roles the Roving Leader is expected to perform: (1) planning and implementing meaningful activities, and generating interest and participation; (2) dealing with a variety of problems that might develop in the course of a group's functioning; and (3) handling various situations that challenge a Leader's role in the group.

The "General Information Test" (Appendix D), designed to test a Roving Leader's overall knowledge of outreach, includes the following aspects: history and background of the Roving Leader program; philosophy and function of the Roving Leader; the Roving Leader and the community; the Roving Leader's comprehension of the inner city; the Roving Leader and group dynamics; and the Roving Leader in the field. The "Situation-Problem Exercise" (Appendix C), designed to test whether Roving Leaders can make sound judgments on problems they are likely to encounter, includes eleven typical situations or case problems a Roving Leader might meet. These cases were developed from hundreds of actual case studies reported by Roving Leaders in urban areas. The Leader has to make two judgments based on information given in each case–*What do you do?* and *What do you want the individual or group in each situation to do?*

Finally the "Roving Recreation Leader's Rating Scale" (Appendix B), based on the Kammeyer Community Leader's Rating Scale, posits eleven qualities considered indicative of successful Roving Leader behavior, to be used by a supervisor to rate Leaders: (1) professional attitude and awareness of recreation's value for the participant; (2) understanding of recreational skills and knowledge; (3) ability to gain confidence and respect of participants and associates; (4) ability to get along with people and draw them into activity; (5) understanding and sensitivity to group needs; (6) versatility of interest and activities ("uses a broad activity program"); (7) ability to adjust to situations ("resourceful"); (8) ability to organize and plan recreation programs; (9) initiative and dependability in conducting program; (10) intelligence and ability to communicate ideas; and (11) maturity of judgment ("uses common sense").

Resourcefulness

The Roving Leader needs to keenly and accurately anticipate changing emphases and situations rather than merely react to them. An important task during initial contact with youth is to determine what *they* feel their major problems are. To be able to offer worthwhile leisure or work activities to youth, a Leader must first assess their overall life situation. For instance, if a young person is hungry, he or she may not be too keen on recreation programs; they want to eat.

Quite often there are protracted problems that can create mental or physical blocks to a youth's interest in recreation or park programs. The youth who doesn't have a place to sleep might relish a bed and six hours' sleep rather than a competitive sport. Another youth, preoccupied with a relative in jail, could probably care less if the roller rink were open. A youth addicted to drugs has this need as a major priority. Seemingly potential users of recreation may simply not be in the mood for them. Other priorities are more important and require immediate attention. The Roving Leader must be aware of such priorities and demands.

The Roving Leader is more than a recreation leader; he or she has to be a human services worker helping youth to solve their primary problems. If a youth is hungry, the Roving Leader could buy him a meal every day. But this wouldn't be a good or lasting solution, since the Leader has many youngsters to work with and his salary would not permit such expenditures. It is also not a good solution because it puts off understanding why this kid is hungry in the first place. There is something grand about feeding a hungry person, but if this is not accompanied by some plan for comprehending or eliminating the basis for hunger, it is short-sighted and somewhat suspect. It's like putting your finger in the dike and ignoring the flood around you. A more immediate and practical answer might be to find the youth a job, or enroll him or her in a work-study program where they can have some money of their own.

Thus, one component of a Leader's bag is *a resource list of potential employers*. The Leader may become a referrer, broker, or linker of services–

and hopefully an "in-person referrer" who personally accompanies youth to potential employers. There are a great many agencies a youth may be referred to for helpful services. However, referrals don't accomplish much, unless contact is made, follow-up assured, and effective services received and sustained.

Assuming the Leader has met the more pressing problem(s) head on, he should then observe whether change or conflict is the result. Conflict may occur from attempts to solve an original problem, or because a greater problem has come to light of which the original problem was merely symptomatic. For instance, hunger is both a problem and a symptom of a larger problem, and must be viewed as such. As a matter of fact,

> The problem solver often deals quite sincerely, innocently, and conscientiously with problem symptoms and not with *the real problem*. In listening to discussions by persons trying to solve a particular problem, much of the dialogue and suggestions deals frequently with related incidents or peripheral concerns; the discussion never really focuses on the crux or real problem. We talk around the problem, not because of a reluctance or hesitation to state it, but simply because we do not *know* what the real problem is . . . we spend most of our efforts in describing, isolating and classifying symptoms. And we usually feel that we are accomplishing something.[3]

The ultimate goal is to effect change so that new systems can be created to provide strategic opportunities for those in need and eliminate interim tactical solutions to pervasive social problems. With determination *and* a realistic framework, the Leader may then consider the next step–planning leisure services for youth.

Developing Youth Programs

Recreation can be defined as a leisure activity a person participates in because of his own desire and because of the enjoyment he derives from it. Recreation activities are wide and varied. As we noted earlier in this volume (Chapter I), public recreational programs for a long time were primarily playground and swimming oriented. Today, however, activities vary from preschool activities to socials, from sports and games to arts and crafts, from creative dramatics to opera, from day camps to resident camps, from sports to ski jumping.

One of the major problems in referring inner-city youths to organized recreation is that the youth may be familiar with only a few activities. An outreach programmer in East St. Louis, Illinois, was asked to initiate a summer recreation program in a neighborhood where 2,000 Blacks resided. He came with his bag of goodies and attempted to introduce twenty-five programs. He found, to his surprise, that the youngsters wanted to participate

---

[3] Joseph J. Bannon: *Problem Solving in Recreation and Parks* (Englewood Cliffs, N. J., Prentice-Hall, Inc., 1972), p. 56.

in only three activities–basketball, baseball, and roller skating. They were either unfamiliar with or disinterested in the other twenty-two.

When a Roving Leader offers youth a recreation activity, it is important that it be a familiar activity and one the youth most likely enjoyed in the past, or else that an approach be made for the youth to feel comfortable with a "new" activity. After participating in an activity–whether new or familiar–that the youth enjoys, it is probable that his relationship with the Leader will be reinforced.

An inability to comfortably handle new social situations, or even new recreation programs, is a source of conflict for many young people–and adults as well. Therefore, any program offered should have a sound purpose and meaning and should be presented in a context that makes sense. It should not be a stop-gap measure or an attempt to "cool it." It has to be more than that, since young people have a keen eye for adult hypocrisy and are sure to deride the latest offering if we are speaking out of both sides of our mouth. These young people are wise to any attempts to impede some action they are undertaking, or to divert their energies from activities they perceive as crucial.

It is possible for the Roving Leader to gradually introduce young people to new activities. First off, they will probably enjoy cooling off in a swimming pool, but if asked to join a neighborhood swimming team they might shy away. As one youth said, "How can we be expected to be competitive swimmers when the only experience we had was jumping into the Mississippi!" There are many recreation agencies that offer activities which inexperienced youth might enjoy. Before simply suggesting such services, however, it is important that the Roving Leader understand the make-up of these agencies and the ways to relate to them.

Using Community Recreational Activities

In most cities, recreation has been offered by public agencies for many decades, with the number of facilities, parks and programs varying among cities. More often than not, facilities and programs are less than what is really needed or requested by city residents. City budget priorities quite often require that police and fire protection, street construction and maintenance, water, sewer, garbage, and other services rank higher than recreation. The amount of money available for leisure activities may be well below what is actually needed. City activities are, for the most part, supported by real property taxes. However, there is an increasing trend to charge fees for many of the newer programs.

While the tendency to charge a fee is increasing, one must be careful about assuming that this is a satisfactory solution to a lack of funds. Since, for the most part, we are concentrating on services for inner-city youth, most of whom will not have much money, we may be short-sighted in charging for activities we wish to attract them to. Some recreation centers in poverty areas have installed turnstiles, charging youth a dime to enter, which permits the kids to use all the center activities for one fee. A dime is not much to most inner-city kids, but charging a quarter for the swimming pool, another fee for the basketball court or roller rink, certainly is. Although a dime might not appear much to the center either, the turnstile does eliminate the need for any staff members to collect fees–a saving in itself.

In addition to such immediate policies, recreation administrators have to seek other sources of funds on an ongoing basis. If the property taxes in the inner city are unable to sustain adequate recreation services for youth, or if recreation receives a low priority in a city budget, there is no sense in having the people of a poor community, especially parents and young adults, carry the burden for a city's inability to offer crucially needed municipal services. An interim solution can be to charge a minimal fee, reduce the number of staff involved in collecting such fees, and allow youngsters inexpensive access to recreation activities. But a longer-term solution must be sought as well; otherwise, the dime fee will be merely perfunctory and will not even offset minimal costs to the center.

One solution is to establish neighborhood advisory councils to offer suggestions for the operation and policies of recreation centers. One of the goals of the Roving Leader might be to engage the parents of inner-city youth, or the youths themselves, in advisory committee work. A large number of centers are experiencing limited use, accompanied by vandalism. Some cities have considerably reduced these problems by involving residents in planning and by providing activities and facilities the people themselves recommend. The most dynamic agencies have even been willing to involve neighborhood councils in making recommendations about who should be hired to administer or direct recreation center programs.

Again, as with fees, one must avoid optimism about solutions such as advisory councils. The impetus for encouraging or requiring citizen involvement came from the War on Poverty, and for the most part, has been a dismal failure as has the War on Poverty itself. While it is not the purpose of this chapter to speculate on why these failed, we do have to recognize that such practical solutions often operate better in theory than in fact.

In order for parents to have some real say in the recreation offered their children, those involved in administering and allocating funds for recreation have to give up some power to parents–this is not likely. On the other hand, parents have to trust those in control to yield some power to them without strings attached. Again, not likely. As Moynihan shows, the failure of maximum feasible participation as a philosophy of citizen participation was that it sought both power and funds from the same source; that is, it expected local and federal government to yield some of its decision-making and policy-making powers to citizens, as well as finance the apparatus developed for citizens to wield such power.[4] It is a rare policymaking unit that would willingly pay for its own diminishment.

In any event, cities usually have a recreation and parks commission appointed by the mayor who sets the policies and rules for governing recreation and parks functions within city limits. All this is far removed from the day-to-day or night-to-night work of a Roving Leader. For the most part, involvement of the Roving Leader with the city recreation program will be at the neighborhood center. A contact may be made with the center director or a program supervisor. Quite often, there will be two key people at the neighborhood center—a man and a woman, each responsible for special activities for their sex.

Traditionally, centers have been open during the week for regular working hours and for limited hours on week-ends. Progressive city centers are opening their doors later. Some are even remaining open all night to accommodate those young people who work during the day and who desire leisure activities during night hours.

Usually the number of Leaders or supervisors at a neighborhood center will be insufficient to give personal attention to each program participant. The Roving Leader should keep this in mind. His job is more than simply taking a youth to the door of the center, or throwing a ball around with him. The Leader must be ready to follow up after the youth begins a programmed activity.

Nonprofit agencies doing a good job of relating to youth are the Y.M.C.A., the Y.W.C.A., the Boys' Club, the Girls' Club, and the Salvation Army. All of these organizations are on a membership basis with referral, for the most part very personal. These agencies survive from donations made by business, industry, and United-Way type campaigns. Budgets may suffer large cutbacks if the annual United Fund drive is not successful. These organizations usually serve a number of neighborhoods or regions in a city. As easy access to these facilities can be a problem, transportation might be a major job for the Roving Leader.

The Roving Leader must identify *all* recreation agencies that have potential value. These include commercial recreation establishments as well. The Leader must not only identify the resources, but must establish a resource book which lists the location of each agency, the agency supervisor, its leaders, their telephone numbers (work and home), a schedule of activities, and when they are offered by the respective agencies. Policies concerning fees and charges should also be part of this resource packet.

---

[4] Daniel P. Moynihan: *Maximum Feasible Misunderstanding: Community Action in the War on Poverty* (New York, The Free Press, 1969).

Attempting to fill a gap between public agencies, non-profit agencies, or commercial enterprises are federal programs which operate on short-term money that may not be available over time. Usually the federally sponsored centers include family services, health services, legal aid, job referral services, food services, and might also include recreation. Again, as in city budgets, federal recreation funds usually receive low priority, or are funded for one-time programs only. In the opinion of most program supervisors, funds have been inadequate. What is really needed are parks, facilities, and programs that offer ongoing services.

As one reviews the President's budget message for fiscal 1974, it appears that even stop-gap federal programs will be severely circumscribed. As of July 1973, we find such program casualties as "housing subsidies for lower-income families, rural electrification, public service employment, special programs in mental health, urban renewal, model cities, manpower training, some aids for education, support for libraries, student loans, improvements and extensions in the national parks, research and development on mass transportation, and training programs in medical and biological research."[5] In essence, the Nixon administration seeks to win the War on Poverty by a "cease fire." Although many of these programs have failed, the problems to which they were addressed remain as urgent as before. It is not likely that recreation, often considered a mere luxury, will fare any better; no doubt it will fare worse.

The crux of the difficulty is that too many innovative programs are supported by one-term grants, thus limiting the likelihood of their being sustained, even if they are successful. It is preferred, though this is not always possible, that programs be ongoing rather than sporadic. One of the bad effects of the almost-defunct War on Poverty was creation of a plethora of one-time programs and projects. While this profusion of social energy in the inner cities was exciting and long overdue, it left strong uncertainty about new programs–they are usually short-lived, whether effective or not, because OEO and comparable foundation grants were intended as seed money, not as sustained sources. Here is a good example of where innovation can breed uncertainty and apathy.

Urban recreation programming is crucially bound up in the financial dilemma of the cities:

> The fate of our cities is still very much in doubt. Urban recreation will increasingly reflect the financial crisis of our cities and will increasingly come to be the exclusive province of the poor, as our cities become homes for the very, very rich and the very, very poor. The rich, with increasing leisure time . . . will continue to be able to purchase their recreation and to enjoy it largely outside

---

[5] Understanding the budget, *The New Republic, 168,* 6 (Feb. 10, 1973), p. 2.

of the city. The poor will become increasingly dependent upon publicly sponsored recreation programs.[6]

Middleton offers a ten-point plan for "re-creating" recreation programs in urban areas–decentralize, particularize, set priorities, synthesize, develop new careers, evaluate, plan, educate, sensitize, and publicize.

We have to *decentralize* the programming function to encourage innovative and high-quality programs, to try to eliminate the lack of imagination and inertia that bureaucracy breeds. This involves not only decentralization of staff and equipment, but an entire realignment of hierarchical command within urban agencies. "The position of the Lindsay administration [in New York City] has been that administrative decentralization must precede political decentralization if we are not to invite chaos."[7] Recreation agencies have to review those decisions now made at upper levels that could be more effectively made by recreation workers in the field. Decision-making must be delegated to those attempting to design comprehensive recreation programs and services for youth.

If programs are to focus on the clients we wish to serve, they have to be *particularly* designed and implemented to suit inner-city youth. Many of the mobile van programs, discussed in Chapter VI, are programs created expressly for youth in areas where no organized facilities exist. In like manner, in New York City other human services workers are assigned to recreation centers to aid in delineating the true needs of their clients by expanding the approach to clients beyond simply recreation or leisure services.

Recreation programming also has to set *priorities* in order to best use the all-too-often limited resources available in urban areas. That is, recreation specialists have to determine whether they can offer a variety of programs on a large scale, or more quality programs on a smaller scale. Questions such as these must be answered to effectively meet particular neighborhood needs within resource constraints.

In *synthesizing* the wide number of services available to inner-city residents, recreation staff can make another contribution toward truly serving their neighborhood clients. For example, Middleton mentions drug education and prevention programs conducted by local schools or local addiction-service agencies, or V.D. and birth control information offered by schools or local health agencies: "We must begin to provide birth control information as an integral component of teenage recreation programming. . . . Only nine years ago the provision of birth control and family planning information

---

[6] From a keynote address by Donald J. Middleton: Crossroads of Urban Recreation, Tri-State Recreation Commissioners and Superintendents Conference, Montclair State College, Montclair, N. J., Jan. 11, 1973.

[7] *Ibid.,* p. 3.

through recreation programming would have been considered a radical departure. It is now an essential."[8]

Recreation programmers must evaluate and scrutinize Civil Service systems and other class and racial barriers which exist to preclude poor and minority group persons from seeking or obtaining jobs in recreation. As with *New Careers* programs, we must take advantage of local expertise and talent and forego much of the mythology about formal education as *the* prerequisite for jobs. It should be evident that local youth or young adults will be highly sensitive to what programs are necessary. These indigenous workers can also serve as models for young kids of how informal street education can be applied to job situations. An analysis of job functions, in terms of what might be better handled by paraprofessionals, is a logical beginning.

As we will discuss a little later, Middleton also stresses the importance of *planning* and *evaluating* recreation programs. Too often recreation programs are either ineffective or repetitive at the neighborhood level. If programs are evaluated and judged ineffective, they should be modified or eliminated. "If we are not able to gauge the impact of our program, then perhaps that program should not be conducted."[9] Comprehensive planning, at all levels of the recreation bureaucracy, must reflect real neighborhood needs, not merely the same old thing each season, year in and year out. Recreation plans should also be integrated, fused, or complemented with other agencies to reduce repetitive offerings and to enhance program effectiveness and relevance.

In *educating* or even politicizing residents about recreation programs, we endeavor to explain what urban recreation is attempting to do, what our limitations are, what their advisory input might be, as well as how such services might be interpreted, perceived, or redirected by residents' participation in or contributions to program design. Especially critical is working to make urban parks and open space safe for citizens, and then educating them to once again feel safe in these often-dangerous "retreats." More generally, a basic task facing all recreation professionals will be educating and enlightening people on the use of leisure time: "For good or bad, the leisure time explosion will create increasing shock waves in . . . urban recreation programming throughout . . . the seventies."[10]

As with the earlier points, recreation programming must be *sensitive*, flexible, and responsive to neighborhood needs. The programming must be useful, exciting, and related to the lifestyles and ethnic backgrounds of inner-

---

[8] *Ibid.*, p. 6.
[9] *Ibid.*
[10] *Ibid.*, p. 7.

city dwellers. We should do away with programs that demean or oversimplify inner-city youth. Finally, for such programs to succeed, of course, we have to *publicize* them. This is especially critical in attempting to obtain support from shrinking municipal funds:

> If recreation programs are going to be able to compete for the decreasing municipal dollar, then they must become demonstrably competitive . . . ; they must be shown to be essential in maintaining the quality of life in our urban area. . . . Many times, our recreation leaders have been reluctant to publicize their programs and in some instances have been incapable of doing it.[11]

In summary, Middleton stresses that we all have to regenerate confidence in the quality of city life and services. The *"re-*creation" of recreation can be an important aspect of such a renewal.

Planning for Leisure Needs

As we think about planning and developing leisure or work programs for youth, there are several aspects involved. First, there has to be systematic *planning,* including a built-in *evaluation* component. No matter how threatening the idea of evaluation might be, it must be part of any ongoing program that seeks to be effective. Sandwiched in between planning and evaluation is, of course, *implementation.* The selection of good staff, and equally good in-service training, are vital to outreach implementation.[12]

Since there is broad agreement that the most accepted Leaders are those indigenous to a neighborhood, one of the Leader's goals might be to develop a "feeder" program to recruit future Leaders from the community. The ideal, of course, is to recruit staff with educational preparation from a junior or community college. For some, a four-year degree in recreation and parks at a university is preferable, although those with even a high school education can be more than acceptable. It is possible that a training program could be a Roving Leader's complete responsibility.

In developing programs for young people, there are specific demographic data that are essential–the number of youths, their age range, their sex, and the geographical region we wish to serve. We even have to consider groups not indigenous to cities, such as hippies, artists, students, or participants in drug subcultures that either develop in ghetto areas or drift into them. As far as locating so-called "problem" youth, there are many sources that can help us identify them: police, probation officers, children and juvenile court officers, school personnel, churches, public and private welfare

---

[11] *Ibid.*

[12] *The Roving Recreation Leader Training Guide: An Inservice Training Source for Inner-City Youth Services Personnel.* U. S. Department of Health, Education, and Welfare, Dirvision of Manpower Development Training, No. HE 5-287-87055 (Washington, D. C., 1971).

agencies, or other recreation staff members. But here too we have to be careful about readily accepting establishment norms of deviancy:

> The word 'deviant,' with all of its negative social connotations, must be considered from a different perspective. It is probably the 'deviant' who is making the most healthy response to his/her oppressive social conditioning and life-destructive environment.[13]

Roving Leaders must challenge themselves by viewing so-called deviant behavior from the viewpoint of the "deviant" as well as from the viewpoint of established professionals.

An analysis of ongoing programs should be made to find out who is already using them and who might be attracted to them. The population we seek to attract are not the kids who already use the center, but those whose leisure activities are far from organized recreation and are judged as detrimental to both the youngster and the community.

Again, this judgment has to be carefully arrived at and justified. No middle-class platitudes about the benefits of sports can interest kids who have the "wilderness" of a ghetto to explore:

> Even in the Middle Ages, when it might be supposed a meadow was within reach of every Jack and Jill, . . . the young had a way of gravitating to unsuitable places. . . . The places specially made for children's play are also the places where children can most easily be watched playing: the asphalt expanses of school playgrounds, the cage-like enclosures filled with junk by a local authority, the corners of recreation grounds stocked with swings and slides.[14]

The Opies feel a child's deepest desire, when it comes to play, is to be "away in the wastelands." Short of coercion, our task is to make organized activities as appealing as this wasteland, *only* if we feel and can justify the destructiveness of that preferred wasteland.

Other recreation centers and playgrounds can also provide the names and relevant data on youth from their specific area, who may be participating in organized programs but require special attention, as well as the names of those who need special attention but don't come to the recreation facility. Learn as much as possible about each youth and brief other recreation personnel who will be working with them. It is one thing to attract youth to a recreation center, and it is another to have outreach efforts jeopardized by in-house staff who aren't really interested in working with such youngsters or who are unfamiliar with the particular issues surrounding youth.

---

[13] Jacqueline Christeve: Social-psychological implications for current clinical practice. *Symposium of the American Psychological Association*, Honolulu, Hawaii, Sept. 6, 1972, p. 3.

[14] Iona and Peter Opie: *Children's Games in Street and Playground* (New York, Oxford University Press, 1969), p. 17.

We have to be concerned not only with training Roving Leaders, but with how to keep the regular center staff advised as well. An outreach effort has to affect the total recreation system; if a component of that system does not reflect the needs of youth, the program is bound to be unstable. This is why staff training is so important for successful outreach projects. A program planner for outreach activities has to do as much as feasible to ensure that substantive staff training is undertaken.

Although much of this discussion applies to most cities, it is also important in program planning to analyze one's particular situation in view of available resources. For example, you have to isolate the problems peculiar to your area, evaluate approaches or alternative solutions, again in terms of available resources. Thus, while the general framework for program planning offered here might be useful, it is equally important that a specific analysis for each situation accompany such generalizations. For instance, does the agency itself have staff or administration problems? Don't avoid these by concentrating only on community data.

Continuous follow-up is necessary to evaluate the efficacy of staff training and special youth programs. In this way, the program planner can determine which youth are still avoiding recreation facilities, or those who might have drifted away after dabbling in our offerings. An immediate and continuous follow-up is integral to a program plan if you hope to achieve any degree of success. There should be some attempt to diagnose the particular problems of each youngster on the basis of available data and activities designed to meet these problems, or referrals made to other social agencies. Referrals are important in outreach work, because the Roving Leader makes few presumptions about dealing with issues best handled by other professionals. Yet, the Roving Leader performs many roles within the confines of his job.

For example, as a *facilitator,* the Roving Leader seeks to keep communication open between youth and recreation staff. As an *evaluator,* the Leader compares or contrasts facts and seeks to evaluate the program's goals. As an *orienter,* the Leader has the youth group define its goals and where they are in respect to these. As a *compromiser,* the Leader is willing to yield his position in order that action may proceed. The Leader can also be a fact-giver, a summarizer, an expediter, an analyzer, a recorder, and so on. Whatever roles enhance outreach work with youth, these are the roles a Roving Leader has to be adept at.[15]

Specific Program Suggestions

Ingenuity and imagination are the main guideposts and limitations to program development. Since we encounter youth in their broad social milieu,

---

[15] These various roles were first explicated by Milton Douglas, one of the co-authors in this book (see chapter III).

many programs are outside of recreation; we do not only concentrate on leisure-time activities for youth. One activity that can be developed for outreach work with youth is an environmental program. Such a program is useful in neighborhoods where a recreation center is not easily accessible. A community environmental program is geared to the immediate needs of youth in a neighborhood. For instance, youths are taken on educational tours of their own community; they visit various institutions, such as schools and museums, to learn more about the area in which they live. In addition, these groups engage in sports, games, fashion or talent shows, as well as arts and crafts. The main criterion of such activities is that they are brought to the youth, not the youth to them. They are brought by the Roving Leader with his "office in his pocket."

The Roving Leader can leave the play equipment in some kids' homes overnight where they can use it. The next day they take out the equipment for others to use. All this occurs in the immediate neighborhood, with the kids responsible for the equipment. They don't have to walk ten or twelve blocks to a recreation facility to play with clay. It's right there in the neighborhood. Such a program can be a community effort, involving parents, school personnel, recreation staff, and other public officials and community leaders.

With a little pressure you can even encourage municipal service agencies, such as the police and fire departments, to donate money to such programs. These departments may not be as responsive to general arguments about "needy kids," as they are to potential alleviation of problems they themselves experience with neighborhood youth. The same applies to local businesses, especially those that are a part of national chains. These firms can be encouraged to offer youths jobs that pay a decent wage, but which do not put someone else out of a job. In a way it's a payoff, but one that is aboveboard and beneficial to both sides.

Trips to special events outside the neighborhood are also popular with many inner-city youths. Possible trips include college or professional sports, movies, museums, sports shows, aquatic shows, the zoo, etc. Special-rate tickets may even be available from some agencies. One concern in planning special trips is transportation. Transportation can be the Leader's car, or an idea popular in some colleges–PAL program (not the *Police Athletic League*). In PAL, college students volunteer to host youths at college events and provide transportation for them.

Of course, in taking youngsters to such events, the Leader must keep in mind the youth's response to these activities. Many of us are familiar with the response of many inner-city children to the thought of going to the zoo. Animals to them mean rats, dead dogs, or mice. Cages represent prisons. Why on earth would they want to take a trip to see caged animals? Or an aquatic show might have "dead-ass"[16] music accompanying it which bores such children. Whatever we offer young people has to interest them or make sense to them if we expect sustained participation on their part.

Another program which is very useful is a scholarship program for youth in outreach groups who might not otherwise have a chance to go to a community or four-year college. Roving Leaders have been somewhat successful in obtaining aid from various colleges for youth who have completed high school or who have an equivalency diploma. High school counselors often do not encourage inner-city youth to continue their education. In fact, an excellent emphasis for a Roving Leader, in terms of education, is to work with high school dropouts, encouraging them to return to school or to obtain a job or an equivalency diploma through a work-study program.

While it is not the purpose of a Roving Leader program to usurp the responsibility of the school system, it is important to offer educational encouragement if none exists elsewhere. The youngsters have got to know there is money available if they don't have tuition, or work-study programs to enable them to continue their education. To many kids this is startling information, something middle-class people find difficult to understand. The world of higher education is a mystery, and the Roving Leader can familiarize young people with its intricacies and personal opportunities.

Educational opportunities are especially lucrative in junior or community colleges. There are many educational opportunities young people pass by because they have not been properly informed. Even the terminology of higher education–credits, convocation, matriculation, and so forth–can turn kids off unless they are familiar and comfortable with them. The Roving Leader can be extremely useful in demystifying education for inner-city kids.

Like it or not, education determines to a great extent what happens to a young person in life. Education, or at least the environment in which it thrusts young people, can help them move into adulthood with greater facility. Education usually offers one of the first opportunities for a person to view life outside his or her immediate environment or value set. Paul Goodman found that most New York ghetto youths, by the time they are in their early teens, have not been more than half a mile from home.[17] The transition from the excitement of the street to the excitement of formal learning is clearly seen in Claude Brown's *Manchild in the Promised Land*. However, the Roving Leader should be very careful not to denigrate street knowledge. It is the very thing he himself is seeking!

The intent of some of the more traditional recreation activities is not only to engage youth in enjoyable activities, but to elicit other behaviors, such as

---

[16] Leroi Jones: *Home: Social Essays* (New York, William Morrow & Co., 1966).

[17] Paul Goodman: *Like a Conquered Province; The Moral Ambiguity of America* (New York, Random House, 1966), p. 85.

teamwork and individual responsibility as byproducts of such programs. This in some way reduces the criticism that recreation is too limited in its fun-and-games approach to youth problems. But these sports and activities *are* popular, *do* require a degree of skill and development, and can have beneficial side effects. Regardless of whether you believe sports prevent delinquency, build character, or not, still they are pleasurable to young people, and for that reason should be available to them.

Although our chapter ends on a discussion of traditional sports and their use in inner-city environments, we want to again stress that the kinds of programs offered in outreach work are almost limitless–depending on the acuity of Roving Leaders in carefully creating and developing programs they feel are essential and on-target for the needs of inner-city youth. The Roving Leader's "bag of goodies" must transcend the traditional, but cannot ignore the joy many youth find in traditional activities:

> Most men are apt to show their interest in the concerns of the poor chiefly by sympathy with their distresses and sorrows. I was disposed to express mine by sympathizing with their pleasures.
>
> *Thomas De Quincey, 1889*

CHAPTER REFERENCES AND SELECTED READINGS

Addison, Gayle, Jr.: *The Black Situation.* New York, Dell Publishing, 1970.

Bannon, Joseph J.: *Problem Solving in Recreation and Parks.* Englewood Cliffs, N. J. Prentice-Hall, Inc., 1972.

Belton, S. I. and Bloomberg, C. M.: Evaluating the In-Service Training Program at Junior Village. Washington, D. C., Howard University, Center for Youth and Community Service, April 1965.

Fast, Julius: *Body Language.* New York, M. Evans and Company, 1970.

Goodman, Paul: *Like a Conquered Province; The Moral Ambiguity of America.* New York, Random House, 1966.

Meyerson, Martin, ed.: *The Conscience of a City.* New York, G. Braziller, 1970.

The Negro American—Parts 1 and 2. *Daedalus* (Fall 1965 and Winter 1966). Journal of the American Academy of Arts and Sciences.

Opie, Iona and Peter: *Children's Games in Street and Playground.* New York, Oxford University Press, 1969.

CHAPTER V

TRAINING FOR THE OUTREACH FUNCTION

"A Little Learnin' Will Help Us Tell Our Story"

PHYLLIS GRUNAUER

OUTREACH WORK is a unique situation for many human service workers. It requires sustained and effective training to ensure that such workers are prepared to handle the critical situations they are likely to encounter. It is not enough to brief workers on what they can expect in the field, wish them well, and send them out. Training requires planning, time, energy, and intelligence. A successful outreach project is no easy matter and should not be approached as such.

In the good old days of training (not really so good or old), most trainers were satisfied when training needs for outreach work were identified and assessed, problems delineated, alternative training programs examined, one selected, undertaken, and evaluated. These evaluations were then used for reassessing needs, and training would begin again. As trainers, we would clarify objectives with management to ensure the trainer and organization were on the same track (sometimes no easy task), involve the outreach trainees in planning the program, advise the trainees' supervisor, learn from previous mistakes, and, of course, encourage feedback.

Although the above simple problem-solving approach is still used in outreach training, we are much more sophisticated now. For example, the trainers must know about systems analysis and management skills. Evaluation has also changed, moving from simple accounts of how many clients were trained, the number of sessions held, and the costs involved, to a more qualitative assessment of the impact of training.

Even with all the attention given to planning for training, the results can be "blown" for reasons beyond a trainer's control. I am reminded of an ambitious training program undertaken in New York City under the aegis of the University of Illinois, Office of Recreation and Park Resources in Urbana. This project involved a planned and researched model to train Roving Leaders for work with inner-city youth. Any possibility of *fully* using the project model disappeared in the face of new agency policies. All the trainer's time spent encouraging the development of such a model was lost because new agency policy did not encompass such research!

Detached Worker Functions

In order to consider training, we have to first review the functions and tasks of detached work, and identify the individuals and groups the outreach worker will "work" with. To inner-city youth, the world only includes authorities, suckers, hoods and frauds. From their viewpoint, it rarely contains open, non-judgmental, accepting people. The trainer must be aware, therefore, that it is difficult for such youth to accept the detached worker's claim that his or her function is merely to be helpful. The inner-city world is a place where a person usually has to be extremely tough to survive, and "softness" in someone they might wish to emulate confuses youth. The movement toward accepting the worker is often accompanied by hostility. The training approach must include methods or tips on how to counter such hostility.

The hard core of inner-city youth in groups, cliques, or gangs rarely responds to agency programs within a facility, so it is necessary to take programs out to them. To reach youth in the streets, Roving Leaders have to be flexible, and they are usually given a great deal of latitude to enable them to obtain flexibility. One weakness of such flexibility, of course, is that there is frequently inadequate supervision, causing many uncoordinated and unplanned responses to field situations. Without adequate supervision, a detached worker tends to represent only himself rather than the policy and philosophy of his agency. The first thing for the streetworker to clarify is his role as agency staff in a professional job. Though he may and should be friendly with youth, he should never be simply one of the boys.

One of the major goals of a worker is to enable youth to make personal decisions more readily and positively. Workers and administrators too often claim success for the number of youths reached and of group activities carried on, rather than for attitude or behavior changes. The latter, of course, are tougher to define or evaluate because they cannot be readily appraised. The Roving Leader should realize the goal of effecting attitudinal changes is linked with what Chris Argyris calls "interpersonal competence acquisition"–that is, providing persons with chances to diagnose and increase their interpersonal competence. Another way of saying this goal is for the worker to cope effectively with interpersonal relationships, rather than become authoritarian. The more closed the individual, the lower the sense of interpersonal competence, the lower problem-solving effectiveness. Training provides a setting for Roving Leaders to test their various behavior styles without risking the negative consequences of field encounters.

There is a paucity of specific procedures for dealing with certain forms of delinquent behavior such as theft, rape, or malicious mischief. This lack of experience-based procedures forces the Roving Leader to use more general techniques such as individual and family counseling, group activities, or job development. Klein feels that if parents could be more influential in the life of youth, and agency representatives could be brought closer to the everyday social reality of youth, some impact might be expected.[1]

One phase of a worker's activity which must be stressed is the value of independent, first-hand verification of all reports received–even if these are from an eyewitness. Inner-city youths, who may be clique or gang members, are often the worst possible informants about their affairs. It is absolutely necessary for the streetworker to check the data firsthand. The streetclub worker goes in where others often fear to tread. The community tends to avoid the streetclub or gang and often pretends the street or gang worker isn't there, or is "captured" by the gang, and is to be denounced rather than supported. The trainer must be aware of this and other community assumptions in designing realistic training programs.

It is essential that a trainer prepare streetworkers for the type of work with gangs that is clear of popular gang preconceptions. When we speak of a gang, by the way, we mean three or more young people who may occasionally indulge in what their community considers antisocial or dangerous activities. Usually the members of these groups view themselves as clubs for both social activity *and* mutual protection. The term "gang" is used more to meet the needs of social agencies and the media than to offer an objective definition. Practitioners, researchers and theoreticians have used "gang" inconsistently, loosely, and often in direct opposition to one another.[2] Walter Miller, a cultural anthropologist, perceives gangs as providing lower-class adolescents with flexible and adaptive knowledge about personal competence, accepted limits of antisocial behavior, the uses and abuses of authority, as well as skills for interpersonal relations.[3] The trainer may find a bit of basic truth in both reflections and include them in a training framework.

Over the past decade, I have evolved several basic precepts on what streetclub workers perceive as necessary to perform their function–all of which need to be integrated into a training design:

Better understanding and practice in group dynamics.

Better channels of communication among themselves, their supervisors, and agency management.

Clear lines of authority within their organization and the administrative levels outside their agency.

Clarity of their roles and role limitations.

---

[1] Malcolm W. Klein: *Street Gangs and Street Workers* (Englewood Cliffs, N. J., Prentice-Hall, 1971).

[2] *Ibid.*

[3] See William C. Kvaraceus and Walter B. Miller: *Delinquent Behavior-Culture and the Individual* (Washington, D. C., Juvenile Delinquency Project, National Education Association, 1959).

Clarity in the support the agency and its subdivisions or subsystems can give them to enable them to carry out their outreach function.

Planning

One of the first steps for a trainer before implementing a program is to obtain permission from management to proceed. This permission generally comes after management is convinced that organizational aims will be furthered by training. After permission is obtained, a team should be established to plan the tentative scope and objectives of the training. Careful consideration should be given to agency political and structural realities as to the inclusion or exclusion of members for the work committee. Questions like, *How are we to select a cross-section of trainees to be involved in planning?* and *How many are needed?*–should be answered before the first planning session.

If management isn't kept informed about the role of training in helping the agency and its staff, incorrect assumptions develop. Training may come to be viewed as a corrective for poor performance, rather than as an opportunity for continuing staff growth and development at all levels. To aid the agency in achieving its objectives, training should actively support such objectives since it is directly related to the tasks and processes of an organization. This is known in the field of training as "organizational linking."

As a trainer, you present your tentative training plan to management, including a description of the special inner-city population to be served, as well as skills, attitudes, behaviors to be developed, and training expectations. You develop the content from previous need identification and assessment. You may use a variety of methods, including observation at staff meetings, or interviews with workers and supervisors on what skills are needed for outreach. In many agencies the trainer also sits in at top-level management or board meetings. This sharpens the trainer's awareness of the various aspects of agency decision-making on its goals and priorities.

Perhaps an informal chart might be useful for drafting plans for agency training. It could include an agency's goals, worker's job description, how to implement these goals, skills needed for the job, and skill gaps. The gaps in skills would form a major portion of the training content. The content is decided on in mutual planning with a planning committee. With the tentative approval of management, you now meet with a selected planning committee for their reactions and suggestions on your initial training design.

This planning session should result in a clear acceptance of responsibility among those present for tasks to be done before the next planning meeting. (Gathering additional information, choosing a time, developing program methods, selecting resource specialists if needed, may also be concerns for the first session.) After the first planning meeting it might be advisable for the trainer to make a progress report to management to keep them up to date. A phone call, memo, or quick meeting may be your best method. You need management's support and approval for training, not merely lip service. You can ensure this if you keep them involved and apprized of training formulations.

In a large agency, there is usually a good deal of ambivalence among workers (unless they are eagerly new) about responsibility for activities which are not clearly part of their original assignment. However, once they have been exposed to plans for training, implementation, and evaluation, they are often your staunchest allies. They can help interpret training goals to their co-workers, administrators, and the community. They also make suggestions to enlarge your planning committee membership. For example, they are usually much more aware of co-workers in a large agency than the trainer is. You can also have them recommend workers with special skills whom you can call on for help.

While it may be comparatively easy to have some training success in a crisis, to have any lasting impact on trainees, and on an agency's perception of training, one needs to PLAN. Mutual planning, in conjunction with the staff planning committee and management, should take about three times as much time as the training itself. This includes consensus on content, methods, materials, practice situations, role-playing exercises, briefing for any resource specialists or outside participants. With all the good will in the world, your planning time may not meet the ideal you need, but hang in there.

Design of Outreach Training Program

The following general outline may be helpful:
1. GATHER DATA. Who is to be in your training group? How much time and what facilities are available? What are your training resources (both people and materials and means)? What precisely is your Task?
2. NEEDS ASSESSMENT. A feeling of frustration, or a job problem may not require training but changes in organizational structure, procedures or classification. Other problems may contain several training needs. Once these needs have been clearly defined, you and your planning staff translate these needs into training objectives.
3. TRAINING OBJECTIVES. These are the specific tasks, format, and programs you design to meet assessed needs. If the need were "to learn the worker role in the outreach function," the training objective might be, "to role-play with the workers a problem of initial approach or contact with a client." Training objectives usually include phrases like "to train, to discuss, to identify. . . ."

4. THE OUTCOME. This is the desired effect, skill development, new information, or changed behavior that training is designed to achieve based on defined objectives and need.
5. EVALUATION OF DESIGN AGAINST CRITERIA. Does the design meet your objectives? Does it allow for involvement by the participants? Are the methods consistent with your objectives? Is it interesting and exciting?

Whatever evaluation form you develop it should include some of these elements:

What learning was generated from it?

What degree of competence was felt to be gained in the skill or content derived from the training?

What feedback for trainers on the training activity can now be used?

Was group process helpful in any way toward achieving training goals? If so, how?

How may future needs or aspects be reassessed in terms of training programs?

Note: Having selected methods for your training, discuss individual trainer roles (co-trainer, team trainers, back-up trainer).

Trainer Responsibility

Workers are usually curious about the trainer, whom they sometimes perceive as overly judgmental about the need for skills before entering the field. The trainer of streetworkers must at least have the following characteristics:

Several years' experience working with minorities.

A warm personality, interest in, understanding of, and respect for the culture of minorities.

An ability to communicate and to listen well; to be supportive and nonjudgmental.

A non-authoritarian manner, open about personal feelings.

A knack for involving individuals in group tasks and responsibilities.

An orientation to the agency and its objectives, as well as an attitude that is supportive toward trainees.

The trainer does more than offer trainees skills; he or she gives the trainees confidence in an ability to do the job well.

The trainer's responsibility is not only to develop skills and confidence, but to train workers as more effective resources for one another. This is especially important when the trainee is from the ghetto, where competition is largely the norm, and new experiences rarely elicit rewarding responses. Our conditioning is very competitive–at home there is often sibling rivalry, in the classroom children compete for teacher's approval, in the schoolyard they play competitive games, and for an adult or teenager there is competition for livelihood. With this background, it is easy to see why there is little room for the individual to develop cooperative, collaborative skills.

This is particularly true for the inner-city youths with whom the streetworker is involved, and the worker himself, if their backgrounds are similar. A series of conflicts develop from the stark comparison between their way of life and the "approved" lifestyle depicted in the media and through education. Youths frequently have a fear of embarrassment because of limited social experiences in their life. As a result, a sense of aloneness and powerlessness and a state of crisis pervade, and reduction of these feelings is dependent on wits or random chance. The young in the poverty cycle frequently feel looked down on and develop defenses against an "establishment" that views them as unable to truly participate in mainstream activities.

To diminish some of these barriers, there are certain training procedures a trainer can use:

1. TRAINER ENTRY. When the trainer starts the session, he or she reveals only enough personal data that are relevant to the immediate task. After a minute or two of personal introduction, the trainer then gives an orientation to the purpose of the training and the ground rules for the exercises. This should take ten minutes at the most.
2. PAIR AND GROUP INTRODUCTIONS TO TRAINING. Instead of the usual round-robin introductions, the group forms into pairs (dyads), each picking a partner he or she does not know. Each member of the pair introduces himself to his partner, and they then share their feelings and concepts about the training, including their interests, expectations and concerns about it. These introductions should take no more than fifteen minutes.

Each pair is then asked to join another pair to form a group of four. Each member of the dyad introduces his or her partner to the opposite pair, giving as much information as he recalls from the previous dialogue. His partner, in introducing him to the other twosome, provides the same information. The new pair does the same with the original pair *(fifteen minutes)*. Following these introductions the trainer asks the new foursome to make a list of their common goals and expectations for training. This segment should take fifteen or twenty minutes. Each foursome then selects from their group a representative to report to the entire group on their shared group expectations and goals. Representatives should not repeat goals covered by previous speakers. *(Depending on number of groups, 10 to 20 minutes.)*

Sometimes I add to the above exercise a list of training expectations, interests, and goals obtained from planning sessions, observations, or staff meetings with trainees. I cover this list with a sheet of paper. When the trainee reports are all written on a flipchart, I remove the cover from my list and we compare findings. This is a sort of "striptease" and can be used to build trust–I reveal what I consider our mutual training goals, and if I have made a mistake in my "feel" for the situation, it is quite open. Mistakes can then be shown as a part of learning and not something to hide.

The trainee is "forcing himself" to participate with others and is ambivalent about "exposing" himself and sharing. (One of his concerns very often is, Do I have enough on the ball to share?) The trainer must do the same and not set himself apart. They may both be anxious over the ambiguity of a situation which makes different demands on their behavior from what is usually acceptable to either of them. Coping with this ambivalence is an on-going ladder to self-maturity for the worker and the trainer.

Divide the training group into pairs to tell each other *why* they came to the session and *what* they hope to gain. Each pair then finds another pair to make a team of four, then repeats the process until groups of eight are formed. These groups of eight remain as the groups gather for training. Twenty-five minutes of this yields a relaxed and comfortable training environment for the trainer to cover the content more easily. This entire session, including introduction, content presentation, group problem-solving activity and wrap-up should take about two and a half hours.

Unless the trainees are too involved to finish during the allotted time, try to end the session within this time. It is helpful to have some sort of agenda displayed in a prominent place:

DIAGRAM I

AGENDA

2:00 P.M.	Distribution of materials. Meeting starts
2:10-2:35	Introductory Exercise
2:35-2:50	Streetwork Function, Presentation
2:50-3:30	Group Discussion
3:30-4:00	Group Reports
4:00-4:30	Wrap-Up

Where do we go from here?

This is a technique to have trainees share responsibility for ending a session on time. When you feel you have reached a goal of a training session, it is usually good to have a closing exercise to summarize the session's activity and provide a basis for a joint decision on the need for another meeting. Below are detailed outlines for various training sessions.

Content of Training Design

It may be useful, in this context, to present two strategies for learning and behavior offered by Malcolm Knowles:

DIAGRAM II

LEARNING AND BEHAVIOR STRATEGIES[4]

	Pedagogy	*Andragogy*
Climate	Authority-oriented Formal Competitive	Showing Mutuality Respectful Collaborative Informal
Planning	By teacher (trainer)	Mutual planning
Diagnosis of Needs	By teacher (trainer)	Mutual self-diagnosis
Formulation of Objectives	By teacher (trainer)	Mutual negotiations
Design (or plan)	Logic of the subject matter Content units	Sequenced in terms of readiness Problem units
Activities	Transmittal technique	Experiential techniques (inquiry)
Evaluation	By teacher (trainer)	Mutual rediagnosis of needs Mutual measurement of program

Session I

Training goals and expectations for the entire training program are included in this first session. The methods to be used are also highlighted. The session should include methods for creating cooperation and trust. Outreach workers are generally used to a pedagogic, didactic approach to learning and frequently feel the trainer is not helping by forcing them to do all the work with group problem-solving methods. Exercises which foster interpersonal dialogue, feedback, trust and development of group and interpersonal skills have already been discussed under "Trainer Responsibility." This type of climate-setting forces trainees to become involved with others in discovering inadequacies and working together to discover means for improvement.

---

[4] Malcolm S. Knowles: *The Modern Practice of Adult Education* (New York, Association Press, 1970).

Session II

The second session is on the outreach worker's role and role limitation. You may wish to let this second session also cover agency goals and structure. However, trainees' anxiety about what they believe the agency expects of them, and their own feelings about performance, might make other learning more difficult. Therefore, I usually cover role expectations before any discussion of agency goals. Materials for this session can include job descriptions, situations or vignettes for problem-solving in groups, or the use of resource specialists from the administrative staff to answer questions on role limitation. You can use the "Interpretation of Contact" form presented a little later in this chapter.

Session III

Agency purpose, goal, structure, program, and procedures can then logically follow Session II. Coordination among youth-serving agencies may be a purpose of your agency. Also the collection of data to evaluate the effectiveness of agency contracted services for programs, the determination of the eligibility for funds, areas of possible programs, and the development and testing of experimental youth programs and approaches may be concerns of your agency as well. Have available in writing, whenever possible, the overall rationale for why your agency exists. This is initiated by top management, or at the very least has their approval. You might have the agency director on video tape presenting goals, programs, or procedures. The director might also be on video tape with organizational charts discussing the agency's structure to enable it to carry out its functions. Questions that cannot be answered immediately can be forwarded to the director or administrator concerned to have an answer by the next session.

Session IV

How does the streetworker fit into the structure? What is the agency expectation for the worker to implement agency purpose? What is the worker's expectation of the agency? What quality and how much technical assistance, supervision, and task-performance development can he expect? This session includes the limit-setting and standard-setting the worker must undertake for work with inner-city youth. At all times, the worker remembers he is not a loner, but an agency representative. He is not omniscient, but knows where he can get answers. A lecture on the function of a streetworker is one approach, or else a video tape by the field director may be used. This is a good time to use role playing about the agency's expectation of a worker, worker expectation of the agency, interpretations of agency policy and function to clients, the community, or other agencies. Just as you and the planning committee previously prepared problem-solving group situations, you can prepare a few role-playing situations or elicit them from the trainees.

Session V

Although climate setting in a formal sense is covered in Session I, in reality it permeates the entire program. Training also relies heavily on the use of group forces. As noted, a prime responsibility of the trainer is to help the trainees become effective resources for each other's learning and practice. Preparation of workers to work with gangs (or groups) includes understanding of group task, maintenance, and individual needs in a group. "Task" refers to the *work* of the group; "maintenance" to the *interrelations* of the members within the group; and "individual needs" to the *relationship* between the group and individual members.

Malcolm Knowles defines a group as possessing the following qualities:
1. A definable membership—a collection of two or more people identified by type.
2. Group consciousness—the members think of themselves as a group, have a "collective perception of unity," a conscious identification with each other.
3. A sense of shared purpose—the members have the same "object modes," goals or ideals.
4. Interdependence in satisfaction of needs—the members need each other's help to accomplish the purpose of the group.
5. Interaction—the members communicate with one another, influence one another, react to one another.
6. Ability to act in a unitary manner—the group can behave as a single organism.

GROUPS tend to mature and build valuable learning and working environments when the members:
assume responsibility for sharing leadership in the group;
have trust, confidence, and respect for each other as persons and as resources for their own learning;
are willing to share their feelings and values with the group so clear communication can be achieved;
participate in accomplishing the group's tasks and are personally committed to betterment of the group;
satisfy their individual needs and achieve personal growth as a result of group involvement.[5]

---
[5] Malcolm S. Knowles: *Introduction to Group Dynamics* (New York, Association Press, 1959).

One of the tasks of training is to experience the difficulties and pleasures of working with adults in groups. The trainees will also perceive these as applying to the cliques, gangs, and groups with whom they work. Knowledge of group dynamics is valuable for building effective teams, committees, or task forces, in training situations or on the streets.

William Schutz in his theory of group development asserts that we transmit and receive three basic needs to and from others–inclusion, control and affection:

Inclusion–we need enough interaction, acceptance and "ownership" of group activities to feel satisfied and fulfilled. A lack of inclusion may lead to withdrawal and isolation.

Control–we need enough influence and power to be self-directing and respected for our competence. We need to receive from others and to give to others recognition for ability or competence.

Affection–we need to be loved–and also to relate easily with others as associates and friends. We need this mutual give-and-take of emotionally involved relationships of varying intensities.[6]

ISSUES that arise as questions related to Inclusion, Control, and Affection (ICA) might include: Can I trust others in this group to support me? Who is in charge here? Can I say what I think; should I say it, and what effect will it have? Who do I feel close to here, and who do I feel distant from?

This order of ICA questions and issues is a way of enhancing group maturity. Before the group is ready to end its tasks or to break up, the process tends to reverse itself to Affection, Control, Inclusion (ACI).

Affection–the group members begin to pull away from relationships in the group that have no real future.

Control–the group again works on the question, "Who is in charge here?"

Inclusion–Finally members begin to ask themselves if they really want to be a part of the group and spend the time and effort to keep it together.

The trainer in this session can be a participant-observer working on the group tasks, interacting while observing, and helping the group mature, and when necessary, to disband.

Session VI

The topic of this session–resources–can be the wind-up for the first training cycle. The two most valuable resources, self and others, and the use of time and time constraints should be re-emphasized. Public, private, community, and other resources might be highlighted again. This might also be

---

[6] William C. Schutz: *The Interpersonal World* (New York, Science and Behavior Books, 1960).

a good time to demonstrate how to conduct a survey. Lecture, demonstration, or role playing–a client or group coming to the worker for help–are some possible methods. Referrals–criteria for worker's decision on who to refer and whom to refer them to, how much information to give to the referred agency, how well the worker is acquainted with referral staff, and what follow-up can be used–are all topics that should be covered with trainees.

At least a half-hour should be allotted for training evaluation, new learning, and attitude and behavior changes by trainees. What was helpful? What hindered them? Were their expectations of the training met? What would they like to see remain in the next cycle of training? What deleted? What feedback do you as a trainer have to reassess for your next training session?

"How-To" Training Techniques

One-Way/Two-Way Communication Exercises

These classic exercises show the differences between one- and two-way communication, and the superiority of the latter. In one-way communication, the outreach worker tells the youth something and this ends the communication. (A lecture or memo are also examples of one-way communication.) In two-way communication, the youth can ask for clarification, elaboration, etc., and both worker and youth can benefit from the increased mutual understanding that develops. (Discussion and question-and-answer settings are also examples of the latter.)

ONE-WAY COMMUNICATION EXERCISE:

The trainer, or someone he selects, acting as a Roving Leader, gives clear directions. The rest of the group (the youth) with pencil and paper follow the explanation of the sender. The group has no communication with one another or with the Leader. *(Set about a five-minute time limit.)* Here is the diagram (or any simple one you wish to use) for one-way communication:

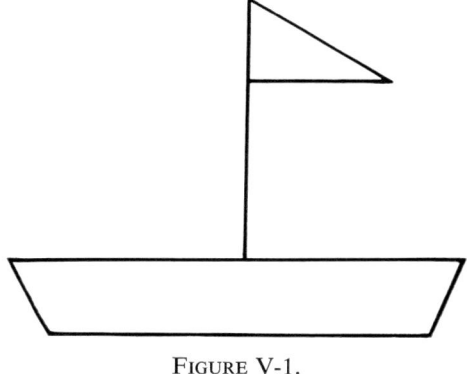

FIGURE V-1.

You, as the Leader, are the only one who looks at the drawing. At the completion of the time limit show the drawing to the group. The group then looks at theirs to be correct; the drawing must be the correct shape and proportion. Ask the group how they felt during the demonstration and how they think the sender felt.

TWO-WAY COMMUNICATION EXERCISE:

Describe your second diagram clearly and completely. This time the "youth" may ask questions and the worker replies. *(Time for this exercise may be 10 or 15 minutes.)* Here is the diagram for two-way communication:

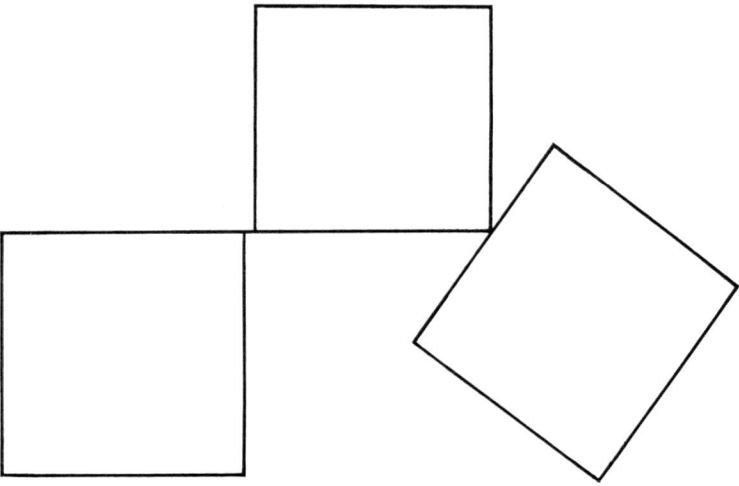

FIGURE V-2.

The following results can be observed:
1. Two-way communication takes much longer.
2. Two-way communication results in greater accuracy in trainee's drawing.
3. In one-way communication, the worker often feels relatively confident; the youth somewhat uncertain or even frustrated.
4. Two-way communication is usually the opposite of No. 3.

Compare the results with a discussion of the relevance of this experiment to oral and written reports and to small group work.

COMMUNICATION AND FEEDBACK EXERCISE:

Select volunteers totaling half of the training group, but not more than ten, and form them into a fishbowl seating arrangement. The members of the outer group can be paired off with a member of the inner group for whom they will serve as personal observers. Observers will face their partners. The inner group is asked to decide on the five most prominent helpful and hindering actions they observed in a previous two-person communication. *(The time limit is about 20 minutes.)* After about 10 minutes has elapsed, time-out can be called so observers can spend 5 minutes with their partner in the fishbowl, giving feedback on his style of communication. The action will then resume for another 10 minutes and will then be repeated with the outside group now in the fishbowl. As a final summation, the group should assess what kinds of feedback were valuable and what kinds were not and record their findings.

FEEDBACK is simply communication with a person (or group) which gives that person (or group) information about how he, she (or it), affects others. The purpose is to enable us to consider changing our behavior. Feedback is *descriptive,* not evaluative or judgmental. It is *specific.* To be told that one is "controlling" is not as useful as to be told that "you did not listen to what others said to you, and I felt forced to accept your suggestions or endure attack from you."

Feedback is *appropriate.* It can be destructive when it serves only our own needs and fails to consider the needs of the person on the receiving end. It should be *requested* rather than imposed. Feedback is *usable* and *timely.* It should be directed toward behavior that the receiver, either youth or worker as the case may be, can do something about. It should be given at the earliest opportunity after the given behavior (depending, of course, on the person's readiness to hear it and the support available from others).

Keep feedback *clear.* Perhaps you could have the receiver try to rephrase the feedback to see if it corresponds to what the sender had in mind. Another criterion is *accuracy.* In a training group both sender and receiver have an opportunity to check with others in the group. They can check to see if it's one person's impression or shared by others. Offer rather than impose feedback. Be open and honest. If feedback is offered in a supportive, responsible way, it can inform you about what is good in your behavior and what is not. It is most helpful when given about and supported by behavioral data.

Interpretation of Contact

The Welfare Council of New York City, as far back as 1950, set up a series of questions to help the youth worker assess his initial contact in the field. This classic self-questionnaire is undoubtedly as applicable today as it was then. The trainer can distribute this questionnaire and use it as an ongoing exercise for the worker in the important function of self-evaluation. In addition, the trainer may find this checklist helpful in interpreting and assessing his own contact with trainees.

Self-Questionnaire

The following questions the worker can ask himself after a group contact. They can also be used as an outline for a record of the contact itself. Check out the details while the contact is still vivid in your mind so specific aspects which may be important are not overlooked:

1. What was I trying to accomplish in this contact? What was the group trying to accomplish?
2. What took place in this contact (what were some of the actions the worker did to accomplish the group's and his own goals)?
3. What were the reactions of the members?
4. To what extent did my methods accomplish what I intended?
5. How could I have improved my methods?
6. Did this contact deepen or retard my relationship with the members or was there no change? Why?
7. What insights did I get into the members' attitudes and behavior?
8. What changes did I notice in the members' attitudes and behavior? How can I account for these changes?
9. On the basis of this and previous contacts, what predictions can I make about the future behavior or attitudes of any of the members?
10. What specific problems did this contact involve that I would like help on?
11. How did I feel personally about this contact? Satisfied, discouraged, hopeful, annoyed, or any other emotions? Why?
12. What do I do next? Why?

The Lecture

In training for outreach, lectures can be useful: (1) when the lecturer has specialized knowledge otherwise not readily available to trainees; (2) if the group is large; (3) if time is limited; and (4) if the information conveyed is straightforward, factual, and descriptive. However, less formal group participation and practice methods may be more effective in developing attitudes and human behavior.

Outreach Situations or Vignettes

You can probably, with your planning group, create a whole repertoire of such problem-solving situations. Here I emphasize gang-oriented vignettes. These are all true situations developed with trainees.

I

You are a new youth worker who has finally made the first real contact with a gang member in your area. The young person requests money for

cigarettes. *In fact, this request has been the opening statement of your contact.*
How do you handle this situation?

To TRAINER: Raise approaches similar to these with your trainees.
Consider whether this is buying acceptance. Discuss ramifications of this action. Jot down comments you find appropriate.
Is this testing or "conning" an outsider? If there is to be a standardization of worker's relationship with group members; does lending money to one individual mean lending money to all gang or group members? In what ways can a youth worker pleasantly refuse a request?

II

You are in the office and police or detectives come in looking for three gang members. Two of the gang members are in the center and one is not.
How do you handle this situation?

To TRAINER: Know what the regulations are for police entering office without a warrant. (In New York City, it is appropriate.) You may raise this to point out the importance of relationships for accomplishing and easing outreach task.

RELATIONSHIPS: How do youth gang or group see you? What is relationship with police captain, youth patrolman, community, gang leadership? What is relationship with community organization, leaders, agencies? Can you call on them for assistance?

Determine all facts pertaining to situation: names of gang members, the charges, where youth will be detained if and when picked up. Also contact stationhouse.

Worker should do some or all of the following: contact agency central office and agency legal office. Take policeman's badge number. Notify parents or guardians of the youth involved.

III

You are a new worker in a center, who recently has been assigned to a fighting gang in an area where no one has worked before your assignment. The reports to your center supervisor have documented incidents of violence to community residents by this gang. Two of the incidents were reported as stabbings.
How would you handle this situation?

To TRAINER: One of your objectives related to this situation is to have group interact to indicate steps in communication with neighborhood people, use of institutions and resources in area to help develop relationships that will enable the worker to quickly check out the validity of the above situation.

In developing relationships:
1. Have worker use area survey in formal and informal way.
2. Contact groups in the area.
3. Identify allies and support for you in area groups:
   a. Who are leaders within group?
   b. within the community?
   c. within the agency?
4. Identify type of group–political, religious, social, cultural, etc. Assess the following:
   a. amount of power of group and of community leadership;
   b. how worker or his agency is seen in the community by the area poverty institution, by delegate agency, and by sister agencies in the public and private sector.
5. Police contact:
   a. Police chief
   b. Youth and community patrolmen.
6. Resources–relate to consultation services, technical assistance, social welfare services.
7. Check out political ramifications on the local scene–both positive and negative.

IV

You are a youth worker in an area where there are fighting gangs, and one gang with weapons is holding a hostage in an abandoned building in your area. You have been called to check out the situation. Your center or unit has had limited contact with this gang.

What do you do?

TO TRAINER: You can use this vignette to stress the worker's need to check out all information and rumors first. Also your central office usually insists on responding to press, radio or TV reporters rather than on having workers give out statements on a dramatic occurrence like this. Speed in carrying out No. 2 of the problem-solving processes below is, therefore, important. You may also use this situation to reinforce the problem-solving approach to outreach.

1. Examine problem, gather and check out information on situation, as follows:
   a. contact gang members, witnesses, neighborhood adults and youth;
   b. verify and interpret information gathered;
   c. give information to your (worker's) supervisor immediately;
   d. deliver information to central agency office.

2. Examine alternative actions:
   a. What is worker's responsibility–can he personally intervene and enter building to see if he can have group release hostage?
   b. Does he talk to group members outside building to have them intervene to release hostage? What is the group acceptance of you as you perceive it?
   c. Does he call police, particularly youth squad?
   d. Does he leave scene, return to office and await instructions from agency?
3. Select priority action based on checked information, resources, supports.
4. Do priority activity.
5. Get feedback and evaluate activity. What you would do or not do in a similar situation. What new learning have you derived from this situation? Use any worker or group "mistakes" as learning rather than for assessing blame or pinpointing scapegoats.

Rogerian Repeat Back

In a conversation lasting about five minutes, each person repeats back what was said (to the previous speaker's satisfaction) before responding. Many trainees will be amazed to discover what poor listeners they are–often because they are so absorbed in what they are going to say when the other person stops talking. This exercise can be used to help resolve a conflict, or simply to demonstrate some very basic problems in communication between two people.

"I Am You" Trainer Involvement Exercise

As means of giving feedback, to an entire group as well as to one person, the trainer assumes the identity of one group member. He tells him "I am you. If I say anything which is not you, you should challenge me, otherwise let me continue." The trainer then asks the group to ask him questions and respond to him as if he is the person whose identity he has assumed. In doing this the trainer needs to be aware of at least three levels of information that person might reveal or allow to be revealed about himself: what he would admit to the group, what he would admit to himself, and what he would hide even from himself. The trainer can give feedback to other group members while responding to them.

Clearing the Air

All group members write down two fears and two expectations they have for the training session. When everyone is finished, all the fears and all the expectations are listed together and discussed.

Some Thoughts on Role Playing

Purpose of Role Playing

To help one person gain insight into another's feelings and attitudes. It is an action-centered emphasis which provides a bridge between theory (or concepts) and actual practice in a nonthreatening atmosphere.

Uses of Role Playing

Can be used in most problem-solving situations in human relations.

Is a method of achieving full participation of audience or discussion group.

Insightful; helps people understand how another person feels in situation.

Reality-testing; tries to see if proposed solution to problem will really work.

Skill-practicing; refines types of behavior required in particular situation by tryout, criticism, retry, and so forth.

Setting Up Role Playing

Have preliminary meeting with players, clarify overall situation and their different roles.

Situation should be meaningful to all participants, and purposes of role playing clear.

A guideline for a situation can be a simple, "What are we looking for?"

Get volunteers; have no one in roles in which they are uncomfortable.

Set "floor" on roles, allowing for flexibility of role playing.

Cut scene when insights have been obtained *(10-15 minutes)*.

Let those "on the spot" talk first–get their perception before their roles are discussed by others; then open talk to all.

Analyze scene carefully for content, *not* for acting. Get ideas for next scenes and approaches of problem.

Comments

Emotional reactions to role playing or action are more accurate than intellectual judgments of how people will behave. The learner can view situations as they would occur in the field, but at the same time avoid negative consequences that can occur in real life.

Evaluation

After implementing a training program, the trainer needs to assess the outcome and start planning for the next phase. Evaluation seeks to measure three components:

Discovery of what change and learning has occurred;

Analysis of how such discoveries apply to other settings and circumstances;

Reassessment of one's own needs and values in view of such learning and application.

In addition to these three aspects, evaluation serves as feedback for the trainer, providing information for continued improvement as an effective facilitator of adult learning. Below are some procedures for evaluation in its fullest application:

Before a training event, it is helpful to know:
  Expectations:
    What do the trainees hope, believe, or fear will happen or not happen?
  Experienced:
    What previous training have the trainees had?
  Responsibilities:
    What are the trainees' leadership roles?
  Relationships:
    What are the trainees' past and future relations with one another?

After a training event, it is helpful to know:
  Emotional reactions (feelings):
    Rating scale
    "Right now, I feel. . . ."
  Information received (understandings):
    What were the three most significant learnings for you today?
    What is clear/unclear?
  Feelings of competence in skill (behavior):
    In administering training design, I feel most adequate in. . . .
    List the skills in which you feel others believe you most competent.
  Group process:
    In what ways did your group work well or not well?
    What person seems to hear me the best?
  Future training:
    What would you like to see done in the next session?
    List the three skills which you now would like to practice.
  Trainer design and administration:
    What could the trainers do to be more helpful?
    In the last session, what was most helpful/least helpful?

Guideposts

Members should not necessarily be asked to sign their names.
Results should always be reported back to the group.

Avoid questions that elicit "yes" or "no" answers.
The sharpness of questions determines the sharpness of answers.
Data are guides, not determinants for you as trainer.
If the group resists using reaction forms, they need to become more involved in the decision to use them and in planning the questions and knowing the use of the results.
Data in written form are only part of the data needed.[7]

In terms of evaluation, how do we test or measure an increase in a trainee's skills? How do we find evidence of improved transferability of learning to actual outreach situations? What is included in this measurement tool? What are the criteria? We should again check with the agency management to see if our norms are shared. That is, are the attainable agency and trainer goals clearly identified and integrally related with the orginization's subsystems and staff needs? When this is clarified, the agency can be more responsive to problems within the agency. Gaps of performance skills begin to surface in the organization's units or subsystems.

With mutual clarification by the agency and trainer about what is needed to competently carry out agency goals and objectives, an organizational competency model can be prepared:

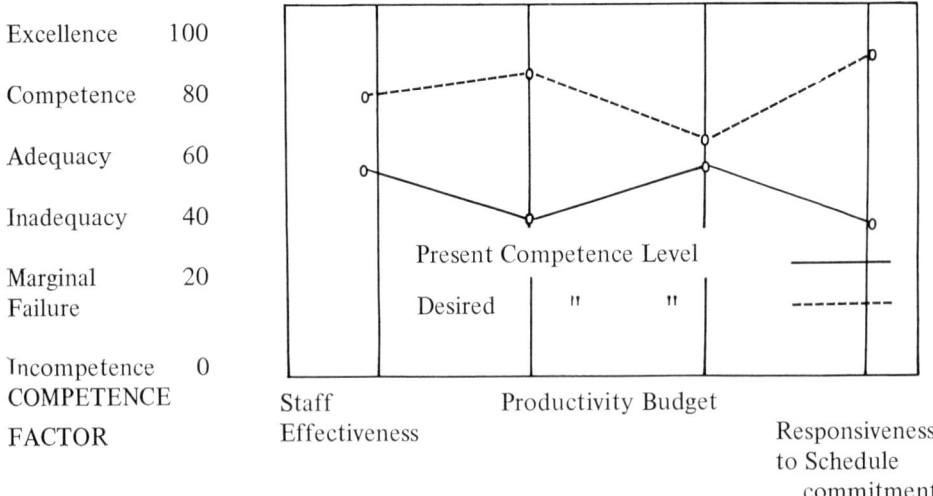

FIGURE V-3. Organizational Competency Model.

The competency model depicts where you're at, where you want to go, and the performance gaps to be eliminated to maximize the end-products. Inci-

---

[7] Matthew B. Miles: *Learning to Work in Groups* (New York, Teachers College, Columbia University Press, 1959).

dentally, the gaps between the agency and street needs often produce a strong motivation to close such gaps.

An individual competency model may be used by the trainee for measuring self-improvement. It may also be used by a supervisor in conferences with the worker. This enables the supervisor and the worker to have a better "fix" on the worker's behavior. I have used it with my training staff as an agenda at group conferences, a measuring device for my perception and theirs of their job skill development. This model better enables me to have a solid feel for the particular training under evaluation:

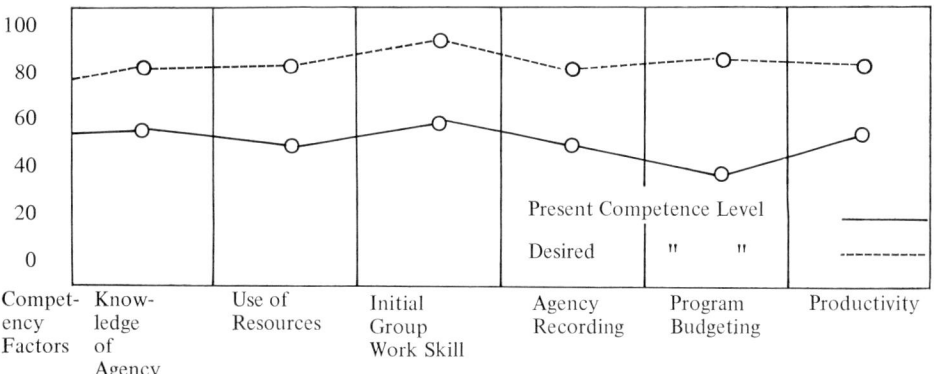

FIGURE V-4. Individual Competency Model.

Evaluation Clinics

A clinic is an evaluation and sharing session in which trainers and (where applicable) trainees with common responsibilities meet to:

    Provide reinforcement to each other's accepted behavioral changes.

    Give support to one another's learnings and values generated during the sessions.

    Explore and develop new skills, methods, formats and devices to enhance one's professional competence.

    Extend workshop learnings to new outreach settings, and experiment with variations on new learning experience.

An evaluation form may combine narration, *yes* or *no* answers, or measurement, as follows:

1. My new learning in this session was:

Nonexistent	Some	A fair amount	A good deal	A great deal	(continuum)

2. What I liked about the training session was:
3. What I did not like about the training session was:
4. What I would like to see continued in the training:

5. What I would not like to see continued in training:
6. Did you like the trainer?
   Why?
7. Did you not like the trainer?
   Why?
8. Other comments, criticisms or ideas.

Summary

Instead of the overall program seen as a series of training sessions, it needs to be thought of as an ongoing *process* whereby objectives are continuously clarified, problems identified and action responses designed and implemented. The outcome of training expected by the organization and that of the trainer should be the same, as well as their clarity on expectations, relationships, support for the worker and for the agency. Factors that contribute to or detract from training should be evaluated and approaches developed which identify critical interdependent elements that must be dealt with to solve the problem.

Training is not only goal-oriented but is also "time-limited," with specific limits on actual time permitted for rendering service. As trainers we are helping staff function more effectively within their agency or social environments. The trainer must also aid his organization to achieve a climate which enhances the growth and development of staff. To judge the effects of what the trainee has learned, the trainer needs to be aware of the individual, group and community systems in which he operates. Attempts to change behavior at one level must achieve reinforcement and complementary changes at other levels.

The trainee-worker needs to share and try out new knowledge, skills, and attitudes in an agency setting that provides support and approval. Those who have not received training also need encouragement to avoid feelings of rejection. Support is necessary to prevent erosion of new learning experiences over time. New skills must be used or they are forgotten. Reinforcing experiences are necessary to stimulate continued use of new skills.

Laird echoes my desire for reinforcement of training—we can change behavior, and we can help each other do so. That is the underlying base for training, particularly in training outreach workers. We have found that:

1. The learner will seek specific rather than abstract goals. Training must be geared to this premise—immediate need satisfaction.
2. The consulted individual will ask specific rather than general questions.

If we don't deal with specific instances, we can philosophize endlessly about the "then and should" and avoid the threatening realities of the "here and now."

Laird writes that "Maybe the Desired Behavior is actually something like this: [the trainer] *will discriminate between generalities and principles—and build his principles upon concrete examples.*"[8]

The involvement of various levels of an organization in need-assessment and problem-solving is often disturbing to traditional leaders in public and private agencies. Where the demands of an agency block the normal development of staff, poor motivation and frustration of organizational goals usually occur. This situation in an agency can be seen in high turnover of staff, low productivity, high costs, waste of programs, and poor service. Training can mitigate many of these problems in outreach projects.

Recent events have reinforced the conclusion, already held by many in urban government, that action must be taken—and swiftly—to avoid continued restlessness in our cities. Urban recreation offers perhaps the greatest potential for immediate, visible results. By providing a direct outlet for excess energies, planned recreation can be a practicable and effective alternative to far more dangerous means of releasing pent-up energies and emotions.

If all people are to effectively use their leisure, programs and services have to be offered on their terms.[9] If people do not use facilities where the service is, for whatever reason, then the service has to "reach out" to them. In any community there are thousands of youngsters not being reached by traditional programs through traditional agencies. Therefore, it becomes a challenge to serve them through an outreach program.

As for recreation programs that do not meet inner-city needs, I feel we have created these difficulties ourselves by not recognizing the *real* needs of the people we serve. We must serve all the people even if we have to go into the streets to serve them.

SELECTED READINGS

Boocock, S. and Schilde, E.: *Simulation Games in Learning.* Beverly Hills, Calif., Sage Publishers, Inc., 1968.

Cartwright, Dorwin, and Alvin Zander, eds.: *Group Dynamics: Research and Theory.* 2nd ed. Evanston, Ill., Row, Peterson, 1960.

Dawson, Helaine: *On The Outskirts of Hope.* New York, McGraw-Hill, 1969.

Gibbons, Donald: *Delinquent Behavior.* Englewood Cliffs, N. J., Prentice-Hall, 1971.

Klein, Malcolm W.: *Street Gangs and Street Workers.* Englewood Cliffs, N. J., Prentice-Hall, 1971.

Knowles, Malcolm S.: *The Modern Practice of Adult Education.* New York, Association Press, 1970.

---

[8] Dugan Laird: Notes from a Training Director, *Training in Business and Industry,* Vol. 9, no. 11 (Nov. 1972).

[9] Based on an earlier paper by John G. Williams: Staff development. Proceedings of National Forum on *Modernizing Urban Park and Recreation Systems,* Houston, Texas, Oct. 1971 (Washington, D. C., National Park and Recreation Association, 1972), pp. 26-27.

Luft, Joseph: *Group Processes: An Introduction to Group Dynamics.* 2nd ed. Palo Alto, Calif.: National Press Books, 1970.

Miles, Matthew B.: *Learning to Work in Groups.* New York, Columbia Teachers College Press, 1969.

Pearl, A. and Riessman, E.: Training the nonprofessional. *New Careers for the Poor.* New York, The Free Press, 1965.

Poston, Richard W.: *The Gang and the Establishment.* New York, Harper & Row, 1972.

Silverman, David: *The Theory of Organization.* New York, Basic Books, 1972.

CHAPTER VI

ADMINISTRATIVE PROBLEMS INHERENT IN THE OUTREACH PROGRAM

"The Boss Had Better Look Out"

JOHN G. WILLIAMS

THE PARK AND RECREATION MOVEMENT in this country, particularly the public phase, for the most part has been directed at middle-class Americans. This statement is not to repudiate the professionals, for they have followed the legislative dictates of politicians elected by a middle-class electorate. Most recreation and park professionals are middle class themselves in terms of their social, economic and educational background, causing an emphasis on middle-class programming. It has only been recently that inner-city residents have realized their electoral power and have generated enough political pressure to demand government services in recreation and parks. As pressure came for recreation and parks services in the inner city, it became apparent that merely transferring or moving a middle-class recreation program, conducted by professionals with middle-class standards and values, was neither acceptable nor adequate for the needs of the inner city. This would be the same as offering middle-class programs in an upper socioeconomic community, where the cultural, educational and financial resources would require much greater sophistication and achievement.

The administrator of a parks and recreation department, or other city or private agency, has many things to consider when planning an outreach program as part of the department's overall programming. He has to first truly understand the purpose and concepts of an outreach program; such understanding greatly determines whether the program will succeed or fail.

As one visits most large metropolitan areas in this country, one becomes increasingly aware of the great number of youth using the streets as playgrounds. What is additionally obvious, though not necessarily atypical, is that with rare exception a recreation facility is nearby. From inquiries about what discourages youth from using such nearby facilities, one meets with some rather fundamental socioeconomic restrictions and taboos. Such restrictions militate against acceptable or realistic involvement in traditional programs offered by recreation facilities. Physical barriers exist–busy thoroughfares are sometimes given as an excuse. Social barriers, primarily intangible boundaries, make open access to nearby facilities difficult. The cultural environment often prevents involvement in traditional programs because of misunderstood behavior patterns. And, all too frequently, so much time is necessary to satisfy the personal needs of these youth, that program expediency dictates alienation rather than incorporation into facility activities.

In many cases, a park and recreation department's programs are nothing more than promoting "fun and games" on its playgrounds and other facilities. As already noted, most of these programs are directed at the middle class and ignore those who need the services most. The profession has not kept up with changing lifestyles or other changes such as working hours, leisure patterns, and an individual's "today" needs. As we shift from a work-oriented society, wherein jobs no longer meet man's higher-lever needs, we turn to leisure and recreational activities to satisfy these same needs. Yet the influencers of leisure and recreation are still concerned with fun and games confined to an out-of-touch environment called the playground. If a change is to occur, it probably won't be in trying to teach the "old dogs" new tricks, but in creating a leisure-service system, with a new role and purpose, starting in the colleges with a new breed of professionals.

A close examination of most leisure programs will reveal that they are nothing more than a list of activities. Granted that in many cases these activities are, for the most part, enjoyable and interesting. But scrutiny of these programs reveals that only those who can readily conform get a great deal out of them and are allowed to participate. I'm not against having participants conform in activities, since one cannot have a successful program unless participants follow the rules and regulations. If just one person or a few disrupt the class or activity, it often becomes necessary to exclude them to permit others who *can* conform and abide by the rules to fully enjoy the activity. The recreation and park profession has been guilty many times of excluding youth from programs because they don't conform. Perhaps we justify such exclusion because of limited staff—we "shoo" them out the door and into the streets to become someone else's problem.

However, the question is still there: What *about* those who cannot conform? What about those who have personality problems, those who act frustrated because they do not have the skills, or significant sophistication, or sufficient talent to obtain satisfaction from the activity, those who, in their frustration, seem inevitably to cause discipline problems? What types of programs do we have for those with little talent or with adjustment setbacks?

If we take a hard look at what our programs are, we realize most are nothing more than a facility with a "cafeteria" of activities where participants choose and participate: (1) if they find an activity they are interested in; (2) if they have the skill and sophistication to obtain satisfaction from the activity; (3) if they conform without disrupting an activity; and (4) if they can participate in a highly organized and structured program. What happens if they don't have the skill, cannot conform, don't like the activities? The choice is simple–they either get out or we kick them out. This situation exists in many cities and is no exaggeration.

The traditional center plays an important role in a community for those with the training and background for participating in highly organized, structured programs and for those with the ability to conform. The ones who grow up in homes with interested parents, learn about the need to conform– not merely for the sake of conforming, but with the knowledge that abiding by rules and regulations is important. Those who do not have these advantages, on the other hand, view conforming as simply another indication that life is a struggle, as another reason to rebel. How, then, can we reach those youths who find our programs uninteresting, too structured, or who cannot conform?

We are realizing more and more that environment often dictates the kind of activities one is interested in and will pursue. Generally speaking, every man has certain basic needs which are met in various ways depending on his environment. Quite obviously, an individual in a high socioeconomic area will have many advantages in education, home life, and recreational opportunity and will find that meeting his basic needs is much easier than for someone in poorer circumstances. Conversely, many inner-city residents in the lowest socioeconomic levels of the community, have not had the educational or financial advantages to satisfy many of their basic needs. In fact, one finds many of them without as much formal education as they would like, out of work, or making so little money they can hardly buy enough food or provide shelter for themselves and their families.

Experience indicates that people tend to gravitate toward areas which fulfill their desire to be needed, understood, and accepted. When these fundamental needs are not satisfied, through opportunities for meaningful involvement and positive interaction, there is a tendency to become isolated from the mainstream with an attitude of defiant self-preservation. For disadvantaged youth with parents who tend to support the rationale of isolation and defiance, the consequent alienation often as not precipitates illegal behavior. This is not to say that these individuals should be content with their environment and not pursue a better way of life; but without a job or enough food, it seems ridiculous to impose a middle-class recreation program, directed by middle-class leaders, on them. This lower socioeconomic group should certainly be offered new and different opportunities. However, the conditions of the community, and the attitudes and ambitions of the people, are not to be changed by simply dangling something better in front of them.

Here are some additional reasons why recreation and park agencies find themselves no longer able to meet the needs of inner-city residents. There are lifestyles that are either unrecognized, neglected, or suppressed by these agencies. For instance, casualness in dress and attitude is the "going thing" among people today, but park and recreation agencies are still bound by traditionally strict patterns of appearance, behavior, and customs. Youth constitute a growing proportion of our population and are beginning to feel the economic and political power they can exert. Different hours of employment and leisure require new patterns in patron availability for recreation and park services; but still agencies persist in keeping things as they were. Further, the depth and variety of programming should be affected by the improved sophistication and greater mobility of people; but this is rarely the case.

The question remains, How does outreach serve these individuals, and through what means? To serve them we are going to have to send our leadership outside the recreation center. We are going to have to serve these hard-to-reach people wherever they gather, helping them use their leisure to greater advantage, to become happier citizens and to make a greater community contribution.

The task of outreach programs is with individuals during their leisure–helping them solve personal problems. Very often the service provided is of a social-service type, in great detail and depth. Although the individual who is very close to conforming does not need the social services that one with real personality conflicts does, he or she will still need some help in adjusting to society and developing a good personality. The Outreach Leader may need to get some support from other agencies in the community, as when he helps inner-city youths find jobs or get back into school.

As these young people begin to solve some of the personal problems affecting their attitudes toward the community and society in general, we try to work with them, teaching them how to use their leisure wisely and how to make the most of their free time. Then, as these youths begin to feel more a part of society and begin to use their leisure in a healthy way, we can take them to the nearest recreation center and fit them into the regular program. Of course, the process of rehabilitating individuals is not quite this simple, since many youths never adjust to society.

As we look at the programs offered in many communities, we can readily see that we have two types: the one extreme is recreation programs at a traditional recreation center, with a program and staff primarily facility-oriented and generally designed for persons who conform easily. At the other end we have a Roving Leader program for youth in conflict, or on the verge of getting into serious trouble.

The next question then is, what about all the individuals who are in between these two extremes? The persons who do not conform and, as a result, are excluded from traditional recreation center programs? And what about those who are not enough of a problem to require a Roving Leader program? In other words, those who do not conform but are not real troublemakers in the community. What opportunities are there for these youth?

For most large cities, leisure needs are estimated as follows: Approximately 15 per cent of the population is financially independent and takes care of its own leisure needs; another 15 per cent is less than five years old or is unserviceable for a variety of reasons; the majority of the population (60 per cent) is served by public or private agencies free of charge or at a very minimal cost. This majority is served through traditional, facility-oriented programs which demand conformity to acceptable standards and social mores. Naturally, within this group there are extremes of attitudes served. The overtly antisocial group, a minority, is served by a Roving Leader program where available, with an emphasis on alleviation of conflict and resocialization through recreation. However, between these two ends of the social spectrum, one finds a remaining ten per cent of the population consisting primarily of youth. These forgotten people balance precariously between a desire and need for socialization and understanding, and the cultural realities which make conformity to the status quo difficult at best and tempt revenge as social redress. It is to these youth the Roving Leader program should also address itself, realizing that to offer them a service which is both understandable and meaningful, recreation opportunities must *reach out* to them. As in all recreation planning, while we have an obligation to provide opportunities for choice, we have a more fundamental responsibility to provide a background against which choices can be made. Here lies the rationale for expanding the Roving Leader program.

When you come right down to it, there are few agencies in a community that are truly interested in troublesome youth. The police department deals with them when they have broken a law, but has no other real interest. The school board is interested as long as they are good students. Other than a few recreation-oriented agencies, the other community services exclude such youth if they cannot conform and comply with middle-class standards. Also, a majority of agencies are open nine to five and close their doors to anyone after hours. Unless there are recreation programs or Roving Leaders, there is really no one interested in helping these youth with their problems and ultimately guiding them into the mainstream of society.

Another barrier preventing agencies from meeting inner-city needs in program services is the vital issue of citizen involvement. Citizens often wanting to have a word or hand in decision-making and program determination feel inadequate when confronted with professional superiority and techniques, a feeling produced not totally from lack of education, but more from lack of experience. Civil Service systems fail to acknowledge the inner-city residents' volunteer service of special skills when considering them for employment. Government restrictions and arbitrary limitations on grants and projects bar interested communities and neighborhoods from participation. Agencies often find the individual's stay in a community is temporary and become wary of involving transient residents in long-range programs. In addition, agencies are often confronted with citizen demands that create hostilities between them. Self-determination of programs by people–both youth and adult–presupposes an education that the citizen lacks.

Nonetheless, the principle of self-determination is playing an ever-increasing role in today's society. Too often the right of people to be heard, regardless of age, race, sex, creed, draft, or socioeconomic status, has been denied by governments at the city, state and national levels. As a result, the "establishment" is not only being questioned, but is being challenged by proponents of local control. The proponents for decentralization argue that there is need for change, but to alter the establishment through conventional channels appears impossible, because in the eyes of the poor and the "have nots" government does not really want to change. Government believes the poor and have nots do not know what is best for them.

The hang-up of providing recreation and park services that meet inner-city needs centers on resources for program planning and implementation. There is a definite failure on the agency's part to recognize indigenous human and natural resources, particularly in youth, that could be used by the agency. Too often lack of financial resources is the excuse for poor programming, and no attempts are made to overcome this limitation. The programming potential of existing physical resources–bars, poolhalls, military bases, industrial warehouses, churches, etc.–is completely overlooked by too many recreation and park agencies. These, then, are just a few of the reasons we have failed.

The best way to improve some of these conditions is to change the environment. This can most effectively be done by greater use and development of the natural leadership in a community. Right here is a most challenging task. After this leadership is recognized and developed, it must start working with the community by recognizing the *now* needs of the community and by shaping recreation programs that will meet these needs.

Specific needs of inner-city residents should be determined by a natural leader from the community *and* the residents themselves. Through outreach work, the recreation program and facilities should be built around inner-city demands, as the natural leaders recognize them. These are the people who are equipped to give leadership and direction to inner-city residents, with help from park and recreation agencies. The recreation profession as a public service agency, has a unique opportunity in that it appeals to all people. It is a non-threatening service–happy and pleasurable to use–and generally it requires only leisure to make it available. Often inner-city residents have more leisure than any group because of unemployment or being out of school, and this fact too offers the park and recreation profession quite a challenge.

We will have to go out into the streets and up alleys to work with these people. Some staff may even require specialized training in group dynamics in their efforts to help these people adjust to society and use their leisure wisely. For the most part, we will work with individuals in small groups. We will need more personal understanding of their problems and, of course, we would require more patience with them. If these individuals are not willing to come to recreation centers, then we will take recreation programs to them. This can be done with Traveling Recreation Leaders who close off streets and create instant playgrounds, or with portable pools and mobile recreation centers.

Operating a mobile or portable recreation program is not simply buying some mobile equipment, furnishing it, staffing it, and sending it into the community. When only this approach is used, the program is doomed to fail and will never obtain the potential of a properly planned mobile program. A

Baltimore News American photograph.

FIGURE VI-1. Summer Fun. Spray devices attached to fire hydrants make for Maxi-Sprinklers.

portable program is much more–it is a different program altogether and requires a different philosophy and approach to implement and sustain it.

Mobile recreation is the tool, and carryover the goal. The emphasis is on instant play areas served by FUN WAGONS, TRAVELING PLAYLEADERS, a mobile NATURE WAGON or PORTABLE POOLS. These facilities are set up in areas of the city where activity is normally unavailable. The TRAVELING PLAYLEADER program involves the use of well-trained leaders who concentrate on involving children between 5 and 12 years of age in the joys of quiet recreation play. Each leader gathers children from "isolated" neighborhoods, finds a safe, quiet area in an alley or a vacant lot, and directs a variety of games and activities ranging from jacks to creative expression. With an emphasis on carryover and minimal equipment, which the leader carries in a duffel bag, the burden is placed on the leader's ability to motivate and create positive attitudes toward leisure and activity. Each leader is assigned five areas to be visited twice a week.

To complement the playleader's efforts, a portable recreation center or FUN WAGON is used. This versatile equipment adds a new dimension to the outreach program by attacking the twin demons of boredom and poverty, by providing wholesome, active recreation where and when it is needed. Not in hard-to-reach parks or activities, not in already overburdened recreation areas, but right in the city streets–the very recruiting ground for the forces of unrest. Beyond that, it provides flexibility–activity for all ages, all backgrounds. The Fun Wagon can be moved quickly, easily and often, covering large areas at minimal cost and with maximum effectiveness. This "portable recreation center" establishes patterns of wholesome activity that can be continued even after the initial stimulus has been withdrawn. It can offer individuals the dignity and satisfaction of helping oneself and one's neighbors in a real and measurable way.

It is, in essence, a complete recreation center on wheels. Within minutes of its arrival, any city street in even the most depressed areas can be converted into a fully equipped recreation center with activities for all. It effectively provides instant recreation in areas where no facilities are available and where help is needed most urgently. Since the programs and activities offered by the Fun Wagon can be continued on a permanent basis after the Wagon itself has left, it provides a positive stimulus to really improve social conditions in impoverished urban communities.

Since Fun Wagon activities are planned and programmed as a complete recreation package, maximum effectiveness can be achieved. The package concept also encourages using community residents as recreation aids and playleaders–either as volunteers or temporary employees. This potential for direct community involvement is every bit as significant as the benefits from the recreation activities to the inhabitants themselves.

FIGURE VI-2. Street Play.

The activities available through the Fun Wagon are broad in scope and encourage participation by youth of all ages. The Fun Wagon includes athletic opportunities as well as more passive pursuits–crafts, puzzles and table games. Such sports as basketball, volleyball, shuffleboard, and duck pins (bowling) are well received. Citywide contests are brought to isolated areas, often for the first time, involving games and toys like "hula-hoops," "yo-yos" and "limbo legs." An expandable puppet stage is available as part of the Fun Wagon, and a public address-phonograph set implements such creative activities as dance, drama and music. A spray device which attaches to fire hydrants brings to concrete and brick jungles the proverbial "sprinkler" in which to frolic (see Figures VI-1 and VI-2 above, and Figure VI-3 on p. 139).

Portable pools can be taken during the summer months into parts of the city, where access to municipal pools is difficult, and provide lessons and free aquatic play for thousands of youngsters; for the most part, these youth never have enjoyed the excitement of aquatic activity.[1]

Another innovation, the NATURE WAGON, was designed for children who have little or no exposure to even the most basic natural wonders of animal and plant life. A specialist travels with the Nature Wagon offering visual and tactile exposure to woodland animals and vegetation. These mobile facilities and talented leaders share positive, constructive, enjoyable alternatives with youth who might otherwise engage in activities which often prove harmful to themselves as well as to society. This service has proved highly successful in educating this ten per cent of our population in understanding their leisure.

It is the objective of outreach programs to provide a way for young, disadvantaged youth to find their all-important niche in society. In the long run, it is hoped that such programming will be unnecessary and obsolete. However, now that the needs are all too apparent and the scope of these needs is so broad, the outreach programs continue to introduce new experiences offering exposure to more creative art (through a mobile ART CENTER) and a greater variety of play activity for the streets.

The reactions to the available equipment and tangible aspects of outreach, such as leadership, are easily observable. However, for success, it is paramount that our presence be felt even more so when the tangible goods are absent. The strength of the "drive for play" in young people is second to none; this drive, coupled with parental demands for proximal recreation in many disadvantaged areas (restrictions and taboos), demands that our goals become carryover in the strongest sense. Using exciting, creative, yet minimal equipment and games, activities during the periods between outreach visits can be times of enjoyable activity rather than of unhappy boredom.

From an administrator's standpoint, there are many problems in establishing an outreach program. The major one, obviously, is the total lack of understanding of the need for such programs and a real apathy by government officials and agencies in dealing with youth. The attitude seems to be one of, *why can't these youth act like everyone else?* And, why can't they participate in *regular* recreation programs? Finally, *why should government have to spend thousands of dollars working with a handful of youth that can't conform, can't live by the rules like everybody else?* "Outreach" is such a novel concept to many, that few people are even aware there are cities and agencies conducting such programs. As a result of these attitudes, no one

---

[1] Herman Silverman: Portable swimming pool—Going strong, *Park and Recreation* (March 1969), pp. 48-50.

FIGURE VI-3. On with the Show!

takes the lead, no one tries to establish a program to help troublesome youth. Rather, they wait until the kids are in *real* trouble and then throw them in jail or some other institution.

With outreach programs, there are few tangible results to indicate what one has accomplished. It can be pointed out that x number of youth were served, but the success of the program can only be measured by the problems that *do not* occur–the group conflicts that are contained without violence, the weapon that does not get used, the dope that is not taken, the crime that goes uncommitted. While these things cannot be ascertained, it is still the responsibility of the outreach program to serve youth in the hopes that such serious outcomes will be avoided.

Obviously, because of its uniqueness, the funding of outreach programs is sometimes difficult. In trying to obtain funding, it is discouraging to point to results. There is little support for government to sponsor such programs. With so many demands on public monies, funding a seemingly novel concept is even harder. Furthermore, there is no one agency with responsibility for such programs, which fact weakens the effect of requests for funds in an agency's budget. It is almost impossible to sell a program without specific tangible impact.

In starting outreach programs, personnel too is a problem. Other than through special training institutes, where and how does a community leader get more information? Aside from a few agencies who have started programs based on trial-and-error efforts resulting from conceptual ideas, administrators find little documentation to help them begin programs. As we seek to establish an outreach program, we find that other service agencies may recognize the need for one, but will do little to help establish it. To be fair, they may not understand what you and I are trying to do; or maybe, they question the competence of our agency in directing such a program. There seems to be some professional elitism on the part of social work and allied professions toward sanctioning only programs which are headed by administrators with advanced degrees. Only time, experience, and tangible results will gain the support of some of these allied professions and agencies.

Sixty to eighty per cent of the Roving Leader's time is spent in social services other than recreation–helping teenagers and young adults solve their personal problems, find jobs, get back in school, or helping one of them with some run-in with the police. Even with a liberal interpretation of the objectives of recreation, this may not seem to be the role for a park and recreation department. However that may be, the remaining 20 to 30 per cent of a Roving Leader's time is spent using recreation to gain the confidence and trust of youth.

It is through recreation activities that the leader can most effectively detect what the kids are *really* like, what their innermost problems are–their concerns, their likes, their hates, as well as many other personality traits. Although a large per cent of a Roving Leader's association with youth is viewed as more social-service oriented, what other agency would have contact with these people during their leisure?

Your staff may resent outreach programs because of budget and personnel constraints. They might need new equipment in other established programs; and you want a new program costing thousands which takes money from *their* requirements. Their attitude may be that this isn't recreation's responsibility, so why should the agency fund it? "Let someone else do it," is the usual comment. Salaries can also create problems. To attract the kind of outreach leader needed, a salary comparable to that of a center director or other middle management member usually has to be offered. Often a conflict arises between the traditional center director and the outreach leader on salary. The center directors feel the outreach leader hasn't all the responsibility he claims. The administrator has to be prepared to defend and explain these differences to his own staff as well as to other agencies, his board, or anyone taking potshots at the program.

In initiating this kind of program, every effort should be made to sell the concept in advance, to show to the existing staff how the program can complement and support them, how the center directors can refer some troublesome youth to outreach leaders and ultimately make their centers function more effectively. It must be shown that it is the responsibility of recreation to serve *all* youth. That is, the park and recreation profession is dedicated to helping people use their leisure and free time to good advantage. Likewise, we should be just as concerned with helping people who are misusing their free time or leisure. Many recreation techniques give the Roving Leader an entrée to gain the confidence of youth and really help them.

One way some misunderstandings can be overcome is to involve the outreach leader in staff meetings or every time the recreation personnel meet, so they can all get to know one another and exchange philosophies and ideas so as to understand each other's problems and see how each can help the other. If the agency has an inservice training program, specific sessions conducted by both outreach leaders and traditional recreation personnel, on what they are doing and the concepts and techniques they use, can reduce ambivalences.

In addition to these exchanges, there are some natural areas in which the administrator can encourage cooperation between the outreach leader and the directors of various facilities in a park and recreation department. When outreach leaders see youth that are ready to fit into community activity, they can seek a good way to involve the boys in the regular recreation program. Maybe it starts with the outreach leader using the gymnasium at the local recreation center during the dinner hour from 6:00 to 7:00 each evening when no one else is in the center for basketball practice, tumbling, or whatever activity. Maybe the next step could be to place the team, coached by the outreach leader, in the regular center basketball league; ultimately, one or two players on the team could sign up on a regular center team to play in the league. Whatever the tactic, the objective is to begin to move the youth into some regular activity.

With time and good administrative direction, the Roving Leader program can become a natural and integral part of a recreation and park agency. It does not take long for the center directors and other staff to see what an asset this service can be to regular traditional programming. Referrals can be made back and forth for youth that need service and those that have learned to operate in the mainstream. As the program begins to become established, the outreach leader begins to make increased contacts with other agencies. These agencies too begin to see the advantages and need for this particular program and to appreciate the ways it benefits and assists them. Better cooperation and support can then develop. All this takes time and keen, shrewd leadership by the Roving Leader.

As to where the outreach leader program should be located, there are many possibilities: the park and recreation department is a logical first choice. Recreation and park professionals understand many of the techniques that outreach leaders must have, and there are many obvious tie-ins with existing programs. Also, recreation and park agencies are not 9:00 to 5:00 operations, but operate in afternoons and evenings when many youth need help. However, more than any other factor as to location, is the attitude and support the program receives from the top administrator. The program can present many problems, but these can be overcome if those in charge really support it. Outreach programs have even been operated successfully as independent agencies, financed by the United-Way type of funds and many other means.

There are areas in which action *must* be taken if the park and recreation profession is going to meet the challenge of providing efficient outreach services in the inner city. First, we have too long grouped people into one category and in one recreation center, without recognizing individual needs, interests and personalities. Second, we have imposed our values and standards in the areas of skills as well as behavior, without regard for the social or economic status of communities. Third, we have not kept up with contemporary trends in our profession as well as in other disciplines and professions. Fourth, we have not involved the people we serve in program planning and problem-solving. Fifth, we have tried to raise individuals' leisure pursuits by rules, regulations and policies, rather than by motivating them to better activities. And sixth, we have become too facility-oriented.

We need to take a program out to the people we serve. It's time to extend an encouraging hand to these individuals. There is still a great need for conventional facility-oriented programs, but they do not serve all the people. We need to reach out and help those who have not discovered the value of wholesome leisure. This "reach-out" program will supplement our facility programs and give them a new dimension, and help each citizen use his leisure wisely for a fuller, more fruitful life.

CHAPTER REFERENCES AND SELECTED READINGS

Bannon, Joseph J.: A creative dimension in recreation training, *Illinois Career Journal*, Vol. 30, no. 1, Autumn 1972.

Guggenheimer, Elinor: *Planning for Park and Recreation Needs in Urban Areas,* New York: Twayne Publishers, 1969.
Jenkins, Shirley: *Comparative Recreation Needs and Services in New York Neighborhoods,* New York, Research Department, Community Council of Greater New York, 1963.
Kraus, Richard: *Recreation and Leisure in Modern Society,* New York, Appleton-Century-Crofts, 1971.
Lowden, Wingo: Recreation and urban development: A policy perspective, *Annals of the American Academy of Political and Social Science,* 1964.
Montgomery, William L.: Programming that reaches the unreachables, *Proceedings of the Congress for Recreation and Parks,* Washington, D. C., National Recreation and Park Association, 1968.
Premo, M. J. (Ed.): *Parks and Recreation in the Urban Crisis,* Washington, D. C., Report of National Forum on Urban Affairs, National Recreation and Park Association, 1969.
Programs for Urban Action, New York, National Council of Young Men's Christian Association, 1968.
Recreation in the Nation's Cities: Problems and Approaches, Washington, D. C., National League, of cities, 1968.
Study of Recreation Needs and Services in South Central Los Angeles. Los Angeles, Recreation and Youth Services Planning Council, 1966.

CHAPTER VII

THE REFERRAL PROCESS

"Outreach's Little Helpers"

DONALD H. PARKIN

THE MAIN CONCERN of this chapter is how an outreach worker functions as part of a total community. As indicated in an earlier chapter (Ch. II), we are concerned with the relationship of recreation to the larger social structure. The referral process encompasses a community's complete resources in varying degrees, depending on the community's circumstances.

Social Systems

The approach in this chapter, so we can apply the referral process, will be that of social systems.[1] Let's imagine a city of 500,000 which we will call King City, U.S.A. This city could be much larger, the size of New York, or much smaller. The size is insignificant. We refer to King City as our suprasystem.

A *suprasystem* is the largest system in any given situation which the systems analyst is primarily concerned with. For example, the world could be a suprasystem with continents comprising subsystems. You could also have nations comprising subsystems if nations were the parts of the world you were primarily concerned with. Nations could also be regarded as subsystems of one continent if, for example, nations in South America were your primary concern. In our situation, our largest system of primary concern is King City, which is representative of any other city you might desire to use. A *suprasystem* has a purpose for existence and may be broken down into several *sub*systems which corporately serve the purpose of the larger system.[2] In Figure VII-1, we show the basic concept of a suprasystem, its subsystems, and the relationships of purpose. Each subsystem has its own purpose which contributes to the purpose of the suprasystem.

The only way the purpose of King City can be achieved is through the combined purposes of all its subsystems. What really is Chicago? Chicago

---

[1] Robert Boguslaw: *The New Utopians* (Englewood Cliffs, N. J., Prentice-Hall, Inc., 1965), pp. 1-7.
[2] Bela H. Benathy: *Instructional Systems* (Belmont, Calif., Fearon Publishers, 1968), p. 13.

146   *Outreach*

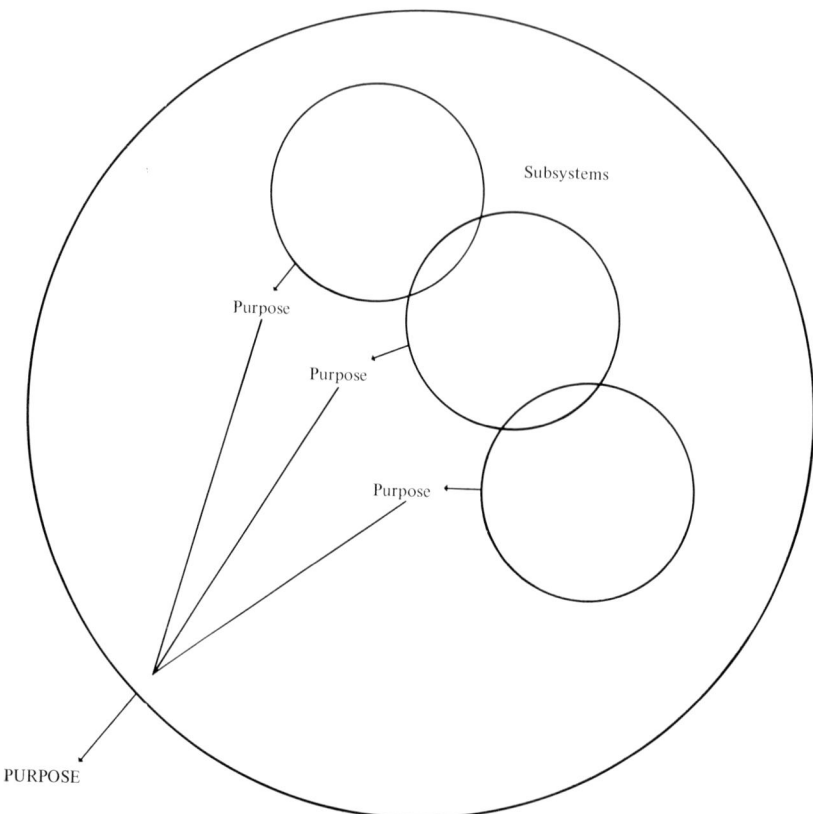

FIGURE VII-1. Suprasystem "King" City.

is a political subsystem, a school subsystem, a recreation and parks subsystem, a social subsystem, an industrial subsystem, and so on. The extent to which any one subsystem or combination of subsystems fails to function, is the degree to which the suprasystem likewise fails in accomplishing *its* purpose. Occasionally, subsystems perceive themselves as the system around which all other systems revolve. In the referral process, the main difficulty with this type of arrogance is that such egotistical systems see little need for other systems to be referred to them or to make referrals from them. It is important we understand the function of purpose and the way each subsystem contributes to the overall purpose of the suprasystem.

When you discuss purpose, you are speaking of output or, as Likert calls it, "end-result variables."[3] The output of a system is closely associated with the accomplishment of purpose. For example, if the purpose of a state cor-

---

[3] Rensis Likert: *New Patterns of Management* (New York, McGraw-Hill Book Co., Inc., 1961), p. 201.

rectional institution is rehabilitation, then output will be measured quite closely with the rate of recidivism; the lower the rate, the more successful the institution. Output and purpose should be concomitant, though quite often they are not.

The Purpose of the Suprasystem

To define the purpose of a city is certainly controversial. However, since we need a purpose, let me offer one you can tear apart. (Whatever purpose you finally devise, plug it in, and proceed with your own city.) For King City the purpose is simply for man, a social being, to live with other social beings. King City provides man with the opportunity to live in a perpetual state of opposing forces between his own needs and those of the immediate society.[4] There are laws regarding animals, mores regarding dead people, and other similar rules regarding nonliving human concerns. However, such concerns are primarily for the benefit of the living.

---

[4] Elliot Aronson: *The Social Animal* (San Francisco, W. H. Freeman and Co., 1972), p. 13.

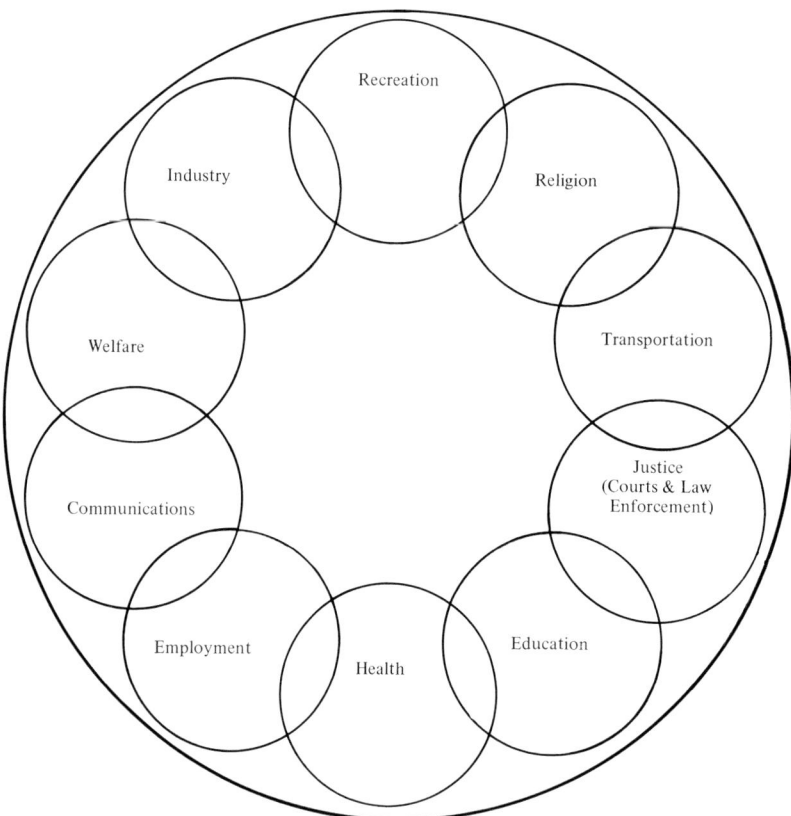

FIGURE VII-2. Subsystems of the Suprasystem "King" City.

If the purpose of a city can be defined–and let's assume you have defined yours–then we can begin to define the conglomerate purposes of the city's subsystems. Figure VII-2 shows some of the social-service subsystems of King City. Social-serving agencies from both the private and public sectors are interspersed in this figure. (These two sectors will be delineated in the last section of this chapter under the heading, How to Identify Gaps in Services.) On a New Towns Project I worked on, we sought to establish a new town with no old-town interference. We had twenty-two subsystems in our proposed city, with two recreation colleagues and myself working on the recreation subsystem. Each subsystem had to establish its own purpose, but each purpose was established in conjunction with the purpose for the New Town. That made sense. If recreation were to be a part of the whole, it had to contribute to the purpose of the whole.

Dysfunction

An important social system principle has emerged: If the purpose of a subsystem does *not* contribute to the purpose of the suprasystem, there is dysfunction.[5] Remember our social being living in a constant state of opposing forces between *him* and all the other *hims?* He's got enough trouble just surviving, without the added difficulty of an impaired social environment because of friction between a subsystem and the larger city. In a utopian new town situation, we could possibly use Skinner's *Walden Two* and schedule our man into nonconflicting situations.[6] Such possibilities are not the mere whims of irresponsible persons. Social systems are not to be confused with automated systems. The systems concept can be approached from different directions. Boguslaw presents some clearly delineated possibilities for the aspirations of utopian automated systems when applied to society:

> One of the more familiar elements of utopian thought is the aspiration to transcend present reality. This aspiration is normally seen as something less than a dream but more than a simple acceptance of the status quo. Utopians are builders who reject their contemporary status quos and reach out for new forms within which to shape their wished-for worlds. David Riesman once described utopia as a plan that now is nowhere but that someday may be somewhere. In the contemporary world, this utopian 'plan' has become known as the process of 'system design.'
>
> But utopian thinking embraces much more than a plan. It contains the implicit notion that societies must be built free from human imperfections. The classical utopians tried to achieve this end by populating their social systems with perfect human beings, perfect social structures, perfect situations, or perfect principles. They were do-gooders in the finest sense of the term. They des-

---

[5] John A. Seiler: *Systems Analysis in Organizational Behavior* (Homewood, Ill., Richard D. Irwin, Inc., and the Dorsey Press, 1967), pp. 17-19.

[6] B. F. Skinner: *Walden Two* (New York, Macmillan Co., 1948).

perately wished to escape from the melancholy world in which they lived into a happier, more moral, more just, or more prosperous one. Their primary concern was people—although some focused their efforts upon saving souls while others focused on filling stomachs.

But the new utopians are concerned with non-people and people-substitutes. Their planning is done with computer hardware, system procedures, functional analyses, and heuristics. . . . Impatience with 'human error' has become a unifying imperative among the new utopians. The theoretical and practical solutions they seek call increasingly for decreases in the number and in the scope of responsibility of human beings within the operating structures of their new machined systems.[7]

The outreach worker would be obsolete if either Skinner's *Walden Two* or the utopian machine systems were to become reality. Fortunately, in King City we are dealing with reality. We cannot manipulate or program the purpose of the suprasystem; only individual subsystems can be manipulated. Therefore in recreation, for example, it is important that the subsystem work as completely as possible to achieve the purpose of the suprasystem. In King City, man is seeking a state of equilibrium between his individual needs and those of his immediate environment. In recreation we deal with man's ever-changing leisure needs.

Equilibrium

When we state that a subsystem can be manipulated and a suprasystem cannot, we mean the suprasystem is the subsystems. As each subsystem comes into contact with man—caught between the opposing forces of himself and the suprasystem–the subsystem can be manipulated. This manipulation can be from within or without and is a continual process in a social system. No matter how dynamic or frequent the changes may be, each social system is constantly seeking a balance between the needs of individuals and the needs of the larger system.[8] Each of these systems concepts is significant for understanding the referral process.

If recreation or any other subsystem could satisfy the whole spectrum of man's needs, individual and social, there would be no need for any other subsystems. When a subsystem attempts to overextend its services, it usually does a poor job of fulfilling its own purpose. For instance, education's purpose and recreation's are distinct, with each contributing toward the larger system. They work together and apart, each system realizing its part of the whole suprasystem. We consequently discover another facet of social systems–that of contributing purposes of individual subsystems to the process of equilibrium. In 1917 or 1918 the National Education Association established seven cardinal principles devised to inform other subsystems of how

---

[7] Robert Boguslaw: *Op. cit.,* p. 2.
[8] John Seiler: *Op. cit.,* pp. 13-15.

education envisioned its purpose in King City. This poor subsystem has been maligned by the inhabitants of King City and by other subsystems for not accomplishing its purpose. However, each system is responsible for accomplishing its own purpose and cannot escape this responsibility by illuminating the failures of another peer system.

If a subsystem is not doing its job, and if it is a powerful system, the equilibrium process may cause a shift in favor of the inadequately functioning system. We have all observed this when a poor political system influences the entire suprasystem. But inevitably man comes to the forefront, the pendulum swings, and the lame-duck system is manipulated. This doesn't mean some subsystems shouldn't put the heat on another subsystem to shape up, but that the primary responsibility of *each* subsystem is to accomplish its own purpose.

Interfacing

Figure VII-3 depicts where subsystems overlap. Interfacing is the area where two systems perform the same or very similar tasks in seeking to achieve their purposes and, hopefully, the purpose of the suprasystem. In this diagram recreation is shown overlapping with other subsystems, but these are not all the subsystems which interface with recreation. To some extent, every social-serving subsystem interfaces with every other subsystem; however, this figure is only to demonstrate the interfacing aspects of social systems. Although this may seem a long introduction to the referral process, this is where the outreach worker from one subsystem encounters outreach workers from other subsystems. Here is a common ground, a point of contact where two subsystems have mutual interests and concerns. It is important for the outreach worker to make initial contacts with other subsystems through interface areas. This establishes respect and unanimity, the old "all for one and one for all" approach. "Those guys in recreation can't be all that bad. They actually do something besides play games and have fun."

Let's practice our interfacing idea. In education one of the seven cardinal principles is "the worthy use of leisure time." To recreation outreach workers this should sound familiar. This is an interface. However, if you have ever engaged in the intricacies of the marriage between recreation and education you know how high the divorce rate is. Both recreation and education usually have choice words for their indolent subsystem peer. The lines are drawn, and the outreach worker has one less social-serving agency for referral.

STOP! Go back to where we discussed the primary responsibility of each individual system to achieve its own purpose. In a social system we are not our brother's keeper. (We may get into trouble with the religious system for such a statement.) In the referral process it is important not to hassle an-

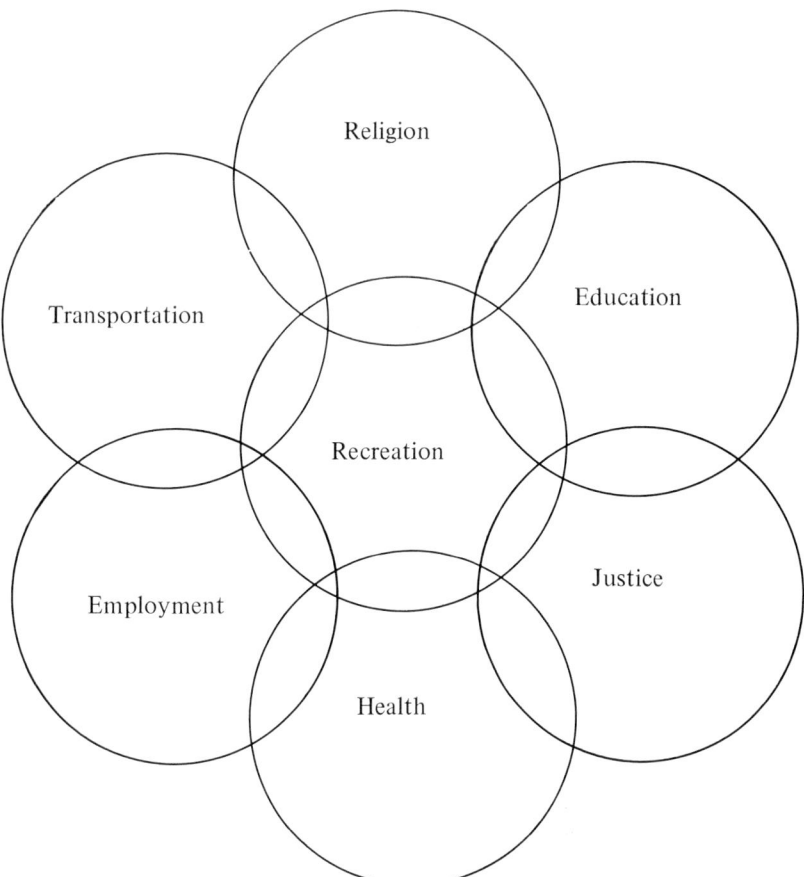

FIGURE VII-3. Interfacing of Subsystems.

other subsystem. The outreach worker must be willing to accept another subsystem's primary purpose, for good or bad, for better or worse.

Keeping Pace With Change
Primary Purpose

Two concepts have been confusingly yet intentionally presented in close proximity to illustrate a point. First, an area of interface–"worthy use of leisure time"–was presented, where education and recreation converged in a common area. Second, we referred to the primary purpose of each subsystem, not areas of common ground. Since primary purpose is the basic reason for a subsystem's existence within the larger suprasystem, each must try to answer the question: "What is my role within the suprasystem?" Also, each subsystem must recognize the autonomy of other subsystems' primary purposes. Without this acceptance of the primary purpose of each subsystem,

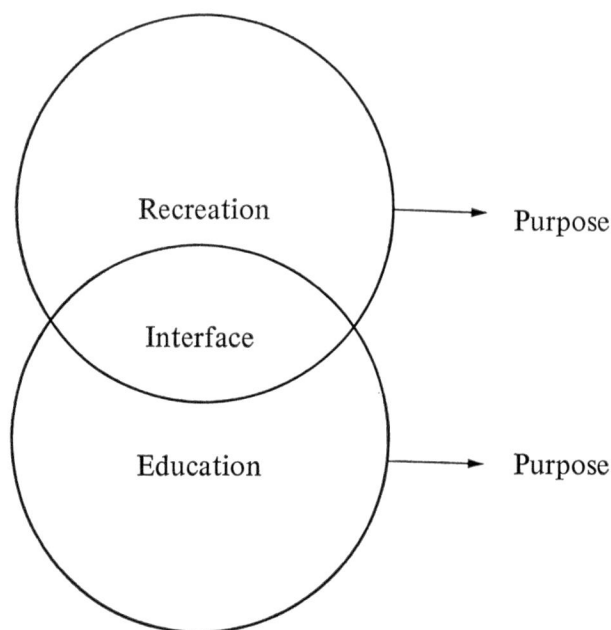

FIGURE VII-4. Primary Purpose—Each System Has Its Goal.

there is no referral process. When an outreach worker encounters a dropout from school, and when the dropout decides to drop back in, the outreach worker makes a referral to the education subsystem. If education is not doing its job (usually they are–it's just peripheral critics not knowing what the score is), this is education's responsibility, not the outreach worker's.

Rate of Change

When dysfunction occurs it is usually because the primary purpose of a subsystem is incongruent with the purpose of the suprasystem. It would appear all we would have to do is simply change one of the systems to fit the other. The suprasystem only changes while the whole system seeks a state of equilibrium. This change is made by all the subsystems in concert with each other. This leaves only one avenue for direct change and that is within the incongruent subsystem. Invariably, subsystems are resistant to change. Each subsystem wants all the other systems to change to meet his primary purpose. Of course, these other subsystems are also resistant to change themselves. When change does occur, it usually is a result of man's functioning individually and corporately to seek a state of balance between his individual needs and the needs of the larger system.

The ability to change is an important aspect of systems. Social systems are in a constant state of flux as they seek a state of equilibrium. Cities in particular are changing and will continue to change as do all systems:

> Now grayped is Gawan gay,
> And lagt his launce rygt pore,
> And gef hem alle goud day,
> He wende for ever more.[9]

This is part of an English poem, "Gawain and the Green Knight," written in fourteenth century. Translated into today's English, we have:

> Now Gawain is gay(ly) arrayed,
> And (he) caught up his lance right (then and) there,
> And bade (literally, gave) them all good day,
> (As) he thought for ever more.

Just for fun try this next line:

"Faeder ūre, bū be eart on heofonum, sī bīn nama gehālgod." This is the first line of "The Lord's Prayer" in Early English. "Our Father, thou who art in heaven, hallowed be your name."

Our English language changes so rapidly that by the time the Merriam Company's unabridged dictionary is printed, it is already obsolete. Approximately every twenty-five years a new unabridged dictionary is published. There were almost 150,000 less words in the Webster's Third than in the Webster's Second edition, plus approximately 200,000 new words out of a total of 450,000.[10]

This diversion was to illustrate change in a part of our system which we like to think of as not rapidly changing. Also, language is touched on for the benefit of outreach workers who would be interested enough to investigate the intricacies of speech communities. To the bum on Main Street in Los Angeles, good English is the language of other Los Angeles bums. Speech communities cut across the boundaries of subsystems on occasion but not always. They are formed by such features as age, geography, education, occupation and social position. Their primary function is communication *within* their own community. This communication process is also used to keep outsiders out. The outreach worker may have difficulty getting inside the speech community. He certainly will have difficulty if he doesn't gain the confidence of the inhabitants. Confidence is not gained by pseudo-mimicry.

The language of speech communities is in a constant state of change. However, if this speech community is also a subsystem, the communication

---

[9] Leonard H. Frey: *Readings in Early English Language History* (New York, Odyssey Press, 1966), pp. 54-55.

[10] Paul Roberts: *Understanding English* (New York, Harper & Row, 1958), pp. 378-403.

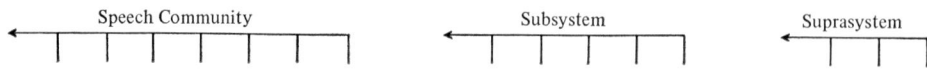

Figure VII-5. Rate of Change—Some Comparisons.

change is not necessarily in proportion to a change in purpose. The outreach worker must not confuse purpose with internal communication. The rate of change between the subsystems and suprasystem is also disproportionate. In Figure VII-5 the three rates of change which the outreach worker must contend with are presented. Some of our violent social conflicts occur when certain subsystems change faster than others and threaten other parts of the system. If the faster changing systems (speech communities included) exert influence on the suprasystem to change and King City *does* change, the slower subsystems must also change their primary purposes. If some systems resist, then incongruence occurs (in more pragmatic terms, WATTS, DETROIT, NEWARK).

There are many fine books on social change mentioned in this chapter.

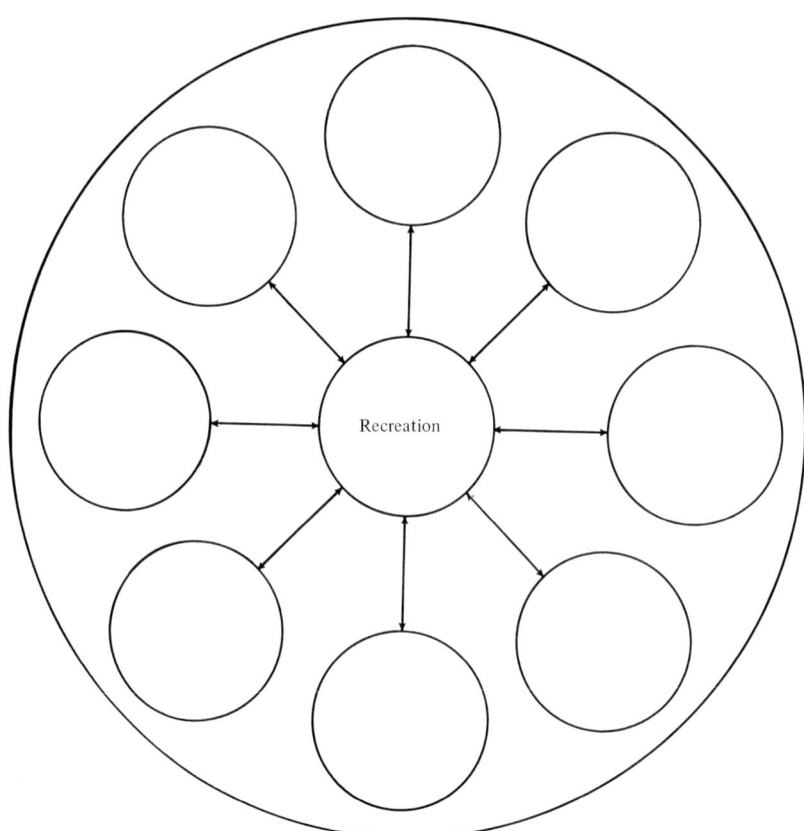

FIGURE VII-6. The Feedback Process in Recreation.

Social change is very insidious, but the outreach worker needs to be constantly aware of it in referral. Those subsystems which do not keep pace with changes in the suprasystem are likely to get "burned" in more ways than one. The recreation outreach worker, as well as outreach workers from other subsystems, must continually monitor the subsystems in their suprasystem, for change.

Feedback

Feedback in a social system is the monitoring process, similar to a coach scouting the opposition. The more he knows about his opponent, the better prepared his team will be. Monitoring is also similar to a speaker or entertainer who constantly measures his audience's responses. Feedback involves perception: the outreach worker may "feel" right about some situations and "feel" completely out of others. In very precise terms, feedback is finding out what's going on in King City and using this information to adjust your approach. Feedback will quite likely dictate changes in tactics by the outreach worker (cf. Fig. VII-6). A referral that was proper last week may not be this week. A winning football coach is one who can go into the locker room at half-time losing and go back into the locker room after the game, having won.

Internal Environment

Change is so complex that the outreach worker should have some knowledge of the forces which cause change. In a social system there are both internal and external forces. The internal environmental forces which bring about change involve the subsystems within the suprasystem. Generally, these forces occur in the interfacing process, though not always. For example, from the beginning of the Reformation in the sixteenth century until our present time, society in general has been in a change toward what Erich Fromm has called a "work ethic."[11] This change occurred from within the social system. When recreation emerged as a bonafide subsystem, society had to make another change from the glorification of all work and no play, to an acceptance of justifiable alternatives to work. Several subsystems have had to change: education, industry, religion, and employment.

In Figure VII-7 both the internal and external environments are presented. Internal environmental change may be singular or multiple, simple or complex, easy to identify or hidden in a maze of apparent tranquility. Internal environmental forces encompass in varying degrees everything discussed so far. When we contemplate the change Martin Luther King, Jr., brought about, we can begin to appreciate the greatness of the man. Einstein influenced physical change, Martin Luther social change; one just as preponder-

---

[11] Erich Fromm: *Escape From Freedom* (New York, Hearst Corp., by arrangement with Holt, Rinehart & Winston, Inc., 1965).

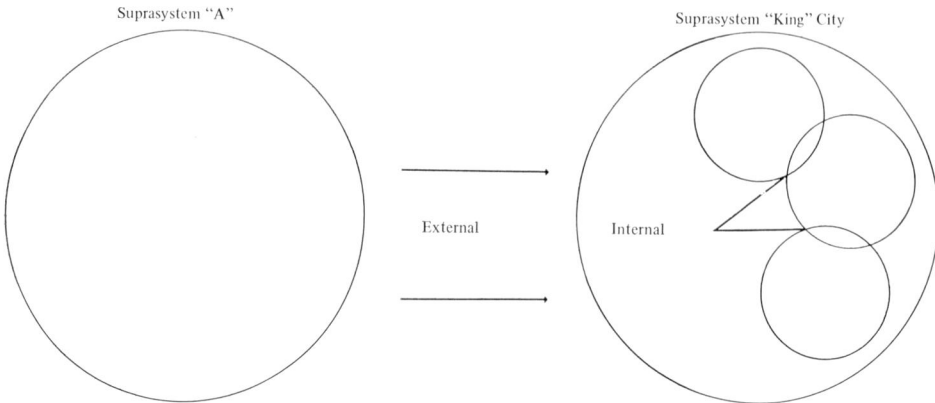

FIGURE VII-7. Internal and External Environments.

ant as the other. The outreach worker as a social-change agent is doing every bit as significant a task as the engineer constructing a dam. In many respects, the outreach worker's referral task is more difficult than the engineer's task since he is dealing with so many intangible, changeable variables. Likewise his end results or output are directly involved with the lives of people.

External Environment

Generally, external environmental force comes from other suprasystems or larger systems. For example, the school-community concept in Flint, Michigan, under the Mott Foundation is one external force which has influenced many other communities. Other types of external forces for King City are state and federal agencies and legislation. Figure VII-8 demon-

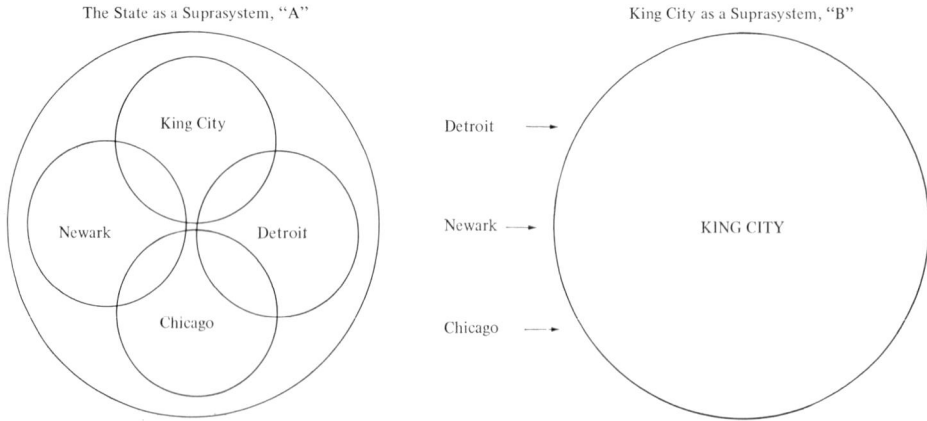

FIGURE VII-8. King City as Both a Subsystem and a Suprasystem.

strates the difference between a city and its environment when viewed as a subsystem within a larger system, or as a suprasystem.

When you deal with the state as a suprasystem, your interest in King City is as a part of a larger system. When you deal with King City as a suprasystem, your interest is in the parts that comprise the city. Consequently, what would be an internal force from Chicago, Detroit and Newark under "A" in Figure VII-8 would be an external force under "B." This is not simply a moot point. The main distinction is that the suprasystem can exert its own influence on internal forces. For example, recreation as a system has control over internal forces, but is at the mercy of external ones. In Figure VII-8, "A," the forces of Chicago, Detroit and Newark upon King City may be controlled by King City seeking legislation from the suprasystem to which all belong. These would be forces such as occurred along the Colorado River and other major waterways which pass through several states. When one state syphons off too much water, the other states hike off to Washington. Under "B," the influences coming from Chicago, Detroit and Newark would be similar to riots, changing morals, or attitudes which are influences outside King City's power to control. With the present mobility of people and the speed via television through which Chicago, Detroit, and Newark "move into" King City, external forces can bring about change almost as fast as internal forces.

Thus, before an outreach worker roves into other subsystems in the referral process, the worker's checklist should include knowledge of:

1. Social systems–systems within King City which affect people.
2. Suprasystem–the larger society of King City.
3. Subsystems–recreation, education, religion, etc., which make up King City.
4. Purpose–why a system exists.
5. Dysfunction–when the purposes of systems within a larger system are either in conflict with one another or with the larger system.
6. Equilibrium–the continual process within a system seeking balance between opposing internal forces.
7. Interfacing–the area where two subsystems perform similar or the same functions.
8. Primary purpose–the *main* contribution of a system.
9. Change–the constant shifting of purposes in a social system.
10. Feedback–the monitoring process by which systems find out what's going on outside their system.
11. Internal environment–the forces bringing about change within a system.

12. External environment–the forces bringing about change from outside the system.

Objectives of the Outreach Referral Program

Merely listing objectives is more difficult than most realize. For reference purposes, Mager's two books will be valuable, plus Kibler, Barker and Miles' work, as well as the two taxonomies by Bloom and Krathwohl which will help further in identifying objectives in both the cognitive and affective domains.[12] The outreach worker has three basic responsibilities in the referral process which the objectives of the program must identify. First, *he must know the purpose of his own system in detail*. This enables him to know what his system cannot do for his client and thus establishes a need for the referral process. To gain adequate knowledge of his system, he may need to analyze his system as a suprasystem. In Figure VII-9, recreation is broken into its subsystems. Not all are included, but enough for one to grasp the point. In large suprasystems like Chicago, the recreation system may be broken down several times. The outreach worker will need to know all the resources available within his own system. This aspect has been taken up in some detail in other chapters of the present volume, and is indeed relevant to the referral process as viewed systematically.

The second responsibility is that *the outreach worker must also know the purpose of the suprasystem in which he is operating*–King City. This in-

---

[12] Robert F. Mager: *Goal Analysis* (Belmont, Calif., Fearon Publishers, 1972); Robert F. Mager: *Preparing Instructional Objectives* (Belmont, Calif., Fearon Publishers, 1958); Robert J. Kibler, Larry Barker, and David Miles: *Behavioral Objectives and Instruction* (Boston, Allyn and Bacon, 1970); B. S. Bloom, *et al.*, eds.: *A Taxonomy of Educational Objectives: Handbook I, The Cognitive Domain* (New York, Longmans, Green Co., 1956); and D. R. Krathwohl, B. S. Bloom, and B. Masia: *A Taxonomy of Education Objectives: Handbook II, The Affective Domain* (New York, David MacKay Co., 1964).

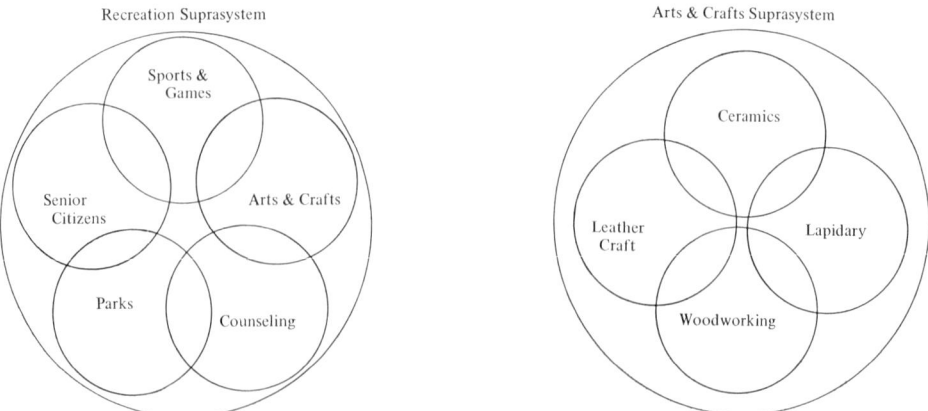

FIGURE VII-9. Recreation and Arts and Crafts Subsystems.

volves an awareness (a low-level affective domain objective) of at least the present "state-of-the-art" of King City. To gain this knowledge, he uses all the tools of the social system process. We can't afford having an outreach worker in King City who doesn't "know" King City. In talking with people from Chicago, Detroit, and Newark, a person quickly realizes the unique characteristics of each city. King City is also unique with its own personality, street language, ethical codes, and political power structure. These are not subsystems, these *are* King City. The outreach worker discovers there are people to be seen with and people not to be seen with in the city. Many other idiosyncrasies are clarified as the outreach worker learns about the purpose of King City:

> *Objective No. 1.* The outreach worker will be able to identify the purpose of his suprasystem in its present state. There will be a monthly evaluation of King City including all outreach workers to compare current changes within the suprasystem. (Each systems designer must determine the rate of change in his system which will consequently affect the frequency of these evaluation sessions.)

The third responsibility is that *the outreach worker must know the purposes of all the social-serving subsystems* interfacing with his subsystem. The outreach worker will be inefficient if he can't differentiate between the educational system's purpose and the religious system's purpose, and so on:

> *Objective No. 2.* The outreach worker will be able to differentiate among the purposes of all social-serving subsystems interfacing with his subsystem. Periodic contacts by the outreach worker will be made with each of these interfacing subsystems so the worker is able to constantly compare and contrast the resources available for referral.

It takes effort to be an effective outreach worker. However, as outreach workers from several different subsystems become involved, each worker's job will be a little easier:

> *Objective No. 3.* The outreach worker will be able to identify and solve problems. Acceptable performance will be determined by his peers based on critical evaluations of simulated case study situations.[13]

> *Objective No. 4.* The outreach worker will list ways of motivating youth. The motivation process will be under constant scrutiny by the entire sub-system staff which will monitor feedback from their own field contacts and knowledge of King City.

> *Objective No. 5.* The outreach worker will construct specific ways of referring motivated clients to the resources of subsystems pertinent to their needs.

At this point the outreach worker begins to see results in the referral process. He has identified a problem, taken measures to solve it, motivated the individual to pursue available community resources, and has a specific plan

---

[13] Joseph J. Bannon: *Problem Solving in Recreation and Parks* (Englewood Cliffs, N. J., Prentice-Hall, Inc., 1972).

for how his client can use these resources. This entire process represents a tremendous amount of work, but too often we get a person all ready for action and then are not able to follow through because of lack of preparation. The motivated client wants an immediate answer to the question, "Now what?" If the outreach worker has done his homework, whatever the problem, he's ready with a referral. For example, the youth worker has a client who is "zapped out" on drugs but is motivated to change. The worker discovers that the client attends a local church periodically, dropped out of school recently, is on probation, works off-and-on as a waitress, was treated at a local clinic for venereal disease, her parents are divorced, and her mother is on welfare.

Knowledge Base

The information gathered on this young woman is what we call the "knowledge base" of any client. Not only must the outreach worker use the systems approach in analyzing the suprasystem and its subsystems, but he must also apply an aspect of learning systems when dealing with clients. Motivation is an entire field of study from theorists such as Maslow to field practitioners. Establishing a base of knowledge will provide the outreach worker with material to assist in the motivation process. The data for the knowledge base are either obtrusively secured or unobtrusively observed. The whole purpose of gathering such information is to motivate a client to accept and follow through on referrals which are beneficial. In the case of this young woman there are several possible referral routes: the church, the school, the probation officer, the social worker, the doctor, or the recreation worker.

Process

We have made many references to "process." Process involves the direction the outreach worker takes in making a referral. The outreach worker starts with himself and his subsystem, moves out into the suprasystem and gains a knowledge of that system; he then identifies a client and the client's needs (knowledge base) and identifies social-serving agencies to meet those needs. BEWARE! Don't start with preconceptions, such as this young woman needs this particular service. Some outreach workers can become so oriented toward a particular subsystem, that subsystem may be viewed as a panacea for all social ills. This process moves from the system to the client. In the referral process, the opposite approach is taken. The outreach worker establishes a knowledge base about his client and then makes referrals in conjunction with the client.

This process will serve two goals. First, it will direct the outreach worker into the related subsystems, objectively seeking information. In the place of a purely academic knowledge of another subsystem, the outreach worker will want to become acquainted with the subtle characteristics sometimes known only to members of that system. You see, an outreach worker can't simply walk into the office of the superintendent of schools and, through a listing of educational objectives, know that system. There is a wide gulf between the academic knowledge of another system and an awareness of the operative functions of the system. The purpose of a system is usually achieved by non-academic procedures. Industrial psychologists have done many studies to determine the influence of motivation, attitude, and other affective and emotional forces. The Hawthorne Studies is a classic example. In the outreach referral program, we need to be aware of this same process going on in King City and its subsystems. The actual achievement of education's purpose is much more difficult to ascertain than merely reading material from the superintendent's office.

The second goal that our suggested process serves is that the outreach worker will become personally involved in the lives of his clients. The outreach worker now becomes an *out-reach* worker, and isn't that what it's all about? In the Bible, Jesus Christ said he came not to be served, but to serve. The outreach worker fills a very similar role—serving the needs of others:

> Different system designers [outreach workers] characteristically begin their work not only with queries about system functions but with different answers to questions such as the following: What is the problem you are trying to solve? Why are you trying to solve it? What *kind* of solution would you accept as satisfactory? How much time and effort are you prepared to devote to the enterprise? How enduring must your solution be?[14]

Common Reasons Clients Are Referred for Service

The list of reasons for referral could be cumbersome and still not be adequate. Let's go back to our young woman. She could have been referred for several reasons: loitering around the school, lifting some coins from her employer, breaking probation, or numerous other reasons. The particular reason may be insignificant as the outreach worker establishes his knowledge base. Figure VII-10 illustrates the use of reasons or the knowledge base in bringing the client to accept and follow through on referrals. There is a fine line within the client when he or she internalizes the learning tasks necessary to follow through on referral. Don't lose sight of the fundamental role of an "out" "reach" worker. He represents a subsystem. He encounters our young woman living in King City who has come into conflict with the purposes of several subsystems in that city. Either the subsystems change (not very likely), or she changes. For her to change she must be convinced the change will help her, as a social being, to meet her individual and social needs as a resident of King City.

---

[14] Robert Boguslaw: *Op. cit.,* p. 9.

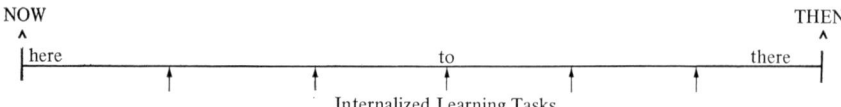

FIGURE VII-10. Knowledge Base and Learning Tasks.

The responsibility of the outreach worker is to identify the learning tasks necessary for our young client to move from here to there or from NOW to THEN. The outreach worker pursues answers to questions like those posed by Boguslaw. The young woman, nevertheless, is the one making the change and only she can do this. The change, to be of permanent value, must be voluntary and internalized. She must see the benefits of the move. Some subsystems threaten their clients to change. To the thief they say, "Stop ripping off the establishment, or we'll lock you up." Without internalizing the learning tasks, the change is only superficial.

Learning Tasks

A learning task is the ideas, attitudes and even facts the client must learn (internalize) to move from here to there. The responsibility of the outreach worker is to present, in very cogent terms and in the most persuasive but not overbearing manner, how the client can change from NOW to THEN.

Notice how extremely practical this is. Society can legislate laws about drugs but cannot legislate rehabilitation. The outreach worker's clients are not compelled to adjust. Let me illustrate the idea of learning tasks close to home. A popular concern today is to be concerned about obesity (being fat). You are fat and want to lose from here to there. Regardless of how you look at it, there is one difficult learning task you must learn (internalize). There are all kinds of gimmicks which you can eat, wear, or ride to keep you from the learning task. But there's only one healthy way–you must learn to tolerate hunger. Our bodies operate in a way very similar to an engine, on the basis of input and output, with one exception: when our input exceeds the output our tanks don't remain full of fuel; we store our fuel as fat for emergencies when we are hungry. Once you have stored up fat, your body must become hungry before it will cannibalize the fat. But most of us *know* the feeling of being hungry. And when you are hungry you *eat*. It is unnatural not to eat when you are hungry. Notice: the fat person must learn–and believe me this is a task!–to be hungry and *not* eat. The biggest problem in losing weight is the learning task. Just as this is true with a fat person, it is also true with our client. She is "here" and until NOW has seen no reason to be "there," or she would be "there" NOW.

Types of Referral by Outreach Workers

Some types have already been alluded to in the course of previous illustrations or in subsystems, but here are a few for perusal:
1. Psychiatric
2. School
3. Employment
4. Health
5. Drug treatment
6. Religious counseling

The type of referral(s) depends on the knowledge base garnered by the outreach worker and the primary purpose of the subsystem into which the referral is made. With our client, when she internalizes the need for a certain type of assistance, then the referral can be made. In some situations, it is extremely difficult to put together a knowledge base which can be used effectively in bringing about the internalization of learning tasks.

Another client was picked up repeatedly for drunkenness. Finally, he was referred to the State Alcoholic Rehabilitation Center where it was discovered he was an alcoholic. The Center dried him out and sent home a rehabilitated alcoholic. Two months later he was back in the Center. Then an outreach worker in the health subsystem started probing obtrusively and unobtrusively. One thing this worker discovered was his client had a son. This little bit of data could help this outreach worker.

Sometimes the type of referral is obvious: with our fat person, a weight reduction program; with our drinker, alcoholic rehabilitation. But not always. Occasionally, the person needing to change is not in a position at the time to internalize the learning tasks. At this point the outreach worker must be very discreet. He directs his client to an agency with the assumption that the agency will motivate the client to change.

How to Contact Other Subsystems

In the present state-of-the-art, most agencies or subsystems tend to retain a jealous guardianship of their primary purposes. We won't argue the reasons either pro or con, we'll just accept them as part of *our* knowledge base. The outreach worker should make the contact as a professional change agent. If the worker has followed through on the systems approach, he will be acting as a professional. "Professional" here is not equated with academic. A high school dropout could make a professional approach as well as a college professor. "Professional" here is synonymous with skilled. The outreach worker knows his system, knows his client, and knows quite a bit about the agency which he is contacting. When this approach is made, the contacted agency realizes they are dealing with a wise outreach worker and will respond much more openly. Also, the outreach worker should go to the agency, not request the agency to come to him. If someone calls me and wants my help, we meet in my office. If the reverse is true we meet in his office.

The outreach worker should not go with a negative attitude or create a negative atmosphere. If a civil engineer came into my office and started ripping apart higher education by telling me what a lousy job the universities are doing, I might become defensive. If he followed his tirade with "by the way, my son is interested in enrolling next fall, could you help him out?" (he is making a referral) how do you think that would set with me? His accusations may be correct, but he has established the wrong atmosphere for a referral. If the agency is not doing an adequate job, don't make the contact. The outreach worker should also bring a copy of the knowledge base. The data in the knowledge base must be kept confidential and only provided with the client's consent.

How to Act as an Advocate for Your Client

An advocate is one who pleads the cause for someone else, similar to a lawyer and his client. As an advocate, the outreach worker represents his client's cause, not his own. A few representative *don'ts* are:

1. Don't use the client as an entrée into an agency for your own gain. For an outreach worker to gain admittance into an agency's office under the guise of representing a client and then off-the-cuff say, "By the way, my wife is a good typist and could you help me get her a job . . ." is taboo!
2. Don't use the client as a premise to espouse your own agency's views.
3. Don't get into arguments with either your client or the referral agency. You may win an argument and lose an agency or a client.
4. Don't pry. If the client or the agency does not want you to know certain things, they have their reasons.
5. Don't overreact or jump to conclusions. Before you assume the policeman on his beat belted your client into unconsciousness, get the facts. As an advocate you want to be sure you are pleading the right cause.

The outreach worker as an advocate is primarily interested in the client's accepting and following through on a referral. The worker continues his role as advocate until his client has completed the trip from here to there and remains "there."

How to Identify Gaps in Services

The usual situation involves more overlaps (interfaces) than gaps. Gaps do occur, however. Problems of an unusual nature, or situations where the problem is extremely complex, may be difficult to categorize. Gaps also occur where a public agency and private agency are performing similar pur-

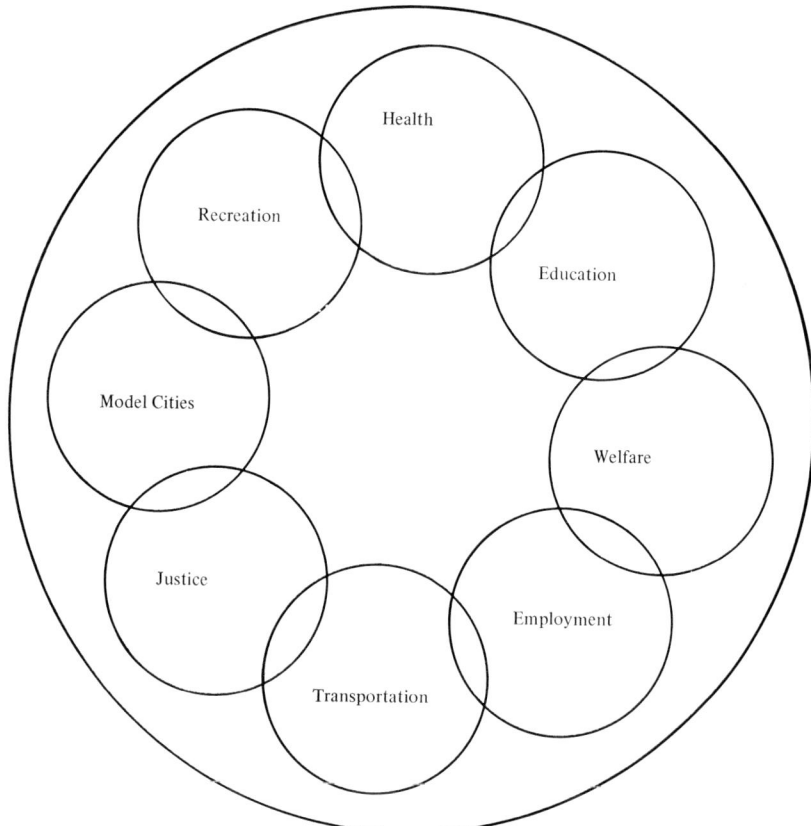

FIGURE VII-11. Subsystems of the Suprasystem (Public Sector).

poses, with each one assuming the other is meeting a particular need, while neither does. Gaps may also occur where an agency must perform two purposes. For example, if there is a Parks and Recreation Department and the director is parks-oriented, the recreation aspect may incur gaps. The reverse is also true.

Figures VII-11 and VII-12 break the social-serving agencies into the private and public sectors. The subsystems of each are representative but not complete, yet you can see where gaps could exist. For example, in the private sector, Partners Incorporated does an excellent job with first-time, middle-class offenders. This is not printed in their brochures but was gleaned from social referral workers with past associations with Partners.

Conclusion

The referral process places a tremendous responsibility on the outreach worker. In most other situations, a worker needs only a grasp of his own system with a cursory knowledge of other systems. The outreach worker in

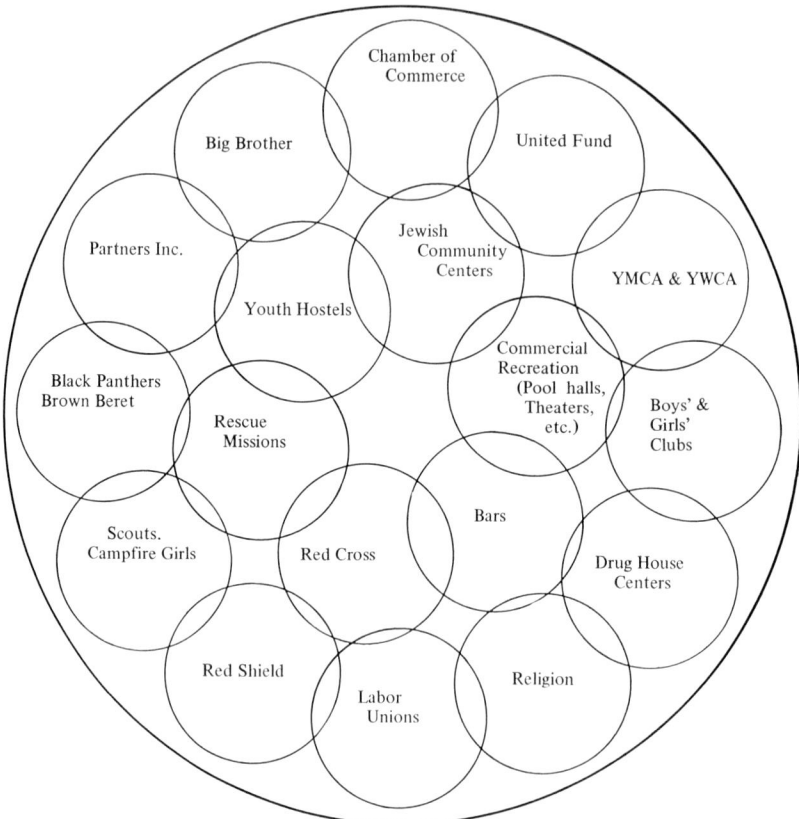

FIGURE VII-12. Subsystems of the Suprasystem (Private Sector).

the referral process needs almost as much knowledge of the other subsystems in King City as of his own subsystem. The referral process is one of giving up areas of social service outside the purview of the outreach worker's own subsystem. The outreach worker is continually attempting to help his client live with other social beings in a constant state of opposing forces between his own individual needs and those of the immediate society around him.

CHAPTER REFERENCES AND SELECTED READINGS

Brager, George A. and Purcell, Francis P. (Eds.): *Community Action Against Poverty*. New Haven, Conn., College and University Press, 1967.

Brandstatter, A. F. and Radelet, L. A.: *Police and Community Relations: A Source Book*. Beverly Hills, Calif., Glencoe Press, 1968.

Geisman, L. L. and LaSorte, M. A.: *Understanding the Multi-Problem Family*. New York, Association Press, 1964.

Hardy, James M.: *Focus on the Family: National Study of Work With Families in the YMCA*. New York, Association Press, 1966.

Kahn, Alfred: *Planning Community Services for Children in Trouble.* New York, Columbia University Press, 1963.

Kaitz, E. M. and Hyman, H. H.: *Urban Planning for Social Welfare: A Model Cities Approach.* New York, Praeger Publishers, 1970.

Perlman, Robert: *Community Organization and Social Planning.* New York, Wiley and Son, 1972.

Perloff, H. S.: New directions in social planning. *Journal of American Institute of Planners,* Vol. 31, no. 4, Nov. 1965.

Reid, William: Interagency coordination in delinquency prevention and control. Social *Service Review,* Vol. 38, Dec. 1964.

Webber, M. M.: Comprehensive planning and social responsibility. *Journal of American Institute of Planners,* Vol. XXIX, Nov. 1963.

CHAPTER VIII

HIGHER EDUCATION IN THE OUTREACH PROGRAM

"The Ivory Tower Has Its Role"

JAMES F. MURPHY

THE TRADITIONAL VIEW of recreation and parks curricula in higher education has been oriented toward maintaining existing institutions as necessary and fundamental to education for leisure. An alternative view perceives the role of higher learning to be more in dealing with *how* a social order may be modified and possibly reconstructed to better serve its members. This "radical" perspective is not concerned with how individuals and institutions might be adjusted and accommodated to maintain social stability, but in fostering honest, insightful, and critical thinkers with an ability to synthesize first-rate analysis of human problems and acknowledge social relationships.

The organization and delivery of leisure service, particularly using an outreach approach, must be viewed within the total spectrum of social, educational, health, environmental and transportation services. The preparation of students as outreach workers must assume a new immediacy in which poverty, racism, urban squalor, malnutrition, and illiteracy are considered part of recreation outreach, since these affect the citizen's ability to participate in organized recreation.

Education (including its dissemination) can no longer be confined to an elite class. There are simply too many day-to-day issues that require educated responses from all segments of a given community. Since education serves as a social mechanism to cope with deficiencies among members of a society, it is by definition undesirable to be uneducated. Modern society has grown so complex that education must be constantly adapted to meet the widely varying needs of both individuals and society.

Grassroots leadership and participation by colleges and universities are crucial if viable outreach curricular objectives are to be developed. These institutions are in a better position to ameliorate the conditions which undermine educational opportunity and foster ignorance and poverty. However, too many four-year universities have become islands or fortresses cut off from their surroundings. The urban university has special responsibilities because of its orientation and proximity to the people. Urban areas are laden with problems of unemployment, substandard housing, illiteracy, school dropouts, etc., and demand particular attention. The detachment of academia from problems of urban communities is a luxury which neither can any longer afford.

The traditional preparation of recreation personnel in colleges and universities has primarily centered on the facility manager. According to Gray, such a "chain-link fence" philosophy "identifies the primary tasks as surveillance of grounds to assure compliance with rules, safety, proper use of facilities and control of equipment; development of a schedule for use of the facility; planning and execution of a program of activities with the staff in face-to-face leadership roles; coordination of maintenance activities to ensure the readiness and sanitary condition of the premises."[1] That is, what happens in the center is what counts.

There is another concept of recreation which perceives personnel as community-change agents. Viewing outreach workers as advocates for the poor represents a *new thrust* in human-service education. The design of such curricula demands that students be prepared for positions where they are expected to serve as agents for community change. The role of the community center director-facilitator is no longer applicable and is largely dysfunctional in recreation and leisure outreach work.[2] Human service advocates are concerned with urban social problems where individual and neighborhood worlds converge.

Advocacy identifies as central the development of people, interaction, community improvement, and preservation of the virtues of urban life, while combating social ills which deprive people of fulfillment. There is a trend away from paternalistic "Big Daddy" leadership and management based on a series of propositions that presupposed people were passive and had to be motivated by rewards and punishments. The move is toward a *participatory style of leadership* for the effective agent of change.

The traditional organizational approach to meeting the needs of people must be altered, and with it a restructuring of the content and style of recreation curricula should take place. The increasing size and complexity of the leisure service bureaucracy and a new emphasis on the importance of human relations demand that leisure-service agencies embrace the style and behavioral approach of the change-agent.

The advocate's role in community life is more suited to respond effectively

---

[1] David E. Gray: The tyranny of the chain-link fence, *California Parks and Recreation*, Vol. 10, no. 10 (August 1968).

[2] James F. Murphy: We are the Human Service field social work warned us against. Speech delivered at Congress for Recreation and Parks, National Recreation and Park Association, Anaheim, Calif., Oct. 5, 1972.

to the pressures of rapid social change, citizen demands for broader participation, and an increasing diversity of lifestyles. The advocate-encourager can comprehend the nature of a society replete with institutions and dominated by the interaction of institutions, and is able to see the need to change the behavior of decadent and unresponsive organizations. Such a process enables the community, the organization, and the recipients of service to develop their *own* capacity for self-renewal and vitality.

Traditional human service organizations need to "de-standardize" their efforts to negate the distortions of life for inner-city residents and create alternative channels for meeting physical, emotional, educational, occupational, and cultural needs. The advocate role of an outreach worker identified recreation and leisure service, along with other human services, as fundamental to alleviating the particular social problems of delinquency-prone youth and assisting in overall social reform in urban communities. Such an approach requires a specialized educational program.

It has been suggested by Gray and others that when we perceive the future of recreation, we will increasingly see recreation and other human services assuming a vital role in areas outside their immediate concerns. For example, recreation programs will have to be devised to impart basic skills and knowledge to help welfare recipients cope with consumer problems, employment opportunities, and social and environmental conditions. While this chapter is directed to specialists in outreach work, these new roles will require that *all* recreators become outreach workers rather than facility-oriented isolationists within their chain-link fences.

According to Kraus, it is essential that recreation and parks facilities be closely integrated with other social services to reflect a multifunctional organization:

> Typically, community-center buildings should be able to serve a variety of age groups with relevant programs: nonworking mothers and preschool children during the day, children of working mothers in day-care centers, elementary school-age children after school, teen-agers and adults during the evenings, retired persons during the day. Centers should provide places where children may do homework and receive tutoring or be part of cultural-enrichment programs. Job counseling, health and family counseling services, legal assistance, narcotics addiction programs, after-care programs for discharged mental patients, sheltered workshops for retarded children and adults, and similar ventures are all part of the potential role of urban recreation centers. Centers may also provide a base for meetings of local organizations, antipoverty agencies, and other community groups.[3]

The multi-service functions of the contemporary community center re-

---

[3] Richard Kraus: *Recreation and Leisure in Modern Society* (New York, Appleton-Century-Crofts, 1971), pp. 449-450.

quire college preparatory programs oriented toward real community needs and problems. The college cannot exist in a self-imposed vacuum and expect to prepare students for the realities of today's urban community. *Accessibility and comprehensiveness* of parks and recreation curricula are necessary. Although they cannot by themselves provide sufficient conditions for assuring that well-trained students will in fact meet the necessary specifications, community colleges and four-year colleges and universities must go beyond technical and special education in preparing students for outreach work. Centers of higher learning must regard *the community itself as a classroom,* engage in urban problems, offer guidance, and assist the disadvantaged in arriving at solutions they themselves determine. Such an approach will serve as an effective intervention model for students whereby the college and the community can more directly identify latent and overt conflicts, as well as felt needs in the community surrounding an urban campus.

The long-range objective of any revised or altered college program designed to train students in outreach work should be to apply the vast resources of higher education to urban problems. Colleges and universities must make a total commitment to ameliorate the degrading conditions of inner-city life.

Higher education is regarded as part of the establishment by the inner-city poor, who view the position of education as largely hypocritical and traditionally non-committal. The poor perceive community service and outreach efforts as diversionary tactics, because institutions often are interested in alleviating misery as long as they can continue to serve those special interests which bring remuneration to the campus. The degree of commitment from community colleges and four-year colleges and universities nestled in inner-city pockets must be salient and binding. It is only through direct meaningful action by higher education that social change can become a constructive force for altering the discriminatory and hypocritical norms and values which pervade American life.

A basic necessity for colleges and universities is reconciliation between the institutions, which most assuredly select but may or may not educate, and the changed demands of society during an era of social upheaval. Educational institutions structured primarily to keep the disadvantaged poor off the streets or to sort them out are doing a disservice to their communities.

Intervention Strategies

Some of the organizational patterns developed by many comprehensive community colleges seem most appropriate for four-year colleges and universities seeking relevant curricula for students interested in working with the poor and "hard-to-reach." Many community colleges are located "substantially" in the community they are serving, thereby aiding their outreach efforts to inner-city poor.

Outreach education incorporates a community-based approach which moves beyond the multiple-use of a physical plant to a total, comprehensive concept of learning and living that uses the full resources of the physical and natural environment within the community context. This approach includes a philosophy which pervades all segments of education and directs the thrust of these toward community needs. Outreach education has the potential of serving as a catalyst by providing leadership to mobilize community resources to solve community problems. This philosophy seeks to aid all children, youth and adults through its educational services and to create an atmosphere whereby a community sees its local college as an integral and helpful part of community life.[4]

A new sense of community identity, participation and involvement is the aim of the Peralta Colleges in Oakland, California. A Student Service Corps carries on a work-study service program of community outreach service and development in the inner city. Community Development Centers provide educational and counseling services. The Centers serve as the locus for the College's outreach effort by functioning as staging areas for programs and services to the general community. Spokesmen for the college district maintain that taking the educational, cultural and human resources of the College into the community "can demonstrate not only how the community college can serve the inner city but how residents of the inner city can be involved as active participants in the task of serving their neighbors."[5]

Gleazer suggests that because of the community college's strategic setting, and its basic aim of extending educational opportunity, it must assume major leadership in creative inner-city development. This belief must be shared by the poor themselves, who see any institution as a threat to their existence, especially if that institution perceives only middle-class values as the norm for all citizens. In a pluralistic society, singular educational objectives are irrelevant and outmoded.

The urban community colleges and their predecessors, the four-year colleges and universities, must revise their structure to more adequately serve as centers for analyzing local community problems and as catalysts and coordinators of action programs. The new lifestyle for higher education, especially for colleges in inner-city areas, needs to be one of community involvement. If institutions of higher education expect inner-city residents to

---

[4] Donald E. Hawkins: *Community Education in a Leisure-Centered Society* (Washington, D. C., American Association for Health, Physical Education and Recreation, 1970), p. 10.

[5] Edmund J. Gleazer: *This Is the Community College* (Boston, Houghton Mifflin Co., 1968), p. 91.

enter into relationships of trust and mutuality of interest, then such institutions are going to have to demonstrate their real commitment to the community.

Formal learning needs to include the community to offer students closer contact with actual situations and break away from a limited lecture-textbook approach. At a National Forum on Careers in Parks and Recreation, Black students questioned the sincerity of faculty-administrative commitment to minority group students, stressing their concern that educational institutions perpetuate training programs that hamper rather than facilitate student entrance and mobility in recreation and parks.[6]

It was further revealed at this Forum that students are ambivalent about their ability to make meaningful contributions to the recreation movement:

> They perceived a disparity between the intent of the educational program and the actual skills and knowledge provided during their academic experience. They pointed out that the present curriculum includes leadership techniques for such community projects as playground activities and community center programs, but offers little instruction in administration, problem-solving and decision-making techniques, program planning and implementation methods, recreation economics and budgeting or urbanology. In light of the trend toward using recreation as a social change agent and a community organization and development technique, students believe that a new philosophical basis for the academic recreation program is needed.[7]

Citizens need to feel those who provide community services are responsive to their needs. Colleges and universities can demonstrate such a responsiveness by revising curricula to allow and encourage students to engage in community work as part of their fieldwork and internship program, or preferably, as part of their regular courses:

> This extension of education into the community can have a positive impact upon preparing students for realistic career choices and residents for assuming productive, meaningful roles within the community. Dialogue and demonstrated commitment to the community are essential if educational institutions are to maintain credibility and relevance in today's world.[8]

Leisure Service Delivery System

Recently expressed citizen awareness has brought serious questioning of the goods and services provided by traditional leisure-service agencies. Inner-city residents have become aware of the disparity between what is promised in involvement and decision-making and what is actually offered by parks and recreation agencies.

Currently, there is a trend toward decentralized local determination and

---
[6] *Ibid.*, pp. 5-6.
[7] *Ibid.*, pp. 5-6.
[8] *Ibid.*, p. 20.

provision of services. This is partly due to increased community involvement in planning and programming and partly to the inability of municipal services to meet the demand. Inherent in the success of this approach is the development of citizen and professional capabilities for delivering goods and services and in ensuring the quality, quantity, availability, and relevance of such.

The entire delivery of public recreation and leisure services has been scrutinized through surveys and investigations of conditions in central cities emanating from civil unrest during the 1960s.[9] Public servants have assumed that all groups are equal in their need for recreation, and that recreation is universally a voluntary experience. These concepts have not worked as operational guidelines for subordinated groups. Blacks, Chicanos, Puerto Ricans, Indians, Chinese, etc., have never been able to engage in recreation programs as freely or with the uniform knowledge and skills of white citizens, because of discrimination, insufficient discretionary income, and inadequate leisure opportunities and services in their communities.

The voluntary nature of recreation has been presumed requisite for participation in public recreation programs, yet has never been voluntary for Blacks and other minority groups. Lack of specialized approaches and outreach efforts in providing recreation for the poor and disadvantaged groups has deprived them of the chance to participate on a voluntary basis.[10]

A National League of Cities study, cosponsored by the Bureau of Outdoor Recreation and Department of the Interior, found that "in most cities surveyed, officials readily admitted that the needs of all population groups were not being adequately met. Only in recent years have cities begun to recognize an obligation to provide recreation for the handicapped and deprived."[11] The survey also started that inadequate and inappropriate facilities have caused resentment by inner-city residents toward leisure-service administrators. The study reached eight conclusions regarding municipal recreation. Two of their findings are particularly relevant to providing recreation and leisure service for disadvantaged citizens:

1. Residents of deprived urban neighborhoods are almost entirely dependent on public recreation facilities, whereas residents of more affluent

---

[9] Some of the more salient studies were: Shirley Jenkins: *Comparative Recreation Needs and Services in New York Neighborhoods* (New York, Research Department, Community Council of Greater New York, 1963); Edwin J. Staley: Determining Neighborhood Recreation Priorities: An Instrument, *Journal of Leisure Research,* no. 1 (Winter 1969), pp. 69-74; and *Recreation in the Nation's Cities: Problems and Approaches* (Washington, D. C., Department of Urban Studies, National League of Cities, 1968).

[10] John A. Nesbitt, Paul D. Brown, and James F. Murphy: *Recreation and Leisure Service for the Disadvantaged: Guidelines to Program Development and Related Readings* (Philadelphia, Lea & Febiger, 1970).

[11] *Recreation in the Nation's Cities, op. cit.,* p. 2.

neighborhoods have a wide range of recreational alternatives. Adequate recreation programs and facilities are considered a high priority among the deprived.

2. Residents of urban slum neighborhoods frequently charge that too much effort is directed toward middle- and upper-income groups, and that recreation planning is performed by persons with no real knowledge of the needs and desires of the deprived. To be successful, recreation programs must be what the people want, not what the recreation department believes is best for them. Increased emphasis on citizen participation can be an essential component for developing meaningful programs.[12]

While many city officials have claimed the recreational needs of disadvantaged groups are essentially the same as the rest of the community, studies by Jenkins and by Staley document the dependency of the poor on public recreation facilities and programs.[13] They conclude that the deprived, particularly inner-city poor, require greater opportunities for recreational and cultural experiences than do the economically and socially advantaged. It was suggested by the National League of Cities in their investigation that "the special needs of the poor require more neighborhood recreation facilities in inner-city areas and more person-oriented recreation programs in which supervisors can work with small groups in meaningful interpersonal relationships."[14]

The Staley study determined there are measurable social characteristics (juvenile delinquency rate, density of population, youth population and median family income) and neighborhood recreation resources (number of full- and part-time professional staff hours, and the acreage and number of recreation centers) which together indicate a comparative need for recreation in given neighborhoods. It is his estimation, after analyzing the recreation services and social needs in south central Los Angeles neighborhoods, that priorities in community-subsidized recreation services should go to those under maximum social pressures. The greatest deprivation in municipal recreation was found in hardcore districts in Los Angeles.

The data from these studies clearly reveal insufficiencies in the quantity of recreation facilities and opportunities, as defined by the needs' criteria, and the relative deprivation of Blacks and other economically disadvantaged groups compared with more affluent groups. Of particular importance, the Staley and Jenkins studies amplify the notion that disadvantaged areas require relatively greater staff-to-clientele ratios, more specifically educated

---

[12] *Ibid.* (paraphrased).
[13] Shirley Jenkins: *Op. cit.*, and Edwin J. Staley: *Op. cit.*
[14] *Recreation in the Nation's Cities, op. cit.*, p. 17.

recreation workers, as well as certain program adaptations. Outreach appears to be one of the most viable and workable approaches for meeting the needs of inner-city people who need the specialized skills and comprehensive programs effectively offered by detached leisure-service workers.

Etiology of the Urban Poor

The problems of job discrimination, inadequate slum housing, juvenile delinquency, adult crime, drug addiction, ill health and overall deprivation are serious social problems confronting America's urban poor. Deprivation generally connotes marginality, in which minimum requirements for health and comfort are rarely achieved.

Low income is a basic characteristic of the urban disadvantaged, and related characteristics have rather obvious humane and educational implications. According to Hunter, deprivation involves lack of money, opportunity, social status, free choice, civil rights, skills, or even hope.[15] Few urban central city residents have become integrated into local civic or social organizations. In most communities more permanent residents made only limited efforts to welcome low-income newcomers. "Both the suburban movement of the past four decades and the recent reaction to 'open housing' proposals demonstrate that their arrival is resented."[16]

The nonwhite poor are irregularly employed: The unemployment rate for Blacks is almost double that of whites, for nonwhite teenagers, the overall employment rate has been as high as 32 per cent, almost one-third of their labor force. Unemployment rates for Chicanos, Indians, Puerto Ricans, Chinese, and other deprived minorities are often greater. In fact, the most serious unemployment is experienced by the young, the female, and the Black. In terms of both frequency and duration, nonwhites not only experience more frequent spells of unemployment, they are more likely than whites to also experience longer duration of such spells of joblessness. An abnormally high incidence of chronic physical and mental health problems is inevitable. Deutsch states that the experiences and perceptions of most impoverished children are constricted and distorted.[17] Although the Black disadvantaged child is less aware of or disturbed by scarcity than his middle-class counterpart, it bears heavily on his family relationships, his attitudes, habits and aspirations.

The typical disadvantaged Black, Chicano, or Indian grows up in an en-

---

[15] David R. Hunter: Can it be done? In C. W. Hunnicutt, ed.: *Urban Education and Cultural Deprivation* (Syracuse, N. Y., Syracuse University, School of Education, 1964).

[16] Elinor F. McCloskey: *Urban Disadvantaged Pupils: Characteristics, Environments and Potentials* (Portland, Oregon, Northwest Regional Educational Laboratory, 1967), p. 10.

[17] Martin Deutsch: *Minority Group and Class Status as Related to Social and Personality Factors in Scholastic Achievement* (Ithaca, N. Y., Cornell University, 1960).

vironment of isolation, constriction, and rejection. He or she lives in an encapsulated community which both shelters and separates them from the wider society.[18] They are confronted with tensions and opposing forces from within and without their community.

In impoverished urban homes children usually assume responsibility for their own meals and those of parents and others in the household. Consequently, strong sibling ties evolved from mutual responsibilities often appear early. The children of impoverished and disorganized families generally roam the streets without supervision at comparatively young ages, where they acquire independence and strong peer-group relationships.[19]

Numerous studies document the general inadequacy of housing in urban areas. Often entire families are crowded into single rooms and pay exorbitant rents. Buildings are generally old and generally in need of repair. Studies by Drake, Pettigrew, Harrington, and others all indicate the high relationship between poverty, poor housing and ill health.[20] Crowded living and sleeping quarters, inadequate sanitation, poor food storage, and insects all tend to produce high rates of illness and death. Data indicate that Black longevity is twenty years less than for whites. The incidence of respiratory and infectious diseases among slum-dwelling children, such as measles, meningitis, diphtheria, and scarlet fever is high.[21]

It has been noted by Herta Riese that the psychological as well as the physical harm of overcrowded living in deprived circumstances have deleterious effects on slum residents. She cites the dearth of opportunity for private reflection and development of imagination as causes for the restlessness and aimlessness of children from destitute environments.[22]

The inner-city neighborhood is as congested as the home and almost equally confining. It appears evident that poverty and housing conditions in inner-city neighborhoods result in a high incidence of both physical and psychological disabilities:

> In summary, the disadvantaged child's world is less quiet, healthy, safe or comforting than that nurturing his middle-class counterpart. Yet it provides a se-

---

[18] Elena Fudilla: *Up From Puerto Rico* (New York, Columbia University Press, 1958).

[19] David P. and Pearl Ausabel: Ego development among segregated Negro children. In A. Harry Passow, ed.: *Education in Depressed Areas* (New York, Bureau of Publications, Teachers College, Columbia University, 1963).

[20] St. Clair Drake: The social and economic status of the Negro in the United States, *Daedalus,* Vol. 94 (Fall 1965), p. 783; Thomas F. Pettigrew: *A Profile of the Negro American* (New York, Van Nostrand, 1964); and Michael Harrington: *The Other America: Poverty in the United States* (Baltimore, Penguin Books, 1963).

[21] Kenneth B. Clark: *Dark Ghetto: Dilemmas of Social Power* (New York, Harper & Row, 1965).

[22] Herta Riese: *Heal the Hurt Child: An Approach Through Educational Therapy with Specific Reference to the Extremely Deprived Negro Child* (Chicago, University of Chicago Press, 1962).

curity of close relationships with siblings and peers, if not with adults. While deprivation may not make the child excessively anxious, it affects almost every aspect of his self-image and his relations with others. It also has overriding influence on his perceptions of need and opportunity.[23]

Impoverished conditions in inner-city environment require particular study and attention by outreach workers, since they represent socioeconomic conditions unlike those in the dominant society. Traditionally, recreation and parks curricula have prepared students for positions which presume a middle-class clientele. An outreach worker requires a different role, set of values, and attitudes and knowledge to more effectively offer leisure opportunity to groups which function for all purposes *outside* the mainstream of American society.

Community Action on the Streets

Outreach work ordinarily involves a threefold approach in an area needing specialized service: (1) street-club, detached or Roving Leader work with young people; (2) community organization and development with local neighborhood leaders; and (3) use of informal facilities as outposts where hard-to-reach youth can meet under continuous and optimum counseling conditions.[24] Essentially, and outreach program is designed to engage human-service workers with young people wherever they might congregate, bring them under the influence and supervision of the workers and attempt to deal constructively with the significant problems in their lives.

While so-called hard-to-reach youth are the special focus of outreach workers, it has become evident that more human-service agencies must begin to use this technique with other urban residents who are alienated from traditional agencies. Their formal atmosphere and often conventional service have little or no relationship to the lifestyle of delinquency-prone, disaffected youth or young adults.

The delivery of service, while trying to effect positive change in antisocial and hard-to-reach youth and to move toward more conventional behavior, should be in concert with the class and cultural norms of the population. The approach of the service should be toward meeting the physical, emotional, educational, employment, and cultural experiences not fulfilled by the dominant external environment, with a view to increasing the capacity for participation and autonomy.

The Chicago Youth Development Project, a privately financed delinquency prevention and control project conducted from 1960-1966, had eight action goals for changing the lives of those in the target area:

---

[23] McCloskey: *Op. cit.*, p. 23.
[24] Frank J. Carney, Hans W. Mattick, and John D. Callaway: *Action on the Streets: A Handbook for Inner City Youth Work* (New York, Association Press, 1967), p. 8.

1. To reduce the absolute amount of illegal and antisocial behavior attributable to the target population in the experimental areas.
2. To change the behavior of individuals and groups in the contacted part of the target population, where necessary, from the less seriously antisocial to the conventional, within the class and cultural norms of the local population.
3. To help individuals and groups in the contacted part of the target population meet their emotional needs for association, friendship and status by providing conventional, organized and supervised activities for them, with a view to increasing their capacity for participation and autonomy.
4. To increase the objective opportunities for youth in the external environment, in education, employment and cultural experiences.
5. To help youth prepare for conventional adult roles by providing guidance in education, work, family life and citizenship through direct intervention in their life processes, especially at times of crisis.
6. To relate the target population to local adults and institutions in positive ways so communication channels between youth and adults may be developed, through which a shared, conventional system of values may be transmitted.
7. To develop in parents and adults a concern for problems affecting local youth, and to organize them to assume responsibility for resolution of local problems.
8. To create a positive change in attitude, in both youth and adults, about the possibility of local self-help efforts to improve the community through active and cooperative intervention in community processes, and thus create a more positive attitude toward the community itself.[25]

It seems apparent that lack of legitimate opportunity for urban minority-group youth, inadequate conventional socialization, disorganization of family and community life, alienation and lack of consensus on conventional values, and latent negative effects of handling youthful offenders through legal channels and institutions all debilitate large numbers of inner-city residents, both young and old.

According to Moore, "study of disadvantaged environments reveals that a matrix of interwoven configurations tends to influence development and support of recreation efforts, and to evoke participation patterns characteristic of the particular milieu."[26] The problem of inadequate social develop-

---

[25] *Ibid.*, pp. 9-10.
[26] Vel Moore: Recreation leadership with socioculturally handicapped clientele. *In* John A. Nesbitt, *et al.*, eds.: *Recreation and Leisure Service for the Disadvantaged* (Philadelphia, Lea & Febiger, 1970), p. 166.

ment for the nation's poor is compounded by inadequate recreation potential:
1. Sustenance difficulties produce a pragmatic orientation; goals tend to be short-term and abilities to defer gratification are limited. Thus, leisure rewards must be relatively immediate and concrete, and they must accompany income security, or else futility is repeated.
2. Restricted childhood play experiences–a possible characteristic of low income areas–implies an undeveloped recreation repertoire. The disadvantaged population seldom has the opportunity to gain leisure know-how in the dominant society's positively sanctioned leisure and play activities.
3. Disadvantaged neighborhoods are distinguished by their lack of recreation services–whether they be public, semipublic, private, nonprofit or commercial.
4. Disadvantaged populations, though often residentially mobile within their own neighborhoods, infrequently travel outside on their own volition. This may be due to deficiencies in transportation, income, knowledge or self-confidence; these factors considerably lessen potential recreation experiences and resources.
5. Cultural differences may develop leisure habits that are inappropriate to an urban setting, or contradictory to the values and norms of the outer society.
6. Minority membership may deter participation in leisure activities because of social pressures and discrimination.[27]

These factors implicate the need for certain adjustments in traditional recreation and group-work practices; some current trends are important and vital to parks and recreation curricula:

Growing demands for minority personnel who are knowledgeable in recreation, sociocultural disadvantage and social group work.

Increasing recognition of community liaison personnel to interpret needs and to arbitrate controversial areas.

Expanding agency efforts to improve human relations programs and services.

Multiplying endeavors to create subprofessional positions suitable to indigenous personnel and two-year college graduates.

Increasing numbers of work-study, apprenticeship and educational opportunities programs.

Spreading demands by disadvantaged populations for improved recreation service and adequately prepared, sensitive leadership.[28]

---
[27] *Ibid.*, p. 167.
[28] *Ibid.*, p. 180.

The role of the outreach worker must be structured to the needs of the community in which he or she is located. In viewing outreach workers as advocates, colleges and universities will be altering the traditional concept of community recreation to conform more closely with social group work, counseling, and community action and health services.[29] It is suggested by Moore that the critical conditions described above will require a gradual change in personnel structure and requirements within the recreation field:

> Emerging recreation positions may be anticipated to include the roving leader, the street worker, the human relations specialist, the urban affairs consultant, the special problems advisor, the program assistant (indigenous), the community coordinator, the specialist in recreation for socioculturally handicapped and so forth. Additionally, there are some indications that the traditional role of the recreation center director will be redesigned with the objective of providing greater opportunities for community involvement and contact while reducing direct facility supervision tasks.[30]

Implications for Recreation and Parks Education

With the tremendous advancements of a post-industrial society, nearly every citizen had difficulty comprehending the effects of social change. The urban poor are particularly disadvantaged in their ability to cope with the ramifications of technological change:

> The rapidity of social change and maladaptation to cultural and technological innovations require that community residents be equipped to deal with social and personal change. Leisure service should be viewed as a social organism—or *human organization*—which manifests the major aspects of the local environment of the residents in order that it may exert a more meaningful influence upon their habits, values, attitudes, and patterns of behavior.[31]

Colleges and universities assuredly face an important challenge in their parks and recreation curricula. Moore suggests that a general program of education include an interdisciplinary selection of courses with the following components:

Human growth and development, sociologically, psychologically, and physiologically.

Socialization and individuation processes.

Mechanism and processes of abreaction.

Urbanization, community organization and neighborhood development.

Sociocultural divergence: characteristics and problems, enculturation and cultural lag, social structure and stratification.

---

[29] James F. Murphy: Community Recreation: A dynamic process, *California Parks and Recreation*, Vol. 28, no. 14, April-May 1972.

[30] Moore: *op. cit.*, p. 180.

[31] Murphy: *Op. cit.*, p. 14.

Program skills and leadership methods as related to sociocultural development and rehabilitation.

Recreation values, organization and management as these pertain to urban recreation service.

Exposure and practice under knowledgeable guidance from practitioners and educators, within the disadvantaged setting, with socioculturally handicapped clientele.[32]

The task of recreation curricula should be to create problem-centered courses which combine the study of the problem with action to deal with it. Students will then come to perceive their own capabilities and learn to contribute where most relevant. This is the domain of the advocate-encourager. A curriculum for human service fields must be action-oriented, dedicated to experimentation with both content and techniques. The needs of students from low-income backgrounds are the same as those of all students—to achieve a purposeful life. The basic objectives of a curriculum for human services are:

1. Provide a new kind of urban higher education for a ghetto population which has been left out of the American dream;
2. Develop and use the energy and talent of the ghetto for an important humanitarian service to urban society;
3. Provide a new path into community service and the helping professions for ghetto residents;
4. Meet the people of the ghetto where they are educationally, and while working to overcome educational deficiencies, launch them into college-level work in community service fields;
5. Educate students through a program of work-study for paraprofessional careers in the human services through a two-year program leading to an associate degree;
6. Explore and develop a curriculum which achieves the closest possible relationship between classroom and fieldwork and draws on all relevant material from the social sciences to create a college-level core program in the human services; and
7. Build an educational institution that will remain in the vanguard of educational experimentation, developing and sustaining equality of opportunity and equality of educational result for all students.[33]

Curricular development, as related to outreach and specialized approaches to leisure services, should emphasize three broad instructional goals:

1. Provide an introduction for all recreation and parks students to con-

---

[32] Moore: *Op. cit.,* pp. 181-87.
[33] Audrey C. Cohen, *College for Human Services* (Washington, D. C., New Careers Institute, University Research Corporation, 1969), p. 15.

temporary cultural, social, economic and political realities as they exist.
2. Provide students with an understanding of the use of recreation as a force for the alleviation of sociocultural disadvantage and alienation.
3. Provide students with community experiences in urban settings in which leisure services are viewed as part of an overall approach to human development.

Unfortunately, only a few courses emphasize the above outreach educational goals, nor are there any fully developed curricula which are explicitly organized to reflect an outreach configuration in recreation and parks. By offering concentration in a major field (with general education coursework), along with field training in useful jobs, a curriculum for human services can provide a program for students who desire action and a chance to improve slum neighborhoods. The extension of the classroom into the community serves as an important first step in bringing needed human services to where people are.

SELECTED READINGS

Cloward, R. A. and Ohlin, L. E.: *Delinquency and Opportunity*. Glencoe, Ill., The Free Press, 1960.

Egerton, John: *State Universities and Black Americans*. Atlanta, Georgia, Southern Education Foundation, 1969.

Folger, J. K.: *Human Resources and Higher Education. A Staff Report of the Commission on Human Resources and Advanced Education*. New York, Russell Sage Foundation, 1970.

Furman, James M.: *Coordination of Higher Education*. Ohio Legislation Service Commission, Report No. 53, 1963.

Gynn, John M.: *Curriculum Principles and Social Trends*. New York, Macmillan Co., 1969.

Harris, Norman Clifton: *Technical Education in the Junior College—New Programs for New Jobs*. Washington, D. C., American Association of Junior Colleges, 1964.

Havinghurst, Robert J.: *Human Development and Education*. New York, Longmans, Green and Co., 1953.

Howard, L. C.: Black consciousness and the identity crisis. *In* Myron Bloy Jr.: *Identity Crisis in Higher Education*. San Francisco, Jossey-Bass, Inc., 1971.

Steinberg, Sheldon S., and Eunice O. Shatz: Junior Colleges and the New Careers Program, *Junior College Journal, 35,* 5 (Feb. 1968), pp. 12-17.

APPENDIX A

THE ROVING RECREATION LEADER'S TRAINING GUIDE

The Roving Recreation Leader Training Guide

AN INSERVICE TRAINING SOURCE FOR INNER-CITY YOUTH SERVICES PERSONNEL

foreword

The need for positive and dynamic social change is most critically felt in working with inner-city youth. The shortage of trained personnel and the dearth of meaningful programs to which youth can respond (especially black youth), reflect the lack of expertise in developing methods of reaching and involving these young persons. The ineffectiveness of current programs is magnified by decreasing numbers of participants and increasing rates of juvenile crime.

A Roving Leader program gives new dimensions to existing programs by proposing a relevant leadership supplement to those offering conventional youth services. Through interpersonal relationships, reeducation, redirection, and face-to-face leadership it is hoped that changes in behavior and attitudes can be achieved.

We have been emotionally and intellectually aware of the problems of youth in the cities for well over a century. The need for the creation and development of new career opportunities for the unskilled and unemployed has received increased recognition since 1965. Inclusion and involvement of community people is essential, not only as a necessary step to effect positive change in existing conditions, but also as a vehicle for establishing new, permanent careers for these persons in the community. The absence of the total impact of a national effort leaves much to be desired.

The Roving Recreation Leader Training Guide represents a unique study made possible through a contract with the Division of Manpower Development and Training, U.S. Office of Education. To our knowledge there were no published models for study or comparison. Therefore, this publication can be considered a pioneer effort. It is anticipated that, because of rapid changes in urban youth work, restudy and revision of this guide will be needed in time. The guide includes nine instructional units covering about 160 hours of instruction.

It is intended that a series of 35 mm. slides, a narration tape, and selected transparencies will be made available to supplement the training guide at some future time for increased effectiveness in the use of the guide.

It is our hope that the multitraining design presented in this guide will serve as a fundamental framework to local, public, private, and church federations, that either provide or have interest in the Roving Leader approach to meeting the needs of the most aggressive, frustrated youth in our Nation's cities.

ARTHUR LEE HARDWICK,
Associate Commissioner, Bureau of Adult, Vocational, and Technical Education

HOWARD A. MATTHEWS,
Director, Division of Manpower Development and Training

acknowledgments

This guide has been prepared with the assistance of many indivduals: Don Henkel, National Recreation and Park Association, served as Project Director; the National Advisory Committee included Edwin Greenidge, Deputy Commissioner, Youth Service Administration, New York, N.Y.; Sidney Lutzin, Professional Service Director, National Recreation and Park Association, Washington, D.C.; George M. NishiNaka, Executive Director, Special Service for Groups, Inc., Los Angeles, Calif.; Clifford T. Seymour, Chairman, Department of Recreation, Southern University, Baton Rouge, La., and John Williams, Director of Recreation, Baltimore, Md.

Sincere thanks is given to the University of Illinois Review Committee: King McCristal, Dean, College of Physical Education; Ernest Anderson, Leader, Extension Education, Cooperative Extension; Anthony Linford, Instructor, Department of Recreation and Park Administration; Allen V. Sapora, Head, Department of Recreation and Park Administration; Paul Hursey, Personnel Services, Affirmative Action Officer; and Lee Carey, Assistant Superintendent of Recreation, Springfield, Ill. Appreciation is extended for the invaluable assistance given by the following persons: Dr. Roy J. Jones, Director of Community Studies Center, Howard University; Dr. Edwin J. Staley, Executive Director, Recreation and Youth Services Planning Council, Los Angeles; Dr. Walter Walker, Professor, Community Organization, School of Social Service Administration, University of Chicago; and Stanley J. Anderson, Adviser on Youth Programs, Children's Bureau, Department of Health, Education, and Welfare, and Former Director, Roving Leader Program, Washington, D.C.

Appreciation is also expressed to the many local government and private agency administrators, and employees and others who willingly contributed their time to provide basic information.

The overall administrative direction of the project staff was provided by Joseph J. Bannon, University of Illinois, Chief of the Office of Recreation and Park Resources. Preparation of this guide was the responsibility of Clarence E. Dade, Jr., University of Illinois, Urban Affairs Specialist, Office of Recreation and Park Resources. Editorial assistance was provided by Mary Kelly Black, Assistant to the Director, Survey Research Laboratory.

contents

	Page
Foreword	A1
Acknowledgments	A2
Introduction	A4
Purpose of the Training Guide	A5
Needs of Inner-City Youth	A5
The Roving Leader Concept	A5
Objectives of the Guide	A6
Definition of Terms	A6
Methodology of Guide Development	A6
Training Units for Roving Leaders	A8
Unit I. Orientation	A8
Unit II. Concept, Role, and Function of Roving Leader	A10
Unit III. The Community and Community Development	A12
Unit IV. Identifying and Understanding Inner-City Youth	A14
Unit V. Group Process	A16
Unit VI. Referral Process and Referral Sources	A18
Unit VII. Programs and Planning	A20
Unit VIII. Field Work	A21
Unit IX. Organizational Staff Training and Development	A24
Appendixes	
A. Agencies and Institutions Participating in the Study	A29
B. Language of Modern Youth	A30
C. Addresses of Film Distributors	A32
D. Sample Job Description	A33
E. Roving Leader Slide Presentation	A34

introduction

The Roving Leader, sometimes called the Gang Leader or Detached Worker, is the individual (male or female) who roams the streets and alleys in urban, suburban, and rural communities, seeks out idle youth, and engages them in constructive activity. Initial contact and rapport are usually established through a game, a sports activity, or an informal recreational activity.

Once the Roving Leader has gained the confidence of youth, he tries to motivate them to return to school; i.e., to a Manpower Development and Training Act (MDTA) occupational training program, or other vocational-technical or college program, or to get a job. In general the Roving Leader seeks to channel the energies of youth into constructive community activities as a means of keeping them from getting into trouble with the law and helping them to develop into responsible citizens. The use of Roving Leaders is another proven way of combating and curbing delinquency in rural as well as urban areas.

Because the role of the Roving Recreation Workers tends to put them in some difficult situations, such workers must know what they are NOT to do, when they should NOT ACT on their own, and how to make use of supervisory assistance.

The information on which this training guide is based was obtained from analyses of Roving Leader programs in 12 cities—New York, Detroit, Los Angeles, San Francisco, Dayton, Ohio, St. Louis, Baltimore, Chicago, Buffalo and Rochester, N.Y., and Washington, D.C. Selection of these cities was made jointly by the National Recreation and Park Association Review Committee and the project staff, University of Illinois, on the basis of geographical location and agency sponsorship, as well as on a preliminary review of their Roving Leader programs.

It is assumed that the information and data obtained from these 12 cities, based on review and analysis, are representative of the techniques and methods presently used by Roving Leaders. It is further assumed that the common elements found in the cities, both problems and solutions, will be generally applicable to cities throughout the country. However, caution should be exercised to avoid overgeneralization from data presented.

Basic information relative to city recreation problems and activities, including data on staffing, was obtained from appropriate recreation department personnel. Such basic data were supplemented in the information received from Youth Opportunity Coordinators and other municipal and county administrators, including Model Cities, planning, human relations, probation, and public schools personnel. Finally, informal interviews were conducted with community leaders, directors of neighborhood civic organizations, and representatives of private and public agencies such as Boys' Clubs, and YMCA's providing or interested in youth services, specifically Roving Leader Programs.

The Roving Leader Project was funded by the U.S. Office of Education under a contract with the National Recreation and Park Association. The project was carried out by University of Illinois, Office of Recreation and Park Resources project staff, under guidelines developed cooperatively. The purpose was to produce a training guide—a source that will assist the agency training officer in developing sound methods and techniques of leadership through an effective preservice training program for Roving Leaders.

This guide provides a nine-unit training program to be conducted over a 160-hour time period. The units are presented in the following order of participant progression:

1. Orientation
2. Concept, Role, and Function
3. The Community and Community Development
4. Identifying and Understanding Inner-City Youth
5. Group Process
6. Referral Process and Referral Sources
7. Programs and Planning
8. Field Work
9. Organizational Staff Training and Development

It is anticipated that after the participants have been exposed to this program, their level of competence will enable them to use this training design as part of their inservice training program for old and newly recruited Roving Leaders.

Purpose of the Training Guide

The purpose of this training guide is to provide a source that will assist the agency training officer in developing methods and techniques of leadership through an effective preservice training program for Roving Leaders.

For the purposes of this guide, the Roving Leader is a worker generally assigned to a specific geographic area within a community for the purpose of strengthening, extending, and stimulating participation of hard-to-reach youth in wholesome recreation programs. A prime purpose of this outreach service is to help delinquency-prone and disadvantaged youth to use their free time constructively and to assist them in utilizing community resources in the educational, health, employment, and related social service areas.

Needs of Inner-City Youth

Although America has been described by Harrington as a Nation of joiners and participants,[1] his description more accurately applied to middle-class Americans. The inhabitants of the "other America," the impoverished and hard-to-reach, rarely seek out or know of organized forms of recreation, such as basketball leagues, pool tournaments, talent shows, arts and crafts classes, and other special interest programs. Their leisure pursuits primarily are hanging out at drugstores, on street corners, in ice cream parlors, and poolhalls. Their recreation usually involves random movements from one place to another, with long stretches of boredom, broken occasionally by crap games and such short-range, excitement-seeking activities as petty stealing, use of drugs, and fights.

Several metropolitan areas are seriously considering the Roving Leader concept and its effectiveness for realistically serving hard-to-reach youth. It has been shown in Washington, D.C., by its Recreation Department; in San Francisco by Youth for Service; in Chicago by the YMCA; and in Buffalo, N.Y., by the Youth Board that a Roving Leader can provide face-to-face leadership different from that normally given by a recreation worker.

When the Giddings Elementary School on the fringe of Hough (Cleveland, Ohio) burned in April 1967, there were rumors that a Maoist gang had caused the fire. Eventually, six youth were arrested and sentenced to reform school:

> . . . They had done it for kicks. They had nothing to do and no place to do it. That was what they told the judge, and the Fire Department's arson investigators, the police and the probation officers all agreed that the kids were bored and not political-racist plotters.... At the same time, lack of money forced the Police Athletic League to cut back its activities for teenagers from the slums. 'We don't have organi-zations to belong to, we have gangs,' explained a ninth grader, at a recent ghetto students' meeting at the Cleveland Board of Education.[2]

The preceding account is an example of administrative and social failure to deal with the needs of inner-city youth.

The Roving Leader Concept

There is a dearth of experience in developing programs that minority youth can respond to, but there is little experience in developing and refining methods of reaching out to involve them. More important, the recreation programs designed to reach and serve low-income, hard-to-reach youth must be concerned with the "how" of reaching them, as well as the "what" of serving them.

The Roving Leader Program represents a somewhat new dimension in providing leadership for hard-to-reach, delinquent-prone youth that has proved to be highly successful. The Roving Leader usually spends weeks, sometimes months, establishing rapport with individuals and groups. He must start at the level of the group. This is not a short-term undertaking. He works with the youth for a long time—sometimes several years. The final test of the Roving Leader's success is when he is no longer needed. It has been amply documented that recreation can be used as one of the positive tools in the control and prevention of delinquency and crime.[3]

---

[1] Michael Harrington, *The Other America*. New York: Penguin Books, 1962.

[2] *New York Times,* April 1967.

[3] *American Recreation Journal,* Vol. 6, No. 1, January-February 1965.

As the Roving Leader concept expands, and as more recreation departments, Boys' Clubs, YMCA's, and other youth-serving agencies use Roving Leaders, it is essential that an effective and coordinated program be developed to train qualified leaders, which includes indigenous leaders from the economically, socially, and educationally deprived communities.

Objectives of the Guide

The objectives of this guide are as follows:

1. To locate, survey, and analyze existing Roving Leader Programs.

2. To produce a course unit design that facilitates training and development of Roving Leaders.

3. To stimulate lay advisory boards and commissions towards realizing the great potential of the Roving Leader, as a relevant leadership supplement to the conventional youth service programs.

Definition of Terms

Roving Leader is a worker generally assigned to a specific area of the inner city for the purpose of strengthening, extending, and stimulating the participation of hard-to-reach youth in wholesome recreation programs and assisting them in utilizing, to the fullest, community resources in the educational, health, employment, and related social service areas.

Outreach defines the function of a social service agency when it reaches out and assists, through face-to-face leadership, persons who were unreceptive or previously excluded from the agency's assistance or who were unaware of the available service.

Indigenous paraprofessional is a resident of the neighborhood, often a member of a minority group, and a *peer* of the participant sharing a common background, language, ethnic origin, style, and interests. Because of his ability to work comfortably with the community, the worker is viewed as a community advocate interpreting its needs, interests, and concerns.

Interdisciplinary concerns involve concepts and methods which transcend one particular discipline. They imply a problem orientation as contrasted to an agency orientation or professional discipline oriented service.

Methodology of Guide Development

Scope and Limitations

Although there are distinct advantages in having a more neutral observer study and analyze any educational or training program, it is fully realized that those involved in supervising or directing streetwork programs are probably more capable of assessing the feasibility and desirability of the final recommendations.

Because it was not feasible to visit and observe all streetwork programs around the country, the project staff selected 12 cities that were most varied in geographical location and agency sponsorship. It is hoped that this guide will be beneficial in pinpointing certain vistas and stimulating cities throughout the country to plan and implement programs using various special techniques and approaches currently practiced by Roving Leaders.

All of the data and information collected indicate that an instrument for training, properly designed, evaluated, and effectively implemented can be a valuable and relevant model for the development of Roving Leaders.

Procedures

A. Selection of a Project Review Committee to review and evaluate information collected by project staff on Roving Leader programs in this country.

B. Visits to 12 cities to observe programs and to interview administrators, workers, and participants in the Roving Leader program in these communities.

C. Review of correspondence, publications, and staff manuals of programs in communities where visitations were not made.

D. Extensive review of the literature in recreation, employment, social group work, group dynamics, and related social and behavioral science fields.

Preparation of Experimental Supplementary Teaching Aids

A. 35-mm color slides

B. Narrative tapes

C. Transparencies

The Interdisciplinary Approach

When we isolate a typical population of urban delinquents, it quickly becomes apparent that one is also dealing with a host of other conditions defined as problems in our society: multi-problem families, school dropouts, unemployed youth, racial minorities, issues of urban renewal and dislocations, and so on, in centrifugal fashion . . . more important to the extent that delinquency is in fact firmly rooted in one or more of the other problems with which it is frequently found to co-exist . . . intervention aimed at delinquency that does not also address itself to crucially related issues is only a partial answer to the problem of delinquency itself.[4]

The following outline is based on an interdisciplinary approach geared to preparing Roving Leaders to utilize the reaching-out technique of serving hard-to-reach youth residing in the urban communities.

---

[4] Martin, John M. and Joseph P. Fitzpatrick, *Delinquent Behavior: A Redefinition of the Problem,* New York: Random House, Inc., 1965, pp. 8, 9.

training units for roving leaders

Unit I. Orientation

For the trainer to organize an effective inservice training program for Roving Leaders he must understand both the origin and development of the concept of providing *direct* leadership to hard-to-reach youth in the inner city. This Unit presents an overview of the multitraining design through which leaders can (1) develop and apply a variety of methods and techniques in performing the task of the Roving Leader and (2) become aware of the behavior and the complicated forces that bear down on the hard-to-reach youth.

The Leader does not belong to the parent agency alone, but he must confer with, refer to, and receive referrals from all youth serving agencies—Youth Aid Division of the Metropolitan Police Department, Juvenile Court, public schools, U.S. Training and Employment Service, public housing, Health Department, Child Welfare Division of Welfare Department, Community Action Agencies and the Neighborhood Development Centers, private agencies, civic groups, and interested citizen groups.

It should be mentioned also that persons working with inner-city youth groups are identified by a variety of other titles,[5] such as:

1. Street-Club Worker
2. Gang Worker
3. Detached Worker
4. Street-Corner Worker
5. Neighborhood Youth-Worker
6. Area-Youth-Worker
7. Special-Service Worker
8. Out-Reach Worker

While these workers differ in approach and methods used, for the purpose of this training guide their intent is the same; namely, to provide direct service of a personal nature to hard-to-reach youth.

[5] Suggested Dictionary of Occupational Titles Codes (DOT 222.110, . . . 095, etc.) YO (Youth) p. 808, *Dictionary of Occupational Titles, 1965, Vol. 1, Definitions of Titles*. Roving Recreation Worker plus Aide; Roving Leader plus Aide; Detached Worker plus Aide; Special Service Worker plus Aide; Street Club Worker plus Aide; Youth Services Worker plus Aide.

The Roving Leader is employed as a field representative to work with hard-to-reach groups and individuals who are known to be problems in the community. Hours are odd in that the Leader continuously maintains contact by frequenting their places of interest and observing their activities. The Leader stimulates these youth to participate in ongoing agency programs, such as making court appearances, school referrals, employment referrals, family and individual counseling, and referrals to other supportive services. This person's role and function vis-à-vis the client is that of counselor, enabler, reenforcer, adviser, intermediator, and friend. The major emphasis is on friendship and flexibility.

There is no structured program the Roving Leader can follow in his work. He has no building in which to carry on a program, but seeks to make use of community facilities as the need arises. He must develop the creative ability to use whatever is available to him at a given time. The leader does not receive on-the-spot supervision as such; therefore, he must take the responsibility for making decisions and acting when necessary.

A. Early Developments

Contemporary Roving Leader work with delinquent groups, under agency sponsorship, probably had its origin in mid-19th century efforts of churchmen and charity workers to deal with young toughs and gangs in city slums. It was not until the Chicago Area Project in the 1930's, that the first organized program was developed in the United States using workers to contact unreached boys directly on the streets.

Shortly after World War II citizens in Washington, D.C., became concerned over the rise in juvenile delinquency. Public concern was finally officially registered in 1953 with creation of the Commisioners' Youth Council which paved the way for the D.C. Roving Leader and first demonstration program. In 1947 the New York City Youth Board was formed; the following year the first program of work with gangs was organized in Harlem. In the mid-1950's, new programs of streetwork were developed in San Francisco and Los Angeles. About the same time other cities started to organize programs to provide detached service to the youth in the streets. Among these cities were Rochester and Buffalo, N.Y., New York City under Youth Board auspices, Chicago under the YMCA, and others. These programs were among some of the earliest efforts to combat delinquency through direct service to street gangs and other hard-to-reach youth, outside the physical structure of a social agency.

It appears that many agency programs which are now traditional or fairly well established *originated* as efforts to serve street groups in their own neighborhoods. Recreational activities, boys' brigades, junior police corps, jobs, intensive club work, and individual counseling have been the traditional (if not systematically developed) means to attract and socialize gang youth. More than 40 years ago, it was recommended that boy workers or "boy-men" be assigned to find, contact, and work with male gangs to "rehabilitate their membership."[6]

A major difference between the Area Projects and social agency gang work programs which came later was in the neighborhood orientation of the Area Project, compared to the specific gang emphasis of the agency programs. Area Projects assumed that effective efforts had to be carried on as part of a larger effort sponsored by the residents of the area. Until just recently, social agencies have focused exclusively on changing the delinquent group per se, seldom utilizing the services of neighborhood persons and giving little attention to changing local neighborhood patterns.[7]

B. Ongoing Programs

The information on programs listed here was obtained from visits made to 12 cities, as mentioned earlier in the guide. However, these data were supplemented by information received from Youth Opportunity Coordinators and other municipal and county administrators, including Model Cities. Human relations, planning, probation, and public school personnel. In addition, Roving Leader programs were identified through a Consultation Conference of YMCA Detached Work Supervisors convened in Washington, D.C., by the Executive Director of Urban Development, National Council of YMCA's. It must be stated that the following list of ongoing programs

---

[6] Frederic M. Thrasher, *The Gang*. Chicago: University of Chicago Press, 1927.

[7] Irving Spergel, *Street Gang Work: Theory and Practice*. New York: Doubleday and Company, Inc. (Anchor Books), 1967.

is by no means complete. However, at this writing it represents those programs that could be identified.

Programs Operated by Young Men's Christian Association:

Canada	**Maryland**	**New York**
Montreal	Baltimore	Buffalo
Toronto	**Pennsylvania**	New York City
Winnipeg	Harrisburg	Rochester
California	Philadelphia	**Ohio**
Oakland	Pittsburgh	Cincinnati
Colorado	**Michigan**	Cleveland
Denver	Detroit	Dayton
Connecticut	Flint	Toledo
Hartford	Lansing	**Oklahoma**
Stamford	**Minnesota**	Oklahoma City
Georgia	Minneapolis	**Oregon**
Atlanta	**Missouri**	Portland
Iowa	St. Louis	**Virginia**
Des Moines	**Nebraska**	Richmond
Illinois	Omaha	**Washington**
Chicago	**New Jersey**	Seattle
Massachusetts	Newark	
Boston	Orange	
	Trenton	

Programs Operated by Municipal and Other Nonprofit Agencies:

City Recreation and Parks Department, Los Angeles, Calif.
D.C. Recreation Department, Washington, D.C.
Special Services for Groups, Inc., Los Angeles, Calif.
Youth Service Agency, New York City
Youth for Service, San Francisco, Calif.
Youth Board of Buffalo, Buffalo, N.Y.
Bureau of Recreation, Baltimore, Md.
Youth Activities Commission, Boston, Mass.
Recreation and Parks Department, Elgin, Ill.

Summary

It appears that the roots of roving leadership practice are to be found deep in the tradition of social agencies in this country. As early as 1848, churchmen and charity workers sought, without much success, to contact "young roughs" and other alienation "youth of the metropolis" through religious or mission streetwork then referred to as "Boys' Meeting." On the basis of this background the Unit discusses the earliest efforts to combat delinquency and alienation through an outreach approach—of going beyond the physical structure of a social agency. Increased recognition has been given recently to the fact that delinquency prevention, treatment, and control require "the participation of those who form a significant part of the social climate of the recipients receiving service." Agencies should realize that innovative and creative methods of providing service to the disadvantaged, hard-to-reach must be their prime consideration in meeting needs of these youth.

Finally, community institutional structures such as schools, labor unions, businesses, industries, social agencies, local citizens' groups, and community planning organizations need to provide more effective communication with low-income, hard-to-reach youth residing in the inner city, as an essential part of their effort to render relevant human services.

Reference List

Barron, Milton, L. *The Juvenile in Delinquent Society.* New York: Alfred A. Knopf, Inc., 1954.
    Parts of this book consider leisure-time use and delinquency. Several theories are mentioned and dismissed as confusing the time juvenile crime occurs with the cause of the crime. The author is also rather severe on the notion that organized recreation answers the needs of potential offenders. The tone of discussion is dated.

Martin, John M., and Joseph P. Fitzpatrick. *Delinquent Behavior: A Redefinition of the Problem.* New York: Random House, Inc., 1966, paper.
    A brief, clear, readable study of delinquency and its causes. The book relies primarily on sociological factors. It contains an excellent bibliography.

Mattick, Hans W., and Nathan S. Caplan. *The Chicago Youth Development Project.* Ann Arbor, Mich.: University of Michigan, Institute for Social Research, April 1962.
    An outline of the detached worker project begun in 1961 in Chicago. The paper discusses the pitfalls and possibilities of this kind of activity. It also considers coordination with existing agencies. The exact nature of its program remains vague, however.

Salisbury, Harrison. *The Shook-Up Generation.* New York: Harper & Row, Publishers, 1958.
    A *New York Times* journalist presents a description of juvenile delinquency in a personalized manner. Mr. Salisbury views the problem as having deep social roots, not only in the lower-income groups, but in suburbia as well. His recommendations call for significant changes in the social fabric of the country. He specifically considers the nonprofessional worker as one method of change.

Thrasher, Frederic M. *The Gang: A Study of 1,313 Gangs in Chicago* (abridged, with a new introduction by James F. Short, Jr.), Chicago: University of Chicago Press, 1963.
    A classic study of gang behavior and the environment in which gangs flourish. The abridged edition of this study (originally published in 1927) contains an excellent introduction showing the relation of Thrasher's conclusions to more modern studies.

Suggested Resources for this Unit

Technical Assistance Specialists

Jim Pratt, Director
Outreach Program
YMCA, 940 W. Main
Rochester, N.Y. 14611

Edwin Greenidge, Deputy Commissioner
Youth Services Agency
38 Park Row
New York, N.Y. 10038

Films

CRIME IN THE STREETS—60 min. (1966)
Indiana University

THE NEGLECTED—30 min. (1965)
Affiliated Film Producers, Inc.

Unit II. Concept, Role and Function of Roving Leader

This Unit deals with the basic concept, role, and function of the Roving Leader program as a problem-oriented service. It also explains the functional relationship between the theory and practice of the Roving Leader providing face-to-face leadership to hard-to-reach youth.

Objectives:

1. To help the Leader develop an understanding of the concept of the Roving Leader program.
2. To understand the functional framework as practiced.

Content Outline:

A. Concept

The Roving Leader program, a problem-oriented service (as contrasted to an agency-oriented or professional discipline oriented service), may be viewed as a fundamentalist orientation to social organization for helping people. The basic idea is to reach out to youth in need by providing face-to-face leadership and at the same time attempting to overcome narrow specialization. The Roving Leader uses the simplest and most direct means possible to provide services of unlimited scope and high personal identity. Through the program of Roving Leadership the Roving Leader is able to mobilize the community's faith in the potential of and capacity for positive change in its most aggressive, deviant youth. It is necessary for a Roving Leader to have the ability to show kindness under trying circumstances. He must also have emotional stability and be a good listener.

B. Role and Function of the Roving Leader

1. To serve as an advocate for youth and to provide service to a community wherein the youth eventually become their own advocates.
2. To provide unlimited service to youth in a face-to-face relationship.
   a. Holding informal sessions in laundromats, ice cream shops, poolrooms, or on street corners.
   b. Accompanying youth to various service agencies to teach them how to negotiate for assistance from appropriate resources (public and private).
   c. Assisting in formal meetings as a means of helping youth develop better ways of solving problems.
3. To serve as an agent to promote communication and exchange of information between students and teachers—in elementary and secondary schools.
   a. Notifying teachers of court appointments, etc.
   b. Arranging for teacher visits to after-school programs in which students participate.
   c. Setting up case conferences to encourage school-community involvement in assisting in the handling of problems and follow through.
4. To assist delinquency-prone, disadvantaged youth in using community resources in recreation, education, health, employment, and other related social service areas.
   a. Involving youth in planning and operation of neighborhood recreation programs.
   b. Conducting registrations for high school equivalency programs, free physical examinations, etc.
   c. Providing referrals to jobs and job training programs (Job Corps, Neighborhood Youth Corps, New Careers, Manpower Development and Training —MDTA,[8] etc.)
5. To assist youth in creating and operating their own programs as a means of developing and increasing their leadership potential for service to the community.
   a. Exposing youths to the world of work both in classrooms and on the job sites.

   b. Planning neighborhood minijob fairs and job clinics with area businesses.
   c. Organizing community beautification projects with youth supervision.
   d. Setting up youth councils—equal representation from all neighborhood groups.
6. To assist in identifying youth service gaps in education, employment and training, health, recreation, and other areas and to suggest ideas for improvement.
   a. Identifying all physical and human resources available in the area for youth service purposes.
   b. Involving the community—youth and adults—in the informal surveys.
   c. Calling on public and private residents to analyze those agency programs and facilities which must be better utilized, expanded, or increased.
   d. Suggesting facilities which may be more adequately used and programs that can be expanded or augmented by new ones.
   e. Mobilizing for action to make better use of existing facilities, expand present programs, and add new and innovative ones.
7. To establish communication and develop rapport with law enforcement, correctional departments, youth organizations, and other community services.
   a. Maintaining an open mind—visiting other agencies in an effort to find ways of solving problems.
   b. Establishing close contact and good working relationships with *local* community organizations and groups; i.e., educational, recreational, civic, civil, special services, in order to facilitate understanding of and working with youth in conflict.
   c. Involving youth and other community residents in a program; asking them to volunteer their services and using them as models for other youth.

Summary

Within this Unit attention is focused on concept, role, and function of the Roving Leader. Even though there are several terms used to describe Roving Leader, and possibly three basic approaches, essentially, the job of the Roving Leader is in part to serve as a communications and interpretations agent between organizations and persons who have resources—but do not know exactly how to render them effectively—and youths who are without access to resources but need desperately to acquire them, and who are unable to negotiate for service on their own. The Roving Leader program is problem oriented and the basic role and function is to modify the delinquent and disturbing behavior of teenagers through *relationship, reeducation,* and *redirection.*

---

[8] Manpower Development and Training Act of 1962, as amended.

Reference List

Mogulof, Melvin B. "Involving Low-Income Neighborhoods in Anti-Delinquency Programs." *Social Work,* October 1965, 10:4, pp. 51–57.

    The author's experience stems from working in Community Action Programs in San Francisco. He gives a cautious view of the involvement of the poor in community action, but he does conclude that it is necessary to support neighborhood groups who will eventually become participants in community affairs.

The Prevention and Control of Anti-Social Behavior of Youth. Los Angeles: Recreation and Youth Services Planning Council, September 1966.

    Even though this manual is intended for those in the Los Angeles area, it presents many useful guidelines for any teacher or youth worker. There are specific cases and also ideas for referral agencies. The book is intended as an inservice training guide for youth service personnel in public schools.

Reaching the Fighting Gang. New York: New York City Youth Board, 1960.

    A report on the activities of the New York City Youth Board's project for dealing with children on the streets. Chapters II, V, and VI give well-written information on gang characteristics and the activities of the detached workers working with them. The book is filled with case histories and should be useful. It is, however, marred by its outdated slang.

Suggested Resources for This Unit

Technical Assistance Specialists

Stanley J. Anderson
Social Science Adviser—Youth Services
Office of the Chief, Children's Bureau
Social and Rehabilitation Service
U.S. Department of Health, Education, and Welfare
Washington, D.C. 20202

Irving Spergel, Professor
School of Social Service Administration
University of Chicago
Chicago, Ill. 60601

Unit III. The Community and Community Development

The community scene today is such that public concerns are constantly changing, and a variety of sociological, economic, and psychological developments are creating new trends and needs to which city agencies must respond. With recent new approaches such as Neighborhood Youth Corps, New Careers, Job Corps, Model Cities and Concentrated Employment Programs, the community has become more involved and as a result the call now is for more innovative techniques to meet the challenge.

The intention here is to present a discussion of community structure and dynamics which is necessary to provide a framework wherein the Roving Leader can see himself as a human service worker. We also want to show that there are five major problems of concern to a community together with various characteristics that help the Leader understand the forces which cause the alienation and frustration of many disadvantaged youth.

Objectives:

1. To acquaint the Leader with the physical, social, economic, political, and cultural structure of the community.
2. To help him define the needs of the community and learn the resources for meeting those needs.
3. To assist the Leader in learning about strategies for change in delivery of services.
4. To use one's knowledge to effect positive change in conditions and services.
5. To involve community people as part of community development in order to effect change in conditions and services existing in the community.

Content Outline:

A. *Definitions of Community*

    1. Geographical boundaries
    2. Interaction of residents and groups
    3. Community resources
        a. Assistance programs (public welfare)
        b. Employment service (State, Office of Economic Opportunity)
        c. Vocational rehabilitation and counseling
        d. Physical health services
        e. Public schools
        f. Legal aid agencies
        g. Retraining programs
        h. Judicial system and facilities
        i. Parks and recreation commissions (and others)
    4. Relationships between agencies
    5. Community as a network of systems
        a. Social
        b. Economic
        c. Political
        d. Service
        e. Racial and Ethnic
        f. Class levels

B. *Characteristics of a Community*
  1. Interaction and participation
  2. Responsibilities, rights, and obligations
  3. Authority lines (political and economic)
  4. Power structure (formal and informal)
  5. Services
  6. Subcommunities (ghetto, slum)

C. *Issues*
  1. Unemployment
     a. Multiple causes of joblessness
        (1) Inadequate education or undereducation
        (2) Lack of vocational skills
        (3) Racial discrimination
        (4) Limited qualifications for specific occupational areas
        (5) Police records
        (6) Fear of failure
        (7) Lack of reliable transportation
        (8) Inadequate child care
        (9) Lack of job openings
  2. Health
     a. Communicable diseases (TB, VD, etc.)
     b. Alcoholism
     c. Drug addiction
     d. Poor mental health
     e. Inadequate sanitation facilities
     f. Health care utilization patterns as determined by socioeconomic group and racial group
  3. Crime
     a. Against persons
     b. Antisocial behavior—drugs—gambling, etc.
     c. Against property
     d. Discrimination and arrests
     e. Community resources and their relationships to crime
  4. Recreation
     a. Resources available
     b. Multiple causes for limited participation
        (1) Lack of public facilities
        (2) Discrimination
        (3) Expense of private facilities
        (4) Legislative budgetary priorities
        (5) Poor leadership
  5. Housing
     a. The development of the ghetto
     b. Open-housing legislation and discrimination
     c. Urban redevelopment and dislocation of people
     d. Landlord-tenant court and eviction proceedings
     e. Mobility rate of poor people
     f. Condition of housing
  6. Education
     a. Multiple causes for increased dropout rate
        (1) Family and individual problems, such as inadequate food and clothing
        (2) Truancy
        (3) Misunderstanding between teachers and students
        (4) Relevance of curriculums (Does it meet the needs of students going to work as well as those going to college?)
     b. Inner-city schools as compared to suburban schools
     c. The public school system (general organization)—Catholic school system
     d. Use of auxiliary personnel (new career aides, etc.)
     e. PTA—its purpose, function, and new potential for service

Summary

This Unit presents the overall structure and process of the community which serve as a general framework of reference within which to deal with a number of basic issues. The sections on unemployment, health, crime, recreation, housing, and education delineate six major problems of crucial concern to every community. The Unit should enable the Leader to identify and define community issues as they affect poor people, disadvantaged youth in particular, not only so that the Leader can be intellectually and emotionally aware of the feelings and needs of the youth he serves, but also that he, as a member of the community, can be more effective.

Reference List

Dentler, Robert A., and Mary Ellen Warshauer. *Big City Drop-Outs and Illiterates.* New York: Center for Urban Education, 1965.
    A study designed to analyze correlations between dropout rates and social and education characteristics in 131 sample cities.

Education of the Deprived and Segregated. Seminar conducted by Bank Street College of Education. New York: Bank Street College of Education, 1963.
    The seminar dealt primarily with questions of elementary education and inschool programs. The last four pages cover programs in connection with law enforcement agencies and other outside agencies.

Gans, Herbert. *The Urban Villagers.* New York: The Free Press of Glencoe, 1962.

A study of Italians in Boston. The group is divided into subcultures, one of which the author contends is responsible for the crimes usually associated with the entire group.

Glazer, Nathan, and Daniel P. Moynihan. *Beyond the Melting Pot*. Cambridge: MIT Press and Harvard University Press, 1964, paper.
> The book contends that the integration process has never occurred. The authors analyze the continued tension that results from this separation and how it affects ethnic cohesion. The study covers five ethnic groups in New York.

Harrington, Michael. *The Other America*. New York: Penguin Books, Inc., 1965.
> Harrington's study holds the distinction of making the urban and rural poor visible to the public. This well-written book gives the ethnic, demographic, and economic characteristics of the poor.

Herman, Melvin; Stanley; Bernard; Sadofsky; and Rosenberg, eds. *Work, Youth and Unemployment*. New York: Thomas Y. Crowell, Co., 1968.
> The book considers the complex causes of youth unemployment. It also considers ways of restructuring social institutions to provide for the use of nonprofessionals. Directions in the use of free time are also considered.

Hutchinson, John. *Principles of Recreation*. New York: A. S. Barnes & Co., 1951.
> Although the book's approach is necessarily dated, it contains sections on youth work. The first part deals with the foundations of recreation and contains useful cultural, social, and economic analysis.

Keach, Everet T., Robert Fulton, and William E. Gardner. *Education and Social Crisis: Perspectives on Teaching Disadvantaged Youth*. New York: John Wiley and Sons, Inc., 1967.
> Contains readings on cultural values and family life, explores problems in schools for disadvantaged youth, and presents programs for disadvantaged youth. The last section describing the programs is very useful as a guide to action. The first section gives good background, in particular Rainwater's piece on the Negro lower-class family.

Suggested Resources for this Unit

Technical Assistance Specialists

Percy Pinkney, Director
Street Work Program
Youth for Service
1160 McAllister Street
San Francisco, Calif. 94115

Walter Walker, Professor
Community Organization
School of Social Service Administration
University of Chicago
Chicago, Ill. 60601

Films

AGE OF TURMOIL—20 min. (1956)
McGraw-Hill, Inc.

IMPACT OF DEPRIVATION ON YOUNG CHILDREN—20 min.
Palmour Street
Modern Talking Pictures Service, Inc.

Unit IV. Identifying and Understanding Inner-City Youth

This section is concerned with understanding youth as they are, in various population groups, so as to be better able to provide the most meaningful service to them relative to their needs. With a basic understanding of the various needs expressed by these groups, which are usually members of minorities such as blacks, Puerto Ricans, American Indians, and Mexican-Americans, the Leader will be able to develop techniques and approaches for working with the power structure as a means toward helping meet certain needs of the youth.

Objectives:

1. To develop in the Leader an understanding of and techniques for serving delinquent and delinquency-prone youth.
2. To help the Leader recognize that behavior is related to feelings and beliefs, and that it is expressed differently by different individuals.
3. To become aware of the wide differences that can exist between "what is being said" and "what is being heard," and reasons for these.
4. To help the Leader develop a tolerance for ambivalence, anxiety, and conflict both in himself and in others.

Content Outline:

A. Population Groups

1. Teenage Gangs
   a. Observation and study of delinquent and nondelinquent behavior
   b. Study of pattern of hanging around
   c. Observation of its relationships with peers and adults
2. Delinquent crime-prone preteens
   a. Poor attendance records in school

    b. Frequent theft and petty larceny charges
    c. Creating discipline problems in school
  3. Disadvantaged from low-income, densely populated neighborhoods
    a. Unemployed or underemployed
    b. High school dropout
    c. Suspicious of white persons
    d. May have police record
  4. School dropouts
    a. Lack of job skills
    b. Police records
    c. Unemployed with sporadic work history
    d. Hang around in poolhalls, carry-out shops and other places

B. Power Structures

1. Formal—elected leaders
   a. Mayor and city council
   b. Ward aldermen
   c. School board
   d. Utility commissioners
2. Informal—inner-city leaders
   a. Black power groups
   b. Civic associations
   c. Street gangs
   d. Policy or numbers backers
   e. Tavern and poolhall owners
   f. Ministers

Summary

This Unit outlines the various population and minority groups residing in the inner city. Much consideration is given to the problems and needs of groups as a necessary undergirding for helping the worker understand that *many kinds* of services must be provided persons with unique needs. It is also made clear that effective techniques become increasingly more important as the Leader develops closer relationships with the disadvantaged, unemployed youth who are usually school dropouts.

Reference List

Bernstein, Saul. *Youth on the Streets.* New York: Association Press, 1964.
    A readable, nonscholarly description of the youth who participate in urban rebellions and possible methods to prevent alienation. The section on action programs gives a many-sided approach.

Carter, Genevieve, "Social Trends and Recreation Planning." *Recreation,* October 1965, 58:8, pp. 378–380.
    The author considers what the trend in leisure time and spending power will mean for recreation. She concedes that most public recreation is aimed at the middle class. The challenge to recreation lies in engaging the poor and disadvantaged in planning and operating programs.

Cavan, Ruth Shonle. *Juvenile Delinquency: Development, Treatment, Control.* New York: J. B. Lippincott Company, 1962.
    A college textbook for study of juvenile delinquency. It summarizes relevant material on all aspects of delinquency, and it contains information on recreation as it related to delinquency, and on the use of street workers and community organizations.

Cloward, Richard A., and Lloyd E. Ohlin. *Delinquency and Opportunity.* Glencoe, Ill.: The Free Press, 1960.
    A sociological analysis of the structure which produces the delinquent subculture. The book is primarily theoretical and relies on other studies for empirical examples.

Drake, St. Clair, and Horace A. Cayton. *Black Metropolis: A Study of Negro Life in a Northern City.* New York: Harcourt and Brace and World, Inc.; paper, Harper & Row.
    A classic study of urban life for the black American. The book contains a history of the black man in America and an analysis of his socioeconomic position. It discusses the "youth problem" and the activities of public and private agencies with young people.

Klein, Malcolm W., and Barbara G. Myerhoff, eds. *Juvenile Gangs in Context: Theory, Research and Action.* Englewood Cliffs, N.J.: Prentice-Hall, Inc., 1967.
    A group of papers from a meeting of the American Sociological Association and the Society for the Study of Social Problems in 1963, the volume includes sections on gang behavior, related pattern of perception and behavior, sociological contexts, and action programs. In the section on programs, reports are given on the Mobilization for Youth, Chicago area detached worker project, and others.

Kraus, Richard J. *Public Recreation and the Negro: A Study of Participation and Administrative Practices.* New York: Center for Urban Education, 1968.
    This report compares the recreation facilities in 24 suburban communities in the New York area. The study carefully contrasts the availability of recreational facilities, the type of users, and the results of the recreation experiences. As expected, facilities in the Black areas are inferior, used mainly by those under 12, and when integrated, often produce racial tension.

Kraus, Richard. "Riots and Recreation." *Journal of Health, Physical Education and Recreation,* March 1967, pp. 42–45.
    The article discussed the role lack of recreation facilities has played in sparking urban rebellion. Better recreation areas in the ghetto may prevent some summer tension.

Lutzin, Sidney G. "The Squeeze Out!—Recreation's Abdication of Responsibility." *Recreation*, October 1962, 55:8, pp. 390–392.
> Recreation has concentrated on agencies which primarily serve the middle class. The author calls for attention to be focused on the needs of the poor.

Office of Manpower, Automation, and Training, U.S. Department of Labor. *Young Workers: Their Special Training Needs.* Washington, D.C.: U.S. Government Printing Office, May 1963.
> An examination of noncollege-bound youth and their educational needs. The report deals with special cases of juvenile delinquency, low-income youth, etc., and contains clearly summarized and illustrated material on the number and characteristics of noncollege-bound youth.

Parker, Seymour, and Robert J. Kleiner. *Mental Illness in the Urban Negro Community.* New York: The Free Press of Glencoe, 1965.
> This survey of 3,000 urban blacks analyzes the relationship between social conditions and mental health. The results indicate that persons designated mentally ill set higher goals than they could possibly achieve and thus suffered anxiety. In addition, the study discovered many subjects with low self-esteem. The study summarizes other academic studies and presents detailed statistical analysis.

Shivers, Jay S. *Leadership in Recreation Service: Principles, Process, Personnel, Methods.* New York: The Macmillan Co., 1967.
> This book gives a detailed explanation of the processes and techniques of leadership in relation to the field of recreational service. Although it is written fundamentally for students in institutions of higher education preparing for the field, it should be of considerable value to practitioners: laymen who volunteer for community service with recreational agencies; educators and government officials who are concerned with the legal aspects for the provision of services in this field; administrators in related fields, that is, group work, sociology, social psychology, and human relations.

Whyte, William F. *Street Corner Society: The Social Structure of an Italian Slum.* Chicago: University of Chicago Press, 1955.
> Description of street corner life in an Italian-American ghetto. The book shows how street corner youth maintain cohesion and their relation to the power structure in the community.

Yablonsky, Lewis. *The Violent Gang.* New York: The Macmilan Company, 1962.
> A sociological-psychological interpretation of gang behavior by a man with many years experience in gang work. The author's summary of relevant materials is very clear. In the final chapter, on coping with the gang, he devotes space to the use of detached workers.

Suggested Resources for this Unit

Technical Assistance Specialists

Grant Haynesworth, Director
Detached Worker Program
Buffalo Youth Board
313 City Hall
Buffalo, N.Y. 14202

Douglas Lindsey, Sr.
Roving Leader
D.C. Roving Leader Program
3149 Sixteenth Street, NW.
Washington, D.C. 20010

Films

THE DROPOUT—29 min. (1961)
International Film Bureau

ANGRY BOY—33 min. (1951)
International Film Bureau

BOY WITH A KNIFE—18 min. (1955)
Los Angeles Community Chest

Unit V. Group Process

In this Unit an attempt is made to give Leaders a basic understanding of the significance of group process in helping to determine values, goals, and expectations of individuals—using tape recordings and role playing as vehicles.

Objectives:

1. To teach Leaders some of the basic concepts used to describe the group process.

2. To give Leaders practice in observing, analyzing, and discussing actual group situations.

3. To help Leaders relate group process to attaining specific goals, both in training and in their jobs as Roving Leaders.

Content Outline:

A. What Makes a Group?

1. Leaders' definitions
2. Theoretical definitions
3. Groups' definitions

B. What Are the Various Groups?

1. The gang
2. In classroom

3. At work
4. For social activities
5. For sports activities

C. Common Factors of Groups

1. Leadership
2. Identity
3. Degrees of participation

D. Two Major Types of Groups

1. Membership groups—groups to which one belongs (formal and informal)
2. Reference groups—groups to which one aspires to be a member of or whose norms influence one's behavior

E. Group Pressure for Conformity or Nonconformity

1. How interchange of ideas in a group can cause members to conform
2. Or not to conform
3. The need for acceptance
4. The positive and active understanding of one's feelings by someone you respect

F. Group Management

1. Goal setting
   a. "Rap" or "bull" sessions to determine direction and focus of the group.
   b. Planning sessions to set programs for each season
2. Natural leaders and the development of leadership
   a. How are "natural" Leaders identified?
   b. How does one gain their cooperation?
   c. What is their relationship to the youth worker?

Summary

The theme of the entire discussion in this Unit is applying what has been discussed to practical purposes and situations. This includes school groups, recreation groups, and other situations encountered by the Leader. Through group sessions, the Leader's job is to get individuals involved in discussions based on their experiences, and to help translate these concerns into useable knowledge, generalized information, and practical decisions.

Reference List

Bion, W. R. *Experiences in Groups.* New York: Basic Books, Inc., 1961.
  A set of papers published over a 10-year period. The author relates group experiences to not only the individual's psychology, but to wider group experiences. There is nothing specific on gang or youth behavior.

Gordon, R. A., et al. "Values and Gang Delinquency: A Study of Street Corner Groups." *American Journal of Sociology,* 1963, 69:2, pp. 109-128.
  A test of three hypotheses about gang behavior, using a semantic differential on gang, nongang lower-class, and nongang middle-class groups, showed little difference in rating deviant behavior, but great difference in attitude toward deviant behavior. The sample was derived from Chicago area YMCA programs and settlement houses.

Lambert, William W., and L. Wallace. *Social Psychology.* Englewood Cliffs, N.J.: Prentice-Hall, Inc., 1964.
  An able and well-written summary of theoretical research in social psychology. The book contains no casework or practical work relevant to the outreach projects.

Liebow, Elliot. *Talley's Corner: A Study of Negro Streetcorner Men.* Boston: Little, Brown and Company, 1967.
  The book contains data collected in Washington, D.C., during 1962-63. It is an attempt to record daily routines of the men on the street. It deals with the relationships between man and children, wives, etc. It is useful as a source on street activities of adults and, by implication, of youth.

Olmsted, Michael S. *The Small Group.* New York: Random House, Inc., 1959, paper.
  A summary of theoretical work on small groups written primarily for an academic audience, rather than the social worker or group leader.

Shepherd, Clovis R. *Small Groups: Some Sociological Perspectives.* San Francisco: Chandler Publishing Company, 1964, paper.
  A summary of the relevant behavioral science theories. The book is directed to both the student of social psychology and interested laymen who must relate frequently in small groups. The last chapter is devoted to using the principles of group dynamics in actual situations.

Spergel, Irving. *Street Gang Work: Theory and Practice.* Reading, Mass.: Addison-Wesley Publishing Co., Inc., 1966.
  This book attempts to join sociological theory with social work experience. The sociology section summarizes prominent theory in a rather conventional manner. The social work section concentrates on control of gang behavior and instilling proper social values.

Suggested Resources for this Unit

Technical Assistance Specialists

Walter Walker, Professor
School of Social Service Administration
University of Chicago
Chicago, Ill. 60601

Irving Spergel, Professor
School of Social Service Administration
University of Chicago
Chicago, Ill. 60601

Films

Getting Along With Parents—14 min. (1954)
Encyclopedia Britannica Films

Getting a Job—16 min. (1954)
Encyclopedia Britannica Films

Learning from Disappointments—11 min.
Coronet Instructional Films

Unit VI. Referral Process and Referral Sources

The focus of the Leader should be that of enabling the youth to use services more effectively. This unit deals with the types of and reasons for referral as well as a sample listing of the different kinds of referral agencies.

Objectives:

1. To help the Leader understand that when the problem lies outside the scope of the program, the youth should be referred to an appropriate agency or agencies for assistance.
2. To develop the ability or clarify a problem.
3. To have the Leader develop ways of stimulating motivated action by youth to accept and follow through on the referral.

Content Outline:

A. *Common Reasons Youth Are Referred for Service*

1. Theft
2. Assault or fighting
3. Disregard for authority
4. Disrupting or interfering with program
5. Immoral acts, etc.

B. *Types of Referral by Leaders*

1. Psychiatric
2. School
3. Employment
4. Drug addiction treatment
5. Others

C. *How To Contact Other Agencies*

D. *How To Act as an Advocate for Your Client*

E. *How To Identify Gaps in Services*

The agencies listed here are only a sample of referral sources. They are listed for your general information and as a sample guide. A more comprehensive source is the current edition of the directory of health, welfare, recreation, and other community services of your city.

Referral Sources

1. Bonabond, Inc.—District of Columbia, 412 Fifth Street, NW.—737-4307.
Program: Job placement, fidelity bonds, bail bond release, counseling, and other supportive services for ex-offenders and others with arrest records. Male and female, 18 years and up.

2. Employment Service—District of Columbia for D.C., 555 Pennsylvania Avenue, NW.—393-6151.
Program: Free public employment service to workers, employers, and disadvantaged workers. Apprenticeship Training and Information Center.

3. Neighborhood Legal Service
Program: Free legal assistance and case representation for poor people and minority group members.

4. Juvenile Aid Division, Police Department
Program: To assist youngsters between 7 and 17 who are involved in delinquent acts.

5. Child Guidance Clinic
Program: Study and treatment of children 18 months to 18 years with personality and behavior difficulties.

6. Juvenile Court Desk
Program: Hearing and disposition of Juvenile Court cases. Cases received through Intake Section, City Probation Department.

7. City Probation Department
Program: Conducts social investigations and super-

vises cases of delinquent minors and certain dependent or neglected children in need of protection by Juvenile Courts.

8. Vocational Schools and Evening Schools

Program: Those programs set up either to certify students for high school completion, or to train them in job or career related skills.

9. Intake and Detention Control

Program: Responsible for intake of juvenile cases in which minor is detained.

There are many others in your local community.

Summary

Most of the discussion in this Unit centers around two major elements of the referral process: delineation and clarification of problems and stimulating motivated action by youth to accept and follow through on the referral. As is pointed out in the sample listing of agencies, it is very crucial for the leader to know about the different resources and select the program which can most effectively attack the problem.

Reference List

Brager, George A., and Francis P. Purcell, eds. *Community Action Against Poverty.* New Haven, Conn.: College and University Press, 1967.

> A group of papers, many of them reprinted from other sources, discussing experiments in community action. The sections on use of nonprofessionals and the poor's relation to social agencies are especially useful. All the articles are tied to specific action projects, many of them demonstration projects resulting from the President's Committee on Juvenile Delinquency and Crime.

Brager, George. "The Indigenous Worker: A New Approach to the Social Work Technician." *Social Work,* 1965, pp. 33–40.

> The Mobilization for Youth's Visiting Homemaker Program as background, the author comments on the faults and virtues of the professional and nonprofessional worker. The analysis is brief and good background reading for the New Careers approach.

Clark, Kenneth. *Dark Ghetto.* New York: Harper & Row, Publishers, 1965.

> A study of ghetto life which rose out of Harlem Youth Opportunities Unlimited. Dr. Clark has not only studied the ghetto but has lived there. The excellent analysis found in this book describes the social, economic, political, and psychological aspects. Delinquency is considered in a special chapter on the pathology of ghetto life.

Kelin, Malcolm W., and Neil Snyder. "The Detached Worker: Uniformities and Variance in Work Style." *Social Work,* October 1965, pp. 60–68.

> A statistical study of several detached worker programs. The authors conclude that there are great differences in the way the workers spend their time and what activities they undertake.

Referral-Guidance Program. Milwaukee Department of Municipal Recreation and Adult Education.

> An outline of a program to give recreation leaders opportunities to refer the disadvantaged to the proper agency.

Reid, William. "Interagency Coordination in Delinquency Prevention and Control." *Social Service Review,* December 1964, 38:4, pp. 418–428.

> A theory of coordination which considers how agencies may exchange resources and ideas without involving additional groups. The article is primarily the formulation of a desirable working program, and does not refer to specific cases.

Riessman, Frank, and Hermine I. Popper. *Up From Poverty: New Career Ladders for Nonprofessionals.* New York: Harper & Row, Publishers, 1968.

> This book considers how the New-Careers approach performs three long range goals: (1) provides work and training for disadvantaged, (2) develops new manpower and human service, and (3) restructures human service agencies to make them more useful to their clients.

Schreiber, Daniel, ed. *The School Drop-Out.* Washington, D.C.: National Education Association, 1964.

> A collection of 16 papers from a symposium of the same name. The papers are well-written and generally critical of the existing school system, especially concerning its relevance to its nonmiddle-class pupils.

The Prevention and Control of Anti-Social Behavior of Youth; An In-Service Training Guide (to aid personnel of recreation and youth service agencies). Los Angeles: Recreation and Youth Services Planning Council, 1966.

> This training guide is intended to serve as both a practical guide and a training manual for the program leader in recreation and youth services agencies in dealing more effectively with antisocial behavior of youth. Although planned as a practical guide for youth services personnel of Los Angeles city schools, it can be used by youth workers in almost any setting.

Suggested Resources for this Unit

Technical Assistance Specialists

Carver J. Leach, Jr., Director
Roving Leader Program
Department of Recreation
1615 Chillum Pl., NE.
Washington, D.C. 20011

Acklin Thiebeaux
Senior Street Worker
Youth for Service
1122 Market Street
San Francisco, Calif. 94103

Daniel Lowery, Field Representative
U.S. Department of Labor
1726 M Street, NW.
Washington, D.C. 20036

Films

Ask Me, Don't Tell Me
Contemporary Films

The Roving Leader in Action
Roving Leader Program Office
Department of Recreation
1615 Chillum Place, NE.
Washington, D.C. 20011

Unit VII. Programs and Planning

Activity, planned or unplanned, is a basic form of communication among gang members. Delinquent youth tend to "act out" feelings or express themselves through activity rather than through verbal exchange and ideas. Through activities the group can be exposed to a relatively well-controlled and productive social environment; i.e., camping, excursions, and work projects are some of the activities that make it possible for youth to improve their social skills and sense of self-respect. In other words, the Leader engages the group in a problem solving effort, through activity and discussion to stimulate changes in attitudes and learn new ways of dealing with problems.

Objectives:

1. To involve parents and group members in planning and executing community activities.
2. To strive for creativity and flexibility in programming based on the needs.
3. To plan each role functioning; how to act and what to say in certain situations.
4. To provide opportunities for program where access is limited.
5. To take quick steps in diagnosing problems and acting to prevent explosive situations.

Content Outline:

A. Planned Activity

1. Plan with members of a gang activities they enjoy and guide them into wholesome activities.
2. Allow group to assist in setting the ground rules; involve members in enforcement.
3. Set up a youth planning council which has equal representation from all groups in the Leader's area.
4. Assign members definite areas of responsibility.
5. Schedule a certain time and area for the youth to use the facilities for activities, as well as for the younger children.
6. Provide opportunities for successful participation, recognition, and acceptance so that each individual's talents may be recognized and accepted.

Examples:
 Arrange skating parties at local rinks by having each individual work on a planning committee.
 Secure complimentary passes for the group to attend sports events and other special activities.
 Help youth plan, organize, and conduct a talent show.

7. Stimulate private and public agencies and others to get involved in the programs.
8. Suggest ideas for expanding use of existing facilities.

Examples:
 Additional lighting—at playfields, playgrounds, and other conducive sites, thus extending hours of operation.
 Closed streets—converting certain streets into play streets by closing off traffic.
 Mobile recreation units—bringing playgrounds and leadership to the children in the form of mobile units to increase neighborhood participation.

B. Unplanned Activity

1. In attempting to control or prevent aggressive behavior, the Roving Leader should size up each conflict situation on its own terms, then select an approach; timing of the worker's action is critical.

Example:
 On one occasion a member of a gang was attacked with sticks by the other members. The worker pretended he thought it was a mock attack. The worker indicated he was leaving for the office early if anyone wanted a ride to the Community Center. They stopped the action immediately, and climbed into the station wagon.

Sometimes a worker's presence is sufficient, if a good relationship has been established.

2. Worker may set up a peace meeting between conflicting groups when communications have broken down.

3. The worker should redirect the less visible types of delinquent activity—such as, stealing, use of narcotics, and truancy—into creative endeavor.

Example:
> A worker once learned that some shoplifting had been going on downtown and that articles such as sports equipment, toys, and painting sets were taken. After discussing the implications of such behavior, the worker asked if anyone had ever painted. Two boys had painted before, and the worker commended them. He then took them to the art museum for discussions of art. The boys became interested and started spending a great deal of time painting. Now the worker plans to exhibit some of their paintings.

Summary

This Unit deals with the techniques and methods of using both *planned* and *unplanned activity* as a means of communicating with gang members and other hard-to-reach youth. In the process of ongoing activities, effort is made to approach problem solving with the youth. It is also pointed out that not only is it necessary for the Roving Leader to introduce these programs, but he must also involve the parents and other residents of the community in planning and operating these programs.

Finally, because delinquent youth tend to "act out" feelings or express themselves through activity rather than words, the Leader must be able to use this medium as a means of improving relationships and re-educating and redirecting the youth.

Reference List

Blake, Mary. "Youth Worker and Police." *Children*, 1961, 8:5, pp. 170-174.
> Suggestions and specific cases of how case workers and police interact. The emphasis is on personal contact between the two and clear communication about the youth worker's activities.

Burchill, George W. *Work-Study Programs for Alienated Youth*. Chicago: Science Research Associates, 1962.
> Reports on nine work programs for alienated youth, including dropouts and handicapped youth. Also of interest are the appendixes which give detailed information on training guides used in the programs.

Caplan, Nathan S. "Factors Affecting the Process and Outcome of Street Club Work." *Sociology and Social Research*, January 1964, 48:2, pp. 207-219.
> A study of streetclub workers to see if they held similar concepts on the dimensions of their work. The statistics presented show that they do share a common framework.

Herman, Melvin, and Stanley Sadofsky. *Youth-Work Programs: Problems of Planning and Operation*. New York: New York University Press, 1966.
> An excellent description of youth-work programs. The book not only covers the interaction of agencies in forming the programs, but specifically considers the recruitment of youth.

Klein, Malcolm, W. "Juvenile Gangs, Police and Detached Workers: Controversies about Intervention." *Social Service Review*, June 1965, 39:2, pp. 182-190.
> Begins by outlining the tendency toward polarization between law enforcement and social work agencies. Their differences are especially pronounced when a detached worker is present. The article does not interpret, but attempts to ask questions that arise between the two groups with references to cases.

Maclennan, P., and W. Klein. "Utilization of Groups in Job Training for the Socially Deprived." *International Journal of Group Psychotherapy*, October 1965, 15:, pp. 424-433.
> Report on efforts at youth training done by Howard University's Center for Youth and Community Studies. The aim of the program was to provide nonprofessionals with training for employment. The problems and techniques used in the program, notably the group care technique, provide valuable insights and information.

Suggested Resources for this Unit

Technical Assistance Specialists

Edwin Greenidge, Deputy Commissioner
Youth Services Agency
38 Park Avenue
New York, N.Y. 10038

Percy Pinkney, Director
Street Work Program
Youth for Service
San Francisco, Calif. 94115

Films

Ask Me, Don't Tell Me
Contemporary Films

Three Steps to Start—26 min. (1955)
McGraw-Hill Book Company, Inc.

What About Juvenile Delinquency?—11 min. (1955)
McGraw-Hill Book Company, Inc.

Unit VIII. Field Work

Field work brings trainees into contact with a variety of people engaged in human services. Roving Leaders must have a working knowledge of the social agencies and other resources in their community. By visiting other agencies and talking with people who render services, the unfamiliar may become familiar and the workers' confidence may be strengthened. Hopefully as a result, the workers' capacity to tune in and understand both community and youth's interest is also strengthened.

Basic Objectives:

1. To acquaint the Leaders with community resources and referral procedures.
2. To help Leaders move from theory to real-life situations.
3. To give Leaders practice in planning and implementing activities.
4. To help Leaders think of contributions they might make to improve services.

Content Outline:

A. Agencies Related to the Problem

1. Welfare Department
2. Salvation Army, etc.
3. Family and Child Services
4. Health and Welfare Council
5. Community action agencies
6. Ghetto schools

B. Minority Group History and Culture

This section of the Unit is designed to provide the trainer with information for use in guiding discussions *in English or other languages.*

1. History of various minority groups (such as blacks, Puerto Ricans, Mexican-Americans) and understanding of forces which shaped their lives.
   a. Slavery (visit museums and freedom schools)
   b. Substandard housing
   c. Job discrimination
   d. Poor police-community relations
   e. Humiliation—remarks of disrespect
   f. Migration of the blacks to the North for jobs—development of slums and scarcity of jobs
   g. Summer riots—1960's
      (1) July 1964—Harlem
      (2) July 1964—Watts
      (3) 1967—Detroit, Newark.
2. How to work with minority group members
   a. Learn language, habits (groups and individual), and culture
   b. Develop sensitivity towards individual feelings
   c. Be reserved in statements; refrain from making derogatory remarks
   d. Think of members as free individuals—don't thrust your values on them
   e. Hold conferences or frank discussions with members of all races to discuss racial tensions
   f. Allow groups opportunity to display their culture

C. The Employment Structure

1. The local employment service
   a. Youth employment branch (Youth Opportunity Program, On-the-Job Training, Vocational Opportunity Program, Concentrated Employment Program)
   b. Manpower Development and Training branch (institutional, noninstitutional)
   c. Unemployment Compensation Board
2. U.S. Civil Service Commission
   a. Qualifications for different jobs
   b. Merit system (promotion)
   c. Agency opportunities
      (1) For professionals
      (2) For paraprofessionals
      (3) For youth—high school graduates and dropouts

D. The Community

1. Neighborhood
   a. Councils, advisory boards
   b. Block clubs
   c. Civic associations and others
2. Citywide
   a. Board of Trade, Chamber of Commerce
   b. City Council
   c. School board
3. Governmental
   a. Probation, juvenile court
   b. Urban renewal
   c. Commission on budget hearings, program proposal, etc.

E. Strengthening the Roving Leader's Capacity To Tune in on Interests of Youth

1. Interests of youth comprises:
   a. Family
   b. Peers
   c. Public, private, and commercial institutions
2. A community inventory taken in five dimensions:
   a. What the youth sees and uses?

b. What gets in youth's way of using systems for their intended purposes?
c. What is available to the youth?
d. What else needs to be made available?
e. How can the Roving Leader help make available and useful the resources a youth needs for growth?
3. Factors related to the inventory task
   a. To strengthen the boy or girl; to help him modify his behavior in a positive direction
   b. To strengthen the operation of the services
   c. To develop, adapt, or modify services needed for dealing with social problems
4. Youth workers must develop methods of operating
   a. Take time to become acquainted
   b. Take time to find out by observation and verification through conversation who has affection or attraction for whom
   c. Take time to note who and what is instrumental in satisfying the needs of the youth
   d. Assess actions in terms of their meaning to the youth
   e. Assess actions in terms of the ranking of persons of influence or the significant others in the lives of the youth
   f. Provide opportunity for
      (1) alternatives of choice
      (2) alternatives of action
   g. Make opportunity significant for others to achieve through engaging him or her in:
      (1) choosing alternatives for the well-being of the group
      (2) selecting alternative actions for the well-being of the group
5. Provide steam outlets for group
   a. *Anxious time*—worker can isolate group (remove from trouble situation)
   b. *Angry times* or frustration reactions
      (1) If reasonable—discuss with offended and offender
      (2) If boiling over—work out physically in gym or pool. Then confront. BEFORE WORKERS ACT THEY MUST THINK!

F. Law and Its Relation to Society

1. Neighborhood Legal Service (Office of Economic Opportunity)—legal issues affecting the poor
2. Legal Aid Society—How legal service is available through court
3. Police Department—policies and practices for handling juveniles
4. Juvenile courts—detention homes
5. Legal departments responsible for evictions and housing code violations and enforcements
6. Have discussions with judges and other officials regarding juvenile offenses—drugs, drunkenness, and general crime patterns in various areas and locations

Summary

The Unit includes a basic framework for organizing field visits and conducting discussions on observations made by the Leaders. Youth service workers must have a working knowledge of how social agencies operate and how their resources may be utilized. Only dramatic and true-to-life curriculum material can be useful to the worker. It is hoped that by visiting the agencies and talking with persons who render services and clients who use them, the unfamiliar may become familiar and the Leader's confidence may be strengthened.

Reference List

Buffalo Youth Board. *Employment for School Drop-Outs.* Buffalo, N.Y.: Buffalo Youth Board, 1962.
   A survey of local employment opportunities for youth who have not completed high school.

Burchill, George W. *Work-Study Program for Alienated Youth: A Casebook.* Chicago: Science Research Associates, 1962.
   A good collection of experiences of programs arising out of the President's Commission on Crime and Juvenile Delinquency. In addition to the cases, the book presents examples of training materials and a list of addresses of the work-study programs.

Cohen, Eli E., and Louise Kapp. *Manpower Policies for Youth.* New York: Columbia University Press, 1966.
   The book contains 14 papers from a symposium of the same name. Of special importance are the papers by Nat Hentoff discussing the question of youth motivation and his observation of the Mobilization for Youth program, and S. M. Miller's warning of the danger of encouraging unemployed youth to train for jobs which do not exist.

National Child Labor Committee. *Youth Employment Programs in Perspective.* Washington: U.S. Government Printing Office, 1964.
   Reports the results of a survey of 39 youth employment programs in 31 communities during 1962–63. The study serves as a guide to youth employment programs and analyzes their effectiveness.

Witmer, Helen L., ed. "Prevention of Juvenile Delinquency." Chapter in *The Annals of the American Academy of Political and Social Science,* 1959, 213 pp. See also R. C. Brown and Don W. Dodson, "Effectiveness of a Boys' Club in Reducing Delinquency," pp. 47–52.

    Compares three similiar white areas in Louisville, Ky., over 10 years and shows a reduction in delinquency in the area which had a boys' club.

Suggested Resources for this Unit

Technical Assistance Specialists

George M. NishiNaka, Executive Director
Special Service for Groups, Inc.
United Way Agency
2400 South Western Avenue
Los Angeles, Calif. 90018

James Pratt, Director
Outreach Program
YMCA, 940 West Main
Rochester, N.Y. 14611

Acklin Thibeaux
Coordinator of Minority Recruitment
Youth for Service
1160 McAllister Street
San Francisco, Calif. 94115

Films

Take An Option on Tomorrow—28 min.
National Business Machines

Who's Delinquent (1960)
RKO Pathe, Inc.

Right or Wrong
  (Making Moral Decision)—10 min. (1956)
Coronet Instructional Films

Unit IX. Organizational Staff Training and Development

Training is clearly one of the administration's most effective means of stimulating the growth of an individual in an organization. The training function has been undergoing a revolution similar to the administrative revolution referred to by so many in recent years. The call in training today is for imaginative and perceptive practitioners. We must as urban program workers, become "problem-oriented" rather than discipline or agency oriented.

This Unit focuses on various training aspects that are both job-related and valuable to the Leader representing his agency as he serves hard-to-reach, disadvantaged youth in the inner city and includes the "how" of dealing with specific problems of antisocial behavior.

Objectives:

1. To help Leaders understand their specific daily work roles.

2. To help Leaders grasp the policies, personnel practices, and mission of both the training program and the agency.

3. To provide Leaders the foundation required for further training and upward mobility.

4. To provide the employing/training agency with the opportunity to evaluate and improve its own function and program.

5. To help them develop an image of youth services workers with which they can identify.

6. To help the Leaders gain perspective regarding their jobs in relationship to other positions in their field and agency.

7. To provide Leaders the knowledge of accident prevention methods and Emergency First Aid procedures.

Content Outline:

A. Agency Table of Organization (use chart)

1. Administrative staff
2. Departmental directors
3. Policies and procedures
4. Line or field supervisors
5. Supervisory responsibility

B. Job Description of Roving Leaders (See appendix D)

1. Duties and responsibilities
2. Relationship with other members of agency—trying to complement another person's role by working together with him in certain cases
3. Attending staff meetings and serving on committees

C. Recording

Recording combines narrative and process types and is used as basis for determining group and individual progress, planning future work, and evaluating effectiveness of the service. Records are also of assistance to both worker and supervisor as they jointly form specific goals for groups and individuals in groups and plan methods of achieving these.

Recording is usually completed on three levels: (1) A daily program record indicates exactly where the worker was and what he was doing at time of contact with his group, (2) a group contact record indicates in detail the many varied aspects of the worker's contact with his group, and (3) the individual contact record is concerned with the worker's continuing contact with individual members of the group. Information from these three levels of recording should provide the basis for the worker's monthly report.

D. Personnel Practices

1. Hiring policies
   a. Jobs that are filled under merit service regulations
   b. Are tests required?
   c. Education and experience required
2. Promotion opportunities
   a. Areas of upward mobility
   b. Requirements for movement to the next step on the career ladder
3. Benefits
   a. Requirements for continuing (i.e., release time, amount paid by agency, etc.)
   b. Agency paid or employee deductions for retirement, life, and accident insurance
   c. Procedures for reimbursement for expenses realized in the line of duty (i.e., mileage, meals, etc.), and others pertaining to your local agency

E. Supervising the Roving Leader Program

1. Administrative
   a. Community relations—gives streetwork operations a base within a firm but flexible network of existing agencies and groups
   b. Staff selection—supervisory decisions are usually influenced by worker's experience, maturity, special skills, ethnic background, and personality
   c. Planning—the amount of direct planning depends on workers' ability and initiative: aim is to prevent worker from spreading himself too thin in serving the youth.
   d. Program evaluation—periodically the supervisor must engage in systematic evaluation of at least parts of program; worker is usually asked to make an evaluation of some aspect of his practice.
   e. Field supervision—supervisor should provide field supervision in addition to that based in office; worker and supervisor may work out improvised plans for this item.
2. Teaching
   a. Use of office and field supervisory conferences and staff meetings
   b. Understanding that the worker approaches his role in terms of knowledge, skills, etc., acquired from previous experiences (i.e., job, social situations, family)
   c. Facilitating a common set of job perceptions between worker and supervisor
3. Support
   a. Having a special understanding and commitment regarding problems of extreme hositility by group members, burn-outs, family crises, and others
   b. Expressing continuing confidence in worker's ability
   c. Being aware of both the needs of the worker and of the group

F. Safety and Accident Prevention

1. Safe practices in public assemblies
   a. Take a look around when you enter a place of public assembly and count the number of exits
   b. As soon as you enter a place of public assembly, locate the two nearest exits to you
2. Field trips
   a. Gain permission of parent or guardian for underage participants
   b. Be sure to plan so there is sufficient time to make the return trip in daylight
   c. Make arrangements in advance for a meeting place if anyone becomes separated from the group
   d. No vehicles should be used for any excursion unless they are in perfect operating condition, the driver is competent, and adequate insurance is in force

G. Emergency First Aid

1. In times of stress many persons may be called on to administer immediate or temporary aid, especially the Roving Leader. (For the purposes of this guide, first aid is defined as the immediate and temporary assistance given to a victim of an accident or sudden illness until the services of a physician can be obtained.)

a. All personnel on staff, including Roving Leaders, should receive formal instruction on first aid and periodic refresher courses as necessary to maintain a high degree of skill in providing emergency assistance.
b. Persons teaching and supervising athletic and recreation activities should have advanced first-aid competence.
c. Specific procedures should be developed for emergency evacuation, panic prevention, and the handling of emergencies at public events, including assemblies, athletic contests, and other spectator activities atended officially by a Roving Leader.
2. To further develop this critical area it is suggested the trainer contact outside resources for a certified Red Cross First Aid Instructor.

H. The "How To" of Dealing With Specific Problems of Antisocial Behavior

The Roving Leader should be able to comfortably deal with all types of people from all segments of society. His work is so diverse that no grouping of people are outside the potential scope of his interaction, including cliques, gangs, and other troublesome groups. *The dividing line between a clique or a play group and a gang is by no means clear,* and in practice such a group is whatever the researcher chooses to call it. Gang, as a technical term, is seldom applied to youth groups except in juvenile delinquency studies, in which it refers to an organized group which has committed delinquency or crime, or is considered likely to do so. There is no yardstick of group characteristics which can be used to distinguish gangs from other kinds of groups.[9]

The Roving Leader is apt to find his planned activities disintegrating into chaos *unless* he takes positive steps to involve members of sub-groups in as many activities as possible. The Leader can influence to a great degree the way these groups behave. He can gradually introduce new (but equally satisfying) activities to the youth involved.

I. How to Deal With Troublesome Groups

1. Use a specific approach
   a. Be friendly and listen to them

---

[9] Gould, Julius and William L. Kolb, *A Dictionary of the Social Sciences.* New York: Free Press of Glencoe, 1964. (See "Cliques," "Gang.")

b. Win their confidence; treat group with respect. Don't talk down.
c. Do not prejudge and act as if they are automatically "bad." Don't tell group how tough they are—this only antagonizes the individuals.
d. Treat each member as an individual and not as a member of a group.
e. Learn the youth's language and idioms.
2. Make sure the group participates in various programs
   a. Listen to demands and requests
   b. Provide reasonable use of facilities and equipment. Provide outlets and activities which meet interests and needs as part of the total group.

J. How to Cope With Gang Activities

1. Basic approaches
   a. Guide the youth into proper behavior or into discontinuing improper behavior.
   b. Be alert and look out for small groups starting; continue observation of area. Watch for agitators and nonconformists.
   c. Know your community and problems involved. Be sensitive to community needs.
   d. Get inside information from alert grass roots sources.
   e. Understand why gangs form. Recognize that there is some rationale for gang life.
   f. Remove reasons which caused the group to organize—try to prevent situations favorable to gang development.

K. Girl Gangs

1. When you see a group of four or five girls always together, talk to them and find out their wants and needs.
2. Engage girls in some constructive activities; e.g., modern dancing. Encourage them to develop some particular talent.
3. Invite successful, celebrated women whom girls admire to come and talk to them.
4. Ask the girls' vice principal to talk to them.
5. Provide activities that meet the needs of girls and are of interest to them; try to develop other interests.
6. Provide activities for individual girls. Give each understanding and let her know the world is not against her.

L. How To Provide Guidance

Sometimes the most effective guidance is that which comes through daily contact. However, the Roving Leader must be alert to these guidance opportunities. Service activities will give the youth an opportunity to participate in community projects and gain a satisfying experience in cooperation and service for others. Special events can be important, as they might focus attention on and provide information about important subjects such as health, safety, and good citizenship.

M. General Guidelines

1. Don't force, just guide. Explain clearly the possible results of good and bad decisions. No long sermons. Don't cause anyone "loss of face."
2. Be open-minded, shockproof, empathic.
3. Respect confidences. Be a master listener. Let the youth know that you are interested in them.
4. Develop a sense of confidence and self-esteem in youngsters.
5. Assess guidance needs through proper diagnostic devices. Understand psychology of guidance and guidance techniques.

Summary

This section deals with helping the Roving Leaders identify the positive as well as negative implications of their educational preparation, the necessity for pre- and in-service training for improving job performance, and for enhancing their capability in providing services of unlimited scope and high personal identity to the hard-to-reach youth. The Unit also provides some insight into the various types of subgroups that the leader must understand and methods he should develop in order to deal with these groups and individuals living in the urban communities.

Reference List

Klein, William, et al. *Leadership Training for New Careers: Non-Professional Counselor, Supervisor and Trainer.* Washington: University Research Corporation, 1966.
  A report on the youth training project conducted by Howard University's Center for Youth and Community Studies. The project is concerned with training the nonprofessional for services in urban areas.

Klein, Malcolm W. "Juvenile Gangs, Police and Detached Workers: Controversies about Intervention." *Social Service Review*, June 1965, 39:2, 183-190.
  Begins by outlining the tendency toward polarization between law enforcement and social work agencies. Their differences are especially pronounced when a detached worker is present. The article does not interpret, but attempts to ask questions that arise between the two groups, with references to cases.

Milwaukee Department of Municipal Recreation and Adult Education. *Referral-Guidance Program.*
  An outline of a program to give recreation leaders opportunities to refer the disadvantaged to the proper agency.

Pearl, A., and F. Reissman, eds. *New Careers for the Poor.* New York: The Free Press of Glencoe, 1965.
  Opening with a clear summary of alternative policies for dealing with poverty, the book presents the case for using the nonprofessional as an aide in community projects. It includes examples of projects, with detailed analysis of costs and methods. Political strategies are also included.

Reissman, Frank, and Hermine I. Popper. *Up From Poverty: New Career Ladders for Non-Professionals.* New York: Harper & Row Publishers, 1968.
  Book considers how the new-careers approach performs three long range goals: It (1) provides work and training for disadvantaged, (2) develops new manpower for human service, and (3) restructures human service agencies to make them more useful to their clients.

Schmais, Aaron. *Implementing Nonprofessional Programs in Human Services.* New York: Center for Study of Unemployed Youth, Graduate School of Social Work, New York University, 1967.
  Maintains that nonprofessional programs on maintained vacancies should be filled with nonprofessionals. Also, training programs should be instituted to assure the effectiveness of the program.

Spergel, Irving. *Street Gang Work: Theory and Practice.* Reading, Mass.: Addison-Wesley Publishing Co., Inc., 1966.
  An attempt to join sociological theory with social work experience gives this book a textbook tone. The sociology section summarizes prominent theory in a rather conventional manner. The social work section concentrates on control of gang behavior and instilling proper social values.

The Prevention and Control of Anti-Social Behavior of Youth. Los Angeles: Recreation and Youth Services Planning Council, September 1966.
  Even though this manual is intended for those in the Los Angeles area, it presents many useful guidelines for any teacher or youth worker. There are specific cases and also ideas for referral agencies. The book is intended as an inservice training guide for youth service personnel in public schools.

Thrasher, Frederic M. *The Gang: A Study of 1,313 Gangs in Chicago* (abridged, with a new introduction by James F. Short, Jr.). Chicago: University of Chicago Press, 1963.
  A classic study of gang behavior and the environment in which gangs flourish. The abridged edition of this study (originally published in 1927) contains an excellent introduction showing the relation of Thrasher's conclusions to more modern studies.

Will, Robert W., and Harold G. Vatter, Eds. *Poverty in Affluence: The Social, Political and Economic Dimensions of Poverty in the United States.* New York: Harcourt, Brace & World, Inc., 1965, paper.

>This book considers the causes, forms, and results of poverty. The editors place the material in proper historical perspective by alluding not only to current proposals and material, but to the Depression and earlier.

Suggested Resources for this Unit

Technical Assistance Specialists

Sam LaBeach
Assistant Regional Director
(Former Supervisor of Roving Leader Program)
Department of Recreation
Washington, D.C. 20011

Stanley J. Anderson
Social Science Adviser—Youth Services
Office of the Chief, Children's Bureau
U.S. Department of Health, Education, and Welfare
Washington, D.C. 20202

Films

First Aid: Fundamentals—10 min. (1953)
Coronet Instructional Films

High Wall—32 min. (1952)
McGraw-Hill Book Company, Inc.

Leaders For Leisure—21 min. (1952)
Playtown U.S.A.

None For the Road (teenagers)—15 min. (1957)
McGraw-Hill Book Company, Inc.

The Roving Leader in Action
Department of Recreation
6115 Chillum Place, NE.
Washington, D.C. 20011

Audiovisual Equipment

16 mm. movie projector (sound)
Tape recorder, standard
Overhead projector, 3M—portable—0-88

appendix a

Agencies and Institutions Participating in the Study

* Youth Service Agency of New York
* New York Urban League (Harlem Street Academies)
* New York City Department of Recreation
* Henry Street Settlement House (Manhattan)
* Buffalo Youth Board, Buffalo, N.Y.
* YMCA of Buffalo, N.Y.
* Rochester-City-County Youth Board
* Youth for Service Agency, San Francisco, Calif.
* Apprenticeship Opportunities Foundation, San Francisco, Calif.
* YMCA of Metropolitan Detroit, Urban Youth Program
* Street Club Service, Bureau of Recreation, Baltimore, Md.
* Model Cities Agency, Baltimore, Md.
* Community Studies Center at Howard University, Washington, D.C.
* D.C. Department of Recreation, Roving Leaders Program, Washington, D.C.
* United Planning Organization, Washington, D.C.
* Special Service for Groups, Los Angeles, Calif.
* Teen Post Youth Centers, Los Angeles, Calif.
Youth Activities Commission, Boston, Mass.
* YMCA of St. Louis, Inner-City Youth Outreach
* St. Louis Urban League, St. Louis, Mo.
Mayor's Council on Youth Opportunity, San Diego, Calif.
  * Institutions and agencies visited.
Dade County Youth Opportunity Program, Miami, Fla.
* Rochester YMCA—Youth Outreach
* Metropolitan YWCA of Rochester, N.Y.
Mayor's Council on Youth Opportunity, St. Paul, Minn.
Commission on Human Relations, County of Los Angeles
Southeastern Tidewater Opportunity Project, Norfolk, Va.
Recreation Department, Park Commission, Memphis, Tenn.
Atlanta Children and Youth Services Council, Atlanta, Ga.
Omaha Human Relations Department, Omaha, Nebr.
Mayor's Council on Youth Opportunity, New Orleans, La.
Mayor's Council on Youth Opportunity, Birmingham, Ala.
Department of Recreation, City of Philadelphia
Recreation and Park Department, Golden Gate Park, San Francisco
YMCA of Metropolitan Minneapolis, Minneapolis, Minn.
City of Elgin Parks Department, Elgin, Ill.

* Institutions and agencies visited.

Louisville and Jefferson County Youth Commission, Louisville, Ky.
Illinois Youth Commission
* Recreation and Youth Services Planning Council, Los Angeles
New York State Youth Commission
* Center for Community Leadership Development, Milwaukee
* Ohio Youth Commission, Columbus, Ohio
Institute of Labor and Industrial Relations, University of Illinois
Oakland Recreation Department, Oakland, Calif.
* Dayton Youth Opportunity Program, Dayton, Ohio
  * Institutions and agencies visited.
* Mayor's Youth Opportunity Program, Columbus, Ohio
Mayor's Council on Youth Opportunity, Cleveland, Ohio
Mayor's Youth Opportunity Program, Akron, Ohio
Dayton Boys' Club-West, Dayton, Ohio
Department of Recreation and Park, Dayton, Ohio
* Los Angeles City Schools Youth Services
* Roosevelt High School, Los Angeles City Schools
* Los Angeles City Department of Recreation and Parks
S. F. V. Youth Foundation, Los Angeles
* Neighborhood Youth Association, Los Angeles
Los Angeles Sheriff's Community Relations
Markham Junior High School, Los Angeles
* Catholic Youth Organization, Los Angeles
* Los Angeles Times Boys' Club
* Division of Delinquency Prevention, CYA, Los Angeles
* Los Angeles County Delinquency and Crime Commission, Palos Verdes Estates
* United Way, Inc. Los Angeles
* Los Angeles County Parks and Recreation
* Mayor's Youth Council, Los Angeles
* Los Angeles County Department of Community Services
* National Recreation and Park Association, Congress, 1968, Seattle, Wash.
* Youth Opportunity Program West Coast Region, Seattle, Wash.
* Department of Recreation, Buffalo, N.Y.
* Office of Dean, Community Education, Federal City College, Washington, D.C.
* Office of Special Projects, Community School Recreation Program, Flint, Mich.
Neighborhood Service Organization, Detroit, Mich.

appendix b

Language of Modern Youth

Language consists of speech and signs. Adolescents use words and signs pictorially, adaptably, and creatively. Such a process is essential to emancipation, to self-identify, and to remodel old values to fit new situations confronting the youth.

It is not possible to include in this guide a complete glossary of terms used by modern youth. It is sufficient to say that the language is well sprinkled with obscenities and clues to the adolescents' preoccupation with their social tasks and interests.

The worker must have the capacity to hear what is said and the context in which the words are used. A potential difficulty for workers is that they hear the language in terms of its meaning to them, and not its meaning for the speaker. A special caution: gang language is almost sacred to gang members—intrusion into something of their own may cause alienation. Do not try to talk the language unless you are completely aware of it all and are accepted by the gang as a "big brother." But to understand it may provide empathy and status with the group.

Selected examples of language used by today's youngsters, but which quickly change, are:

1. *Acid head*—user of LSD.
2. *Bitch'en*—very good, enjoyable, exciting.
3. *Blood music*—black jazz.
4. *Bloods*—blacks.
5. *Boss*—great, wonderful.
6. *Busted*—arrested.
7. *Cat*—a boy or a man.
8. *Chicken scratch*—hypo marks on arm, railroad tracks.
9. *Cheese points, kiss-ups, brownie points*—refers to "boot licking" activities or attitudes.
10. *Coins*—money, bread.
11. *Cool*—excellent, desirable.
12. *Cool it*—
    a) hide, escape, get out.
    b) cut it out, stop offending action.
13. *Play it cool or be cool*—poised and in control of situation.
14. *Crazy*—cool, better than good.
15. *Crib*—house, home, where one lives, pad.
16. *Custom*—real cool, usually referring to a guy. Enthusiastic term.
17. *Cut-out*—leave.
18. *Dig*—look, hear, or understand.
19. *Ding*—"freak," idiot (referring to a person).
20. *Dropping reds*—taking barbiturates, usually red or yellow in color, used to provide "kicks" or to get "high."
21. *Dud*—not any good, bad, of no value, blah.
22. *Dude*—a "square;" a boy; can mean any person to whom one is referring.
23. *Fall-out, man,* or *jump*—flake off, leave.
24. *The finger*—sexual contact.
25. *Fink*—squeal or to inform on someone, blabbermouth, troublemaker.
26. *Fire-on*—punching someone, beating him up.
27. *Flake-off*—depart, leave.
28. *Flip-out* (on LSD)—go out of your mind, crazy.
29. *Funky*—square: "It's a little dirty in here"—this is "square".
30. *Fuzz*—police or authority, the man.
31. *Gig*—a dance or party.
32. *Grip*—steal.
33. *Hang it up*—stop.
34. *Hassle*—"don't hassle me"—don't give me any trouble.
35. *Hawk*—spit.
36. *Hip*—knowledgeable to a certain set of facts; in the know.
37. *Hit*—(on a butt) drag on a cigarette.
38. *Jam*—private party.
39. *Jack him up*—tell him what the score is; beat him up; or tell him to "shape up."
40. *Later, man*—forget it, don't bother me now, get over it.
41. *Lice*—police.
42. *Lighten up*—don't be so hard on me.
43. *Make it*—go home, leave.
44. *The Man*—the big one, the head, leader, or "me."
45. *Mickey Mouse*—dinky, kid stuff, not for real.
46. *Now ain't that foul*—dirty.
47. *Out of sight*—"bitch'en," very good.
48. *Pad*—house, home, where one lives.
49. *Pardner*—close associate.
50. *Punk*—
    a) referring to a hustler or "pimp,"
    b) one who doesn't understand, whimp,
    c) homosexual, male
51. *Pansy*—sissy, male homosexual.
52. *Ruco*—authority (Mexican term): "Here comes El Ruce" (police, teacher, etc.)
53. *Reds*—depressants, also redbirds, red devils, pinks.
54. *Reefer*—a marijuana cigarette.
55. *Scag*—heroin.
56. *Scat*—heroin.
57. *Sniff*—to inhale the vapor or powder of a drug or other material to achieve a "high."
58. *Shoot*—to inject a drug into the bloodstream.
59. *Snow*—cocaine.
60. *Speed*—amphetamines.
61. *Speedball*—mixture of drugs to achieve special effect, usually a mixture of a stimulant and depressant.

62. *Spike*—the syringe needle.
63. *Smack*—heroin.
64. *Square*—a nonuser.
65. *Steamboat*—pipe for smoking marijuana.
66. *Stick*—marijuana cigarette.
67. *Stoned*—under influence of drug.
68. *STP*—a potent hallucinogenic.
69. *Strung* out—having narcotics habit.
70. *Tea*—marijuana.
71. *Ten-cent bag*—a $10 unit of drug.
72. *Tie*—any cord to tie around arm or leg to make vein stand up for easy injection.
73. *Tore up*—under influence of drug.
74. *Tracks*—small scars on arms or legs from syringe.
75. *Trip*—result of taking drug, usually of hallucinogenic type such as LSD.
76. *Turned on*—under influence of drug.
77. *Twist*—marijuana.
78. *Ups*—amphetamines, stimulants.
79. *Weed*—marijuana.

appendix c

Addresses of Film Distributors

Affiliated Film Producers, Inc.
164 East 38th Street
New York, N.Y. 10016

Association Films
(YMCA Motion Picture Bureau)
347 Madison Avenue
New York, N.Y. 10017

Athletic Institute
Merchandise Mart Plaza
Chicago, Ill. 60607

Audio-Visual Center
Syracuse University
Collendale Campus
Colvin Lane
Syracuse, N.Y. 13210

Bray-Mar Productions
276 DuShane Drive
Buffalo, N.Y. 14223

Campus Film Library
14 East 53rd Street
New York, N.Y. 10022

Carl F. Mahnke Productions
(University of Iowa)
Des Moines, Iowa 50318

Columbia University Films
1125 Amsterdam Avenue
New York, N.Y. 10024

Contemporary Films
267 West 25th Street
New York, N.Y. 10001

Coronet Instructional Films
Coronet Building
Chicago, Ill. 60601

Edcom Productions
285 West 6th Street
Mansfield, Ohio 44902

Encyclopedia Britannica Films, Inc.
Wilmette, Ill. 60091

Health & Welfare Materials Center
10 East 4th Street
New York, N.Y. 10017

International Film Bureau, Inc.
57 East Jackson Boulevard
Chicago, Ill. 60604

Los Angeles Community Chest
729 Figueroa Street
Los Angeles, Calif. 90017

McGraw-Hill Book Company, Inc.
Text-Film Department
330 West 42nd Street
New York, N.Y. 10036

Modern Talking Pictures Service, Inc.
2000 L Street, NW.
Washington, D.C. 20036

National Film Board of Canada
680 Fifth Avenue
New York, N.Y. 10019

Playtown U.S.A.
Athletic Institute
Chicago, Ill. 60601

RKO Pathe, Inc.
1740 Broadway
New York, N.Y. 10019

Sid Davis Productions
1418 North Highlands Avenue
Hollywood, Calif. 90028

Stan Loewy Safety Films
P. O. Box 520
Colton, Calif. 92324

Sun Dial Films
341 East 43rd Street
New York, N.Y. 10017

United World Films, Inc.
221 Park Avenue South
New York, N.Y. 10003

Wilding Picture Productions, Inc.
1345 West Argyle Street
Chicago, Ill. 60640

appendix d

Sample Job Description

1. *Name of Position:* Roving Leader
2. *Supervisory Control:*
   The services of the Roving Leader should be supervised by the director of the program or a designated staff member; i.e., field supervisor.
3. *General Description of Duties:*
   The function of a Roving Leader usually assigned to a specific geographic area within a community is that of strengthening, extending, and stimulating participation of hard-to-reach, disadvantaged inner-city youth, who were unreceptive to or excluded from receiving the agency's assistance or who were unaware of the availablility of the service. The Leader combines awareness with creativity of approach that enables him to provide a calibre and type of service related to that of a counselor, advisor, consultant, coach, and friend.
4. *Specific Description of Duties:*
   The duties assigned to Roving Leaders will vary among different agencies or groups of agencies depending on the nature of their services and the target youth being served, but essentially the Roving Leader's duties are as follows:
   A. Provides face-to-face leadership to hard-to-reach youth that is distinctive from that provided by normal playground or agency staff.
   B. Identifies youth with problems and works with them towards effecting changes in attitudes, actions, and outlook, through various programs and activities providing opportunity for relationship, reeducation, and redirection.
   C. Familiarizes himself with the resources of the community that provide services which his agency does not supply.
   D. Visits target neighborhoods and attempts to spend time with families in the area in order to get to know their problems.
   E. Locates candidates for specific recruitment projects as they are needed.
   F. Performs outreach for followup purposes on individual youth, getting information from them or bringing them back to the service center if that is required.
   G. Develops and maintains communication with civil agencies, civic organizations and related services.
   H. Prepares necessary records and reports on the youth's status with regard to:
      (1) Family (size, number of children, ages of family members, how many living at home, etc.).
      (2) Occupational status (work situation in terms of job, relative underemployment, unemployment, etc.).
      (3) Health (physical, emotional, and mental condition of each member of family).
      (4) Income (sources and amount of income).
5. *Qualifications for Roving Leader:*
   General Qualifications —
   A candidate for the position of Roving Leader should possess a significant knowledge of the neighborhood or community in which he desires employment. He should be able to meet and deal with people, particularly youth from a disadvantaged and/or delinquent background. He should possess a high degree of sensitivity, and be able to observe an individual and evaluate where the person "is." The Roving Leader must be a person capable of acting as liaison between all the diverse segments of the community or neighborhood.
   Specfic Qualifications—
   A. College training is desirable but not required; work experience should demonstrate a capacity to work with youth.
   B. High school education or equivalent with on-the-job training in youth work or a related area.
   C. Completion of a Special Training Institute for Roving Leaders that includes academic instruction as well as supervised on-the-job training.
   D. Ability to communicate in the vernacular of the street.
6. *Suggested Selection Criteria:*
   A. Brief written statement (two paragraphs) on why Roving Leaders in the neighborhood are important to disadvantaged youth.
   B. An oral interview to determine interest, motivation, ability to meet and deal with hard-to-reach youth and ability to take oral directions.
   C. Evaluation of education, work experience, and community involvement.

appendix e

Roving Leader Slide Presentation (Slide-Tape Narrative)

(1) ROVING LEADER SLIDE, A TRAINING AID PRESENTATION
"NARRATION"
Vince Sanders

(2) What does one see when he looks at the inner city? . . . Our eyes see many things. . . . For example—the kids on the corner. Whether you're in Chicago, Milan, L.A., or Sao Paulo, you'll see them in all sizes and colors digging each other and surviving in the streets, alleys, and on the playgrounds.
They usually find their own play and if it sometimes gets a little rough, well, that's like real life in the city!

(3) We know that it's overcrowded . . . and that people live close together. . . .

(4) Opportunities for fulfilling the basic needs of life are few and far between.

(5) Families, or what's left of them in the inner city, have their problems. . . . Their needs are not being met.

(6) One of the greatest problems is housing. As the homes deteriorate—some are even condemned—they still must be lived in . . . for there is little opportunity to move to something better.

(7) The pent up emotions of many almost reach the boiling point . . . for there seem to be no immediate answers to the problems at hand. . . .

(8) And conditions most of the time don't improve. . . . Actually they get worse. . . . Problems of sanitation and health become interwoven with the countless other problems of the inner-city residents.

(9) What happens then? The people take to the streets in search of the answers. That is where the action is!

(10) When we seek action we find it. . . . And this action expresses itself in many different forms. . . .

(11) With darkness of night for protection . . . the troubled youth strikes out against the closest thing to him. . . . This attack is really an attack against society, and its failure to respond in a time of need.

(12) And what started with a couple of individuals now begins to meld into street corner gang activities.

(13) For lack of meaningful recreational opportunities . . . the gangs begin to challenge each other. . . . Power and control of the turf becomes the prime goal . . . and once in this groove . . . it becomes hard to move in more constructive directions. . . .

(14) Power . . . Power . . . Power. . . . This is the cry of troubled inner-city youth . . . as they seek recognition and answer to their problems.

(15) In reckless search of power . . . the time bomb explodes. . . .

(16) REVOLT

(17) CONFRONTATION

(18) MORE TROUBLES ARE MET HEAD ON WITH NO IMMEDIATE ANSWERS.

(19) In a dynamic program of action designed to get to the guts of one of the major problems of innercity residents . . . that of providing meaningful recreation. . . . The Roving Leader Training Guide project was established.

(20) This guide was not prepared in an ivory tower . . . it was constructed in the problem areas of the big cities of the United States—New York, Dayton and Columbus, Ohio, Buffalo, Rochester, Baltimore, Washington, D.C., Chicago, Detroit, St. Louis, Los Angeles, and San Francisco.

(21) The Roving Leader concept . . . as presented in this guide . . . will show you today's role of the Roving Leader and his function in meeting the recreation challenge of the inner city.

(22) The Roving Leader must reach out and touch youth in need . . . for the troubled youth have not found the way to meaningful recreational activities alone.

(23) Reaching out means getting out into the neighborhoods.

(24) It means . . . meeting the youth on the street corners.

(25) The Roving Leader serves as an advocate for youth. . . . He promotes student-teacher communication . . . channels participation toward existing community resources . . . develops youth leadership in wholesome directions.

(26) The Roving Leader provides face-to-face leadership. He should analyze recreational services and stimulate ideas and methods for improving existing situations. To get the job done it is necessary that he communicate and work with the agencies of the community.

(27) The Roving Leader must understand his community, its geographical makeup,

(28) the interaction of people, and the needs of the residents of the neighborhoods. He must know the existing community resources . . . and the cooperative agency relationship that must exist to get the job done.

(29) The community where the Roving Leader works is a network of systems. Its patterns of social, economic, political, services, racial and ethnic groups, and class levels are all connected together and must be understood.

(30) The community issues may revolve around these:
- Jobs and Training
- Housing
- Recreation
and
- Education

(31) The community power structure has formal, elected leaders including the mayor, the city council made up of aldermen, school boards, utility commissioners, and others.

(32) The community power structure does not end at city hall. . . .

(33) It includes militant groups, neighborhood civic associations, street gangs, policy backers, and tavern and poolhall-owners.

(34) The Roving Leader must identify every facet of the power structure and do his best to work with each.

(35) The Roving Leader must then go into the neighborhood, establish rapport, and IDENTIFY and UNDERSTAND inner-city youth.

(36) He must meet them on their terms . . . in their environment.

(37) Having established rapport, the Roving Leader must then set out to meet the challenge. . . . To get the job done, he must work towards participation by the members of the community power structure. . . . Social planning must take place. . . . The rights and obligations of all the people must be upheld. . . . In so doing, he must adhere to the lines of communication and authority.

(38) Typical of the problems are gangs, delinquency among pre-teens, low income, and school dropouts.

(39) But what makes up a group? What are the various groups with which the Roving Leader must deal?

(40) There are two familiar types of groups. . . .

(41) The first type is a friendship group.

(42) The second type is a membership group.

(43) The Roving Leader has to understand the group process. . . . He learns very quickly that it is a fine goal to have group action take place in a proper setting and in a democratic manner . . . with high interest.

(44) But in reality, interest may be low, and getting through to the youth is a long, difficult process.

(45) By understanding group techniques, he gradually can make headway. But in making progress, he must be ever ready to meet the challenge of *GROUP PRESSURE.*

(46) This group pressure takes many forms, and its ultimate results may take varying directions.

(47) Programing is an important skill of the roving leader.

(48) Programing has several basic objectives.

(49) These objectives are:
- Planning activities with individuals and groups.
- Establishing planning councils which involve the youth of the neighborhoods.
- Defining the responsibility lines.
- Showing people the way to available opportunities.

(50) In making his contact, the Roving Leader will become involved with youth in some *unplanned activity*. He then observes what the real situation is . . . and at the proper time selects the right approach to deal with the situation.

(51) It is the Roving Leader's job to help youth and to provide opportunities for youth.

(52) He should attempt to redirect delinquent activities into creative endeavor.
Examples of Roving Leaders' action include involvement with youth in the activities of . . .

(53) Football . . .

(54) Group games and . . .

(55) Bowling . . . a very popular activity.

(56) The Roving Leader can build close associations with the youth he serves.

(57) Active interest follows after a close association is developed between the participant and the Roving Leader. The interest carries over into other recreational activities which are then introduced.

(58) These activities might include swimming . . .

(59) or track and field . . . and many other activities.

(60) He teaches youth to play together. . . . How to get along with their fellowman.

(61) The Roving Leader provides the building blocks of leadership necessary to assist youth in forming a stable foundation for the future.

(62) The opportunities are created to find meaningful and gainful employment as well as recreation.

(63) Unemployment is a great problem in the inner city as is the problem of inadequate recreational facilities and programs.

(64) The Roving Leader also has the job of referral. He should know how to contact and deal with the various community agencies that can provide assistance to youth in . . .

(65) education, employment and training, health, welfare, legal assistance, recreation, and psychiatric assistance.

(66) Referral examples include . . .
summer job programs
PROJECT TELL

(67) Manpower Development and Training Programs (MDTA)
Office of Economic Opportunity
Neighborhood Youth Corps
Model Cities
Employment Service
Head Start
and others.

(68) To assist the Roving Leader in getting the job done, it is important that he recognizes that he is a member of a team and responsible directly to a field supervisor.

(69) The Roving Leader's job description includes everything that has been shown in this presentation and EMPHASIZES . . .

(70) Pre- and inservice training, face-to-face leadership, services of an unlimited scope, and the establishment of personal identity with hard-to-reach youth.

(71) The Roving Leader must remember that youth service workers must have a working knowledge of the community and social agency work . . .

(72) and that by visiting the agencies and talking with persons who render services, the unfamiliar will become familiar and the Leader's confidence and value strengthened.

(73) The Roving Leader must become
PROBLEM ORIENTED
rather than
discipline oriented.
The Roving Leader Guide will provide insights as to how this is done.

(74) By putting into practice the methods emphasized in your Roving Leader Guide—*success is possible . . . and probable!*

(75) There are thousands of youth waiting for you. . . . Many are hiding . . . afraid to face reality . . . unable to negotiate for services on their own . . . without the necessary skills to land and hold decent jobs.

(76) You must show them the way . . . THROUGH FACE-TO-FACE-LEADERSHIP. . . . The challenge is yours! . . . Do with it what you will!

(77) Photo.

(78) Credit Slide.

APPENDIX B

ROVING RECREATION LEADER'S RATING SCALE*

Name of leader .... Name of Dept. ....

Length of employment ....

Rated by .... Position ....

Instructions on Use of the Scale

In rating a leader, it is necessary to have clearly in mind the definitions of the qualities upon which he is to be rated. After you have thought carefully about a leader in terms of one of these qualities, use the rating words as a guide and place a check (✔) at some point on the line which represents your estimate of the standing of the leader with regard to this quality. The check mark, indicating your opinion, may be located anywhere along the scale line.

Sample

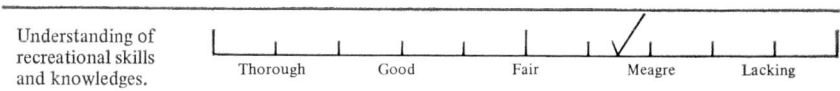

Rating the Leader

Since the ratings made of the leader on the eleven items in the Roving Recreation Leader's Rating Scale represent *your* evaluation with reference to specific skills and abilities, it is desired that you give each leader an overall rating of 1, 2, 3, 4, or 5 which will reflect total effectiveness as a roving recreation leader. Place this rating in the space provided in the box below. Use the following as a basis for the classification on this scale.

---

* Prepared by Shirley J. Kammeyer, State University of Iowa, Iowa City, Iowa, and reprinted by permission.

Chart I. Roving Recreation Leader's Rating Scale

Directions: Place a check (✓) *anywhere* along the scaled line.
Use the rating words as a general guide.

1. Roving leader's professional attitude and awareness of the program value for the participants.	Superior attitude; Sincere devotion to recreation ideals	Almost always enthusiastic	At times indifferent to professional ideals	Temporary interest	Interest only in salary
2. Understanding of recreational skills and knowledges.	Lacking	Meagre	Fair	Good	Thorough
3. Ability to gain and hold confidence and respect of participants and associates.	Superior ability to gain confidence; want to emulate him	Good ability to gain confidence and respect	Inspires fair degree of confidence	Noticeably lacking in ability to command respect	Inspires no confidence or respect
4. Ability to get along with people and draw them into neighborhood activity.	Warm and personable; gets along with anyone	Almost always effective in working with people	Friendly and effective about half of the time	Temperamental and difficult to work with	Unapproachable most of the time
5. Understanding and sensitivity to group needs.	Complete lack of understanding of his group	Decided lack of understanding	Fair ability to see major group problems	Good understanding	Thorough and complete awareness of group needs
6. Versatility of interests and abilities; utilizes broad program for neighborhood participants.	Extremely narrow	Limited to a few	Fair number of interests	Above average number of interests	Exceptional scope of interests and abilities
7. Ability to adjust to situations and is resourceful.	Superior ability to adapt to any conditions	Good adaptability	Successful in some situations; but not with all	Noticeably lacking in adaptability	Completely unable to cope with new situations
8. Ability to organize and plan the neighborhood program.	Acts only under direction	Noticeably lacking in organizational ability	Fair ability to organize	Good organizational ability	Superior ability to plan and organize
9. Demonstrates initiative and dependability in conducting program.	Always reliable; energetic; superior ability to initiate	Almost always industrious in administering program	Spasmodic or occasionally indifferent	Needs constant urging	Unreliable; lazy; no initiative
10. Intelligence and ability to communicate ideas.	Slow to grasp obvious	Subtle points require explanation	Fair understanding of situations	Nearly always grasps situation	Keen and quick to understand
11. Demonstrates mature judgement; common sense.	Exceptional maturity and good judgment	Good judgment and common sense	Fair; usually shows good judgment	Frequently shows poor judgment	Lacks mature judgment

1–Means an excellent leader, one who is outstanding from the standpoint of all that is involved in a good recreation leader.
2–Means a good leader, one who fully possesses the qualifications for good leadership, but who is not outstanding.
3–Means a fair leader, one who is neither particularly good or weak.
4–Means a fair leader, but one whom you would not hire if you could do better.
5–Means a weak leader, one whom you would not recommend for employment in recreation.

LEADER'S OVERALL RATING

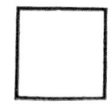

APPENDIX C

THE ROVING RECREATION LEADER'S SITUATION-PROBLEM EXERCISE*

Instructions:

This exercise is composed of twenty situations or "case reports." Each of these situations presents a problem to be solved. You are asked to make two judgments based upon each of the situations.

The first judgment is WHAT DO YOU DO? In making this judgment, concentrate upon the *first* step or action that you would take in each situation. Then, circle the answer (A, B, C, or D) which best expresses your choice of action.

The second judgment is WHAT DO YOU WANT (the individual or group in each situation) TO DO? Then circle the answer (A, B, C, or D) which best expresses the behavior you feel you want from the individual or the group.

Please remember:

1. Concentrate upon *first* steps concerning your actions.
2. Concentrate upon what action you want concerning the behavior of the individual or the group in each situation.

Case A

John V. is a member of a gang which has just begun to use the neighborhood center's basketball courts. You do not know any of the members too well yet. The second time the gang uses the basketball courts, you learn that John has been smoking marijuana.

1. WHAT DO YOU DO?
    A. report John's behavior to the police or the narcotics bureau.
    B. talk to John and point out the harm he is doing to himself.
    C. do and say nothing now; you wish to develop closer friendships.
    D. kick John out of the group and tell him not to come back.

2. WHAT DO YOU WANT JOHN TO DO?
    A. tell you where he gets the drugs, so you can tell the authorities.
    B. refer himself to the proper facilities for the needed treatment.

---

* Developed by Dr. Joseph J. Bannon, Marilyn Fortin and Dr. Doyle Bishop, Office of Recreation and Park Resources, University of Illinois, Urbana, Illinois.

C. begin to think of you as a friend or person who will help him.
D. leave the group and not come back until he is off of marijuana.

Case B

As a roving leader, you have been working with a gang of teenage girls who call themselves the Whips. You and the gang happen to meet outside the Community Center. The gang is very upset because the Community Center officials have refused to let them use the gymnasium. You know that this is one of the nights that the Community Center is open to the entire community. The girls feel that they have been unfairly treated because they are girls. You check with the Community Center Director and learn that the gym is very small, therefore, only a few people can use the facility at one time. This particular night when the girls arrive the gym is filled to capacity.

3. WHAT DO YOU DO?
   A. see if the Community Center Director will make this one exception and let the girls in this time.
   B. explain the reason for the rules to the members of the Whips.
   C. have the girls begin to campaign for the construction of additional facilities at the Center.
   D. get the girls to take part in activities in other locations in the city.

4. WHAT DO YOU WANT THE GIRLS TO DO?
   A. understand and appreciate the needs for rules to govern the operation of the gym.
   B. be allowed into the gym by Center officials.
   C. get interested in art, crafts, and drama.
   D. get involved in an action program for the construction of a new facility.

Case C

The Ravens are a gang which has been causing trouble in your area. They have been involved in many gang fights. Many of the members have been arrested for petty theft, truancy, possession of narcotics, etc. The Ravens come to you while you are at the neighborhood center, and request the use of the neighborhood center's game room. You think you smell beer on one of the gang members' breath, but he does not act as if he is drunk.

5. WHAT DO YOU DO?
   A. say you'll check on it; if the gang does use the game room, notify the police that there could be trouble.
   B. explain that you will have to check on it and ask them to wait while you do.

C. tell them *No* because you know that in the past all they have done is to cause much trouble.
D. say no; although you would like to, the neighborhood center just will not allow them to use the room.

6. WHAT DO YOU WANT THE GANG TO DO?
    A. make a promise to you that they will not cause any trouble at the center.
    B. disband their gang and individually join other recreation groups at the center.
    C. leave the neighborhood center quietly, and not cause any trouble there.
    D. wait quietly while you check to see if they can use the game room.

Case D

Sally, a high school junior, is a member of a recreation program in your area. You have known her for six months, but have had contact with her only as a member of the recreation group. She comes to you wanting a part-time job so she can afford to move in with her married sister to finish high school. She tells you that she and her family, which consists of a mother and five brothers and sisters, just do not get along. Her grades in high school are very poor.

7. WHAT DO YOU DO?
    A. tell Sally that her school work comes first, and to come to you after she finishes high school.
    B. get to know Sally and her family better so you can better assess Sally's problems.
    C. help Sally to understand some of her mother's problems with raising a large family alone.
    D. send Sally out for some interviews for part-time jobs that you have heard of.

8. WHAT DO YOU WANT SALLY TO DO?
    A. move in with her sister and away from her family after getting a part time job.
    B. make up her mind that she should work hard in school to get her high school diploma.
    C. give you the chance to know her and her family situation better before she does anything.
    D. decide that she will do volunteer work at a hospital to keep herself away from home more.

Case E

As a roving leader, you have been working with a gang called the Niters for a year. Many members of the Niters have been arrested for car theft, vandalism, drug use, etc. While you are attending one of the gang meetings, Bobby R. tells you that the gang is going to rob the gas station in the next block. You explain that since you are now aware of this, you will have to notify the authorities. However, six of the gang members say they will pull the job anyway. They leave the meeting and proceed to the gas station. Upon their arrival, they rough up the attendant. While they are looting the station, the owner returns. The gang members then become frightened and flee the scene of the crime.

9. WHAT DO YOU DO?
   A. you call the police and tell them about the attempted robbery of the gas station.
   B. you call the police, explain the situation, when the gang members are caught, you do what you can to assist them.
   C. leave the scene of the crime so the police will not know you are aware of the incident.
   D. since you want to maintain your rapport with the gang, you do nothing.

10. WHAT DO YOU WANT THE GANG TO DO?
    A. realize that you are their friend and will not squeal on them.
    B. realize that this behavior is not acceptable to you and that they will not do it again.
    C. realize that you cannot approve this kind of behavior.
    D. realize that they are wrong and should receive severe punishment.

Case F

You are on the playground with a group of teenagers you have just met. They are members of a gang called the Street Boppers. The group has been boisterous and somewhat disruptive. After a while the gang comes to order and they begin to ask questions about the program that is offered on the playground. While this discussion is going on, the "Jackets," a rival gang from the other side of town comes along. The situation becomes tense and it looks like there will be a gang fight. However, through your effort, you get the gangs to talk to one another and as a result, the rival gang leaves. A police officer then arrives on the scene and orders the Street Boppers to leave the playground. The policeman becomes belligerent and some roughness takes place.

11. WHAT DO YOU DO?
   A. ask the Street Boppers to leave the playground. After they have left, identify yourself to the policeman and explain the situation to him.
   B. tell the Street Boppers they are not being treated fairly and to stand up for their rights.
   C. at this point there is nothing you can do but leave the playground; you want no trouble with the Street Boppers or the police.
   D. you can do nothing at this point; however, later you contact a TV news reporter who is your friend and tell him of the police brutality.

12. WHAT DO YOU WANT THE GANG TO DO?
   A. argue with the policeman and inform him of his unfairness to the gang.
   B. leave the playground as quickly as possible.
   C. leave the playground immediately but plan to "deal" with the policeman at a later date.
   D. understand that law and order must prevail and that the policeman has his job to do.

Case G

As a roving leader you have been helping a gang called the Byrans for a year. The Byrans are a group of Black teenagers, ages 19 to 21, living in the southeast section of the city. The majority of the gang members are school dropouts and the remaining still in school have very poor grades. At one of the meetings of the gang, Mike tells you about his experience in trying to get a job promotion. He says that the establishment is not fair to Blacks. In your discussion with Mike you find out that he has done poorly on written promotional exams and in most cases he has not finished the exam. You know that Mike is a dropout. After discussing Mike's problem with local school authorities, you find that his reading and writing ability is poor.

13. WHAT DO YOU DO?
   A. ask Mike for the names of his supervisors and then discuss with them their prejudices.
   B. tell Mike you understand the situation and that most companies in the area are like that.
   C. get the neighborhood group into a civil rights discussion, point out the ways they can influence change in the situation.
   D. ask Mike's supervisor to see his examination for promotion; assess his needs with the school counselors, and encourage Mike to attend night school to improve his reading and writing ability.

14. WHAT DO YOU WANT MIKE TO DO?
    A. be able to discuss the situation and "keep his cool."
    B. become more proficient in reading and writing skills so he can pass the promotional examination.
    C. begin to think of ways to encourage his supervisors to give him a "fair shake."
    D. nothing until you have talked with his supervisors, then possible court action against the supervisors.

Case H

Officer B. reports to you that he has often seen a group of from eight to ten boys hanging around Tom's Diner. The policeman suspects this group of minor vandalism in the neighborhood; and he thinks that the boys should be involved in some organized recreational activities to "keep them off the streets."

15. WHAT DO YOU DO?
    A. go to Tom's Diner and ask Tom to relay an invitation to the gang to form a basketball team at the neighborhood center.
    B. go to Tom's Diner and try to persuade the boys to join a recreation program at the center that you feel would be right for them.
    C. go to Tom's Diner and hang around; try to get to know the boys individually and as members of the gang and find out their interests.
    D. tell Officer B. that you cannot check this out; if you have a connection with the police and word of it gets around, you cannot do your job.

16. WHAT DO YOU WANT THE GANG TO DO?
    A. become involved in a recreation program at the center.
    B. decide to break up as a gang and not cause any trouble.
    C. decide to continue as a gang but stop their vandalism.
    D. begin to think of you as a good guy who can maybe help them.

Case I

Victor T. is a member of a gang called the Young Chops. Victor is now on probation for assault and battery. The Young Chops are in the process of having one of their meetings at the neighborhood center. Victor is present at this meeting, and is talking very loudly and trying to disrupt the meeting. At one point, he asks you why you are there and comes toward you as if he were planning to start a fight with you.

17. WHAT DO YOU DO?
    A. stand up and tell Victor that you are stronger than he is and that he had better leave the center now or you will beat him up.
    B. tell Victor firmly that if he wishes to cause trouble, he will have to leave; remind him that he has a lot to lose by starting a fight.
    C. get up from your place, leave the room, and quickly get to a phone and call the police to help you control or get rid of Victor.
    D. tell Victor that it is the policy of the neighborhood center not to allow anyone in their rooms who behaves like he is now behaving.

18. WHAT DO YOU WANT VICTOR TO DO?
    A. walk out of the meeting and not return to any of the gang's meetings at the neighborhood center.
    B. start a fight, so you can prove to the group that you can handle yourself with a tough guy.
    C. be arrested by the police and have his probation taken away for causing so much trouble.
    D. think about what he is doing; decide to stay and not disrupt the meeting or decide to leave.

Case J

You make a visit to Jeff R.'s home in the month of December. Jeff's home is in a large apartment building. As you enter the apartment, you notice that this apartment is very cold. You learn that the heating system broke down three days ago, and that all of the tenants have no heat. No one has been around to fix the heating system yet. Some of the tenants have called the janitor for the building.

19. WHAT DO YOU DO?
    A. find out who owns the building, and talk to him about this problem.
    B. organize a tenants' union to go on a rent strike if the problem is not solved soon.
    C. call the police and report this situation to them; suggest they arrest the landlord.
    D. contact the Salvation Army about the need for warm clothes and blankets in this building.

20. WHAT DO YOU WANT THE TENANTS TO DO?
    A. nothing because you can handle this problem by yourself.
    B. decide to withhold their rent from the landlord.

C. receive clothes and blankets to keep themselves warm.
D. nothing until you have talked to the landlord.

Case K

You have been working with a gang of 10 members called the Tigers for six months. Many members of the "Tigers" have been arrested for petty theft, assault and battery, possession of narcotics, etc. While you and the gang are standing on a street corner, Jerry B., a gang member, tells you that they are going to "pull a job" on the drug store in the next block. You try to talk them out of this. You tell them that since you know of this, if they do pull the job, you will have to notify the police. However, you cannot persuade them, and four of the Tigers go down the street and throw a rock through the drug store window. These four grab what they can carry, and then get scared and run away.

21. WHAT DO YOU DO?
    A. since the four actually hurt no one and got no money, you do nothing; you are their friend.
    B. you call the police and tell them what happened; when the four are caught, you do what you can for them.
    C. you and the other members of the Tigers leave the area quickly so that you will not get blamed.
    D. you call the police and tell them you have just noticed that the drug store was broken into.

22. WHAT DO YOU WANT THE GANG TO DO?
    A. realize that there are some things which they may do that you cannot "go along with."
    B. realize that they were wrong to break into the drug store; promise not to do that again.
    C. the six members decide that the four members who broke into the store are out of the gang.
    D. realize that you really are a friend and helper who will not "fink" on them.

Case L

You are on the corner with a group of ten teenagers you have just met. They are members of a gang called the Rattle Snakes. The group has been kidding around and being normally noisy. As they begin to settle down, they ask questions about the activities at the neighborhood center. At this moment, a rival gang of seven members comes along. For a moment, it looks as if there will be a fight. However, you and the gangs talk things over; finally, the rival gang leaves. Suddenly, the police arrive and begin to force the Rattle Snakes to leave the corner. There is a little roughness on the part of the policemen.

23. WHAT DO YOU DO?
   A. advise the boys to leave the corner so no one will get hurt or arrested. Afterwards, explain to the policemen that you are a roving leader and tell them what was happening.
   B. since the policemen are treating these boys unfairly, you tell the Rattle Snakes to stand their ground and not to let these policemen treat them like dirt.
   C. in a situation like this one, there is nothing that you can do except to leave the scene, because you want no trouble with either the policemen or the Rattle Snakes.
   D. you can do and say nothing immediately. However, later, you talk to a friendly newspaper reporter and tell him all about this incident of police brutality.

24. WHAT DO YOU WANT THE GANG TO DO?
   A. tell the policeman that he is not being fair and that the gang have their rights.
   B. leave the scene as quickly as possible so that they don't get hurt or or arrested for anything.
   C. realize that you cannot go against the policeman's order; and that there are "other ways of handling the police."
   D. understand that the policeman is right and that he is just doing his job.

Case M

You have been working with a group called the Rams for nearly six months. The Rams are a group of eight Black teenagers from the ages of 16 to 19. Most are dropouts; the few still in school are doing poorly; and most are unemployed. At one meeting of the group, Joe tells of his experiences in job hunting. He claims that all white employers are prejudiced and will not give any Black a fair deal. You ask a few questions, and learn that Joe obtained application blanks from several companies, but did not fill any out. You know that Joe is a dropout. From past conversations with the school authorities, you also know that Joe's ability to understand reading and his ability to express himself in writing are both very poor.

25. WHAT DO YOU DO?
   A. ask Joe the names of the companies he went to; then contact these companies and point out to them their illegal personnel practices.

B. sympathize with Joe, tell him you know he got a rotten deal; but somehow guide the discussion away from a discussion of only Joe's problems.
C. get the group into a civil rights discussion; point out the ways they can influence our society and white-owned companies in particular.
D. ask to see the application blanks; then ask Joe if you may use them to show the group how to understand and fill out application blanks.

26. WHAT DO YOU WANT JOE TO DO?
    A. be able to talk over his problems in a calm and unemotional manner.
    B. learn how to understand and fill out application blanks to give him a better chance to get a job.
    C. begin to think of ways he can influence society and white-owned companies to give him a fair deal.
    D. nothing until you have talked with the companies involved; then possibly legal action against the companies.

Case N

Katie's Sweet Shop is a hangout for a group of teenagers who call themselves the Falcons. You have often met this group there just to talk. Because of your work, this group is presently involved in some programs at the neighborhood center. At one of these chance meetings, you learn that one member of the gang has just been arrested for carrying a concealed weapon. The Falcons think this is just an excuse used by the police so they can arrest whomever they want to arrest. They do not feel that carrying a concealed weapon is wrong.

27. WHAT DO YOU DO?
    A. somehow guide the discussion away from what happened to only one member of the gang. You are primarily interested in the members of the gang who are with you now.
    B. continue this discussion, but tell the gang your views and the reasons for your views about carrying a concealed weapon–point out that possession can lead to use of a weapon.
    C. tell the group that possession of any concealed weapon is against the law, so they had better not carry any weapons or else they stand a good chance of getting in trouble.
    D. since you wish the gang to think of you as a friend, you strongly agree that the police used possession of a concealed weapon as an excuse to pick up the gang member.

28. WHAT DO YOU WANT THE GANG TO DO?
    A. think of you as one of their gang, and a true friend and helper to all of them.
    B. realize that the arrested member's behavior was wrong; it was against the law.
    C. think about this subject; be aware of your views and the reasons for your views.
    D. end their discussion of this subject of the carrying of a concealed weapon.

Case O

You are at the neighborhood center when you notice three members of a Negro gang called the Young Chops leaving the center. You remember that this is not one of their scheduled nights to be at the neighborhood center, and the center has fairly strict rules about only scheduled groups being there. The three members seem very upset about something. You say, "hi," and ask what is wrong. They tell you that they wanted to watch the girls play basketball in the gym, and Mr. Jackson, the director of the center, told them they had to leave. They tell you that they think Mr. Jackson is prejudiced against Blacks.

29. WHAT DO YOU DO?
    A. go and talk to Mr. Jackson and tell him that the boys think he is prejudiced; ask him to explain his actions.
    B. explain the center's rules apply to everyone, not just Blacks; explain the reasons for these rules.
    C. tell the boys that since Mr. Jackson is the boss, they had better leave now before they get into more trouble.
    D. tell the boys that they had no business watching the girls when they were playing basketball in the first place.

30. WHAT DO YOU WANT THE THREE BOYS TO DO?
    A. understand the reasons for the center's rules; and that the rules apply to everyone.
    B. form a discussion group to talk about prejudice and what they can do about it.
    C. leave the neighborhood center and only come back on their scheduled nights.
    D. go with you to confront Mr. Jackson with their feelings that he is prejudiced.

Case P

You have met a few members of the Rovers, an eight-member gang of boys from the ages of 16 to 20. When you have talked with them, they seem interested in some of the programs at the neighborhood center. You learn that the gang sometimes hangs out in a small alley between Lolly's Liquors and Dizzy's Delicatessen. You have talked once with both of the owners of these businesses, and told them of the roving leader program. Although the owners do not think your ideas will work, they think something has to be done. They do not like "those hoodlums" to hang out in the alley because their loud talking keeps some of their customers away. Since you wish to continue your contact with the Rovers, you go to this alley. The boys are there. They seem interested in several programs carried on by the neighborhood center. At this point, two members begin to argue about whether playing basketball or woodworking would be what the gang would like to do. During this argument, Dizzy comes out and threatens to call the police unless everyone leaves.

31. WHAT DO YOU DO?
    A. since you do not wish to cause either Dizzy or the gang members any trouble, you strongly encourage the eight boys to leave the scene right away.
    B. since Dizzy's behavior toward the boys is unfair this time, you stick up very strongly for the boys and tell Dizzy firmly to leave them alone.
    C. tell the group to leave so they will not get into trouble. Afterwards, you remind Dizzy who you are; tell him what you and the boys were discussing.
    D. tell Dizzy that you think that calling the police would be a very unwise thing to do now, because it probably would cause a fight.

32. WHAT DO YOU WANT THE GANG TO DO?
    A. begin to think of you as a good guy and a friend of theirs.
    B. begin to think of you as a fair guy who will stick up for them.
    C. wait quietly while you try to talk Dizzy out of calling the police.
    D. leave the scene quickly so they will not get into any trouble.

Case Q

You have been working for six months now with a group of teenage girls who call themselves the Kittens. Their club meeting is held on Wednesday nights at the neighborhood center. At one meeting, you notice that two of the girls are absent. You ask the others if the two girls are sick. They tell you that these two girls were just arrested for shoplifting that afternoon. The group goes on to express their feelings about the arrests and shoplifting. You hear such things as: "Those stores are richer than we are–Ann and Jackie were not hurting them much," "Stores usually expect some shoplifting," "Everybody does it," and "Ann and Jackie were just unlucky to get caught."

33. WHAT DO YOU DO?
    A. continue the discussion of shoplifting; ask if anyone ever had something taken from them–how did they feel; let the group know your feelings and the reasons you feel as you do.
    B. tell the girls that shoplifting is wrong and cannot be allowed to go unpunished; tell them that Ann and Jackie got exactly what they deserved and are not to be pitied.
    C. since you wish the girls to think of you as one of their group, you agree with their statements that it is a shame that Ann and Jackie were caught for shoplifting.
    D. in some way, try to get the girls off of this subject; there are better uses of the time for the group's meeting than a discussion of what happened to only two members.

34. WHAT DO YOU WANT THE GROUP TO DO?
    A. think about shoplifting; be aware of your views and the reasons for your views.
    B. make a promise to you that from now on they will not do any shoplifting.
    C. end their discussion of the subject of shoplifting and the two girls' arrests.
    D. think of you as one of their group, and a true friend and helper to them.

Case R

You have been working with a group of five young teenagers who call their gang the Teenies. You and the Teenies happen to meet outside of the YMCA building. The girls are very mad because the YMCA officials have just refused to let them use the swimming pool. You know that this is one of the two nights that the YMCA pool is open to the general public. The girls feel they have been unfairly treated because they are girls. You check with the YMCA leaders and learn that because the pool is small, only a certain number of people can be allowed to use the pool in the interests of safety. This rule has to be followed even when the pool is open to the public. Tonight when the girls arrived, the pool was filled to capacity.

35. WHAT DO YOU DO?
    A. try to influence the YMCA officials to let the group of girls into the pool this time.
    B. explain the YMCA's rules and the reasons for these rules to the five girls.
    C. try to interest the girls in another activity that you think will distract them.
    D. ask the girls to help you plan a community action program to build a larger pool in the area.

36. WHAT DO YOU WANT THE GIRLS TO DO?
    A. understand the rules of the YMCA concerning the use of the pool.
    B. be allowed into the swimming pool by the YMCA officials this time.
    C. become interested in doing something other than going swimming.
    D. help you plan some action to get a new swimming pool for the area.

Case S

Through your work with a group of teenage girls, you hear of a fifteen-year-old girl, named Alice, who is unmarried and pregnant. You decide to contact her and see if she needs help of any kind. You learn that her parents have kicked her out of the house, and that she is living with a married sister. You visit her there. From talking with her, you learn that she is seven months pregnant. She has seen a doctor only once during her pregnancy. She has no definite plans for the future. She is not sure whether to keep the baby or not, and she does not know how she will support herself and the baby if she does decide to keep it. Also, she is not happy living with her sister and brother-in-law who live in a four room apartment and have three young children of their own. She thinks they consider her a burden. Alice tells you that she needs help from someone.

37. WHAT DO YOU DO?
    A. you encourage Alice to tell you who the father of the baby is. If she does, you contact the father and encourage him to marry her.
    B. you continue to visit and talk with Alice; you try to get her to accept her situation, and to make plans for herself and the baby.
    C. you refer Alice to an agency such as Children and Family Services, because you know they have the facilities to help Alice.
    D. you encourage Alice to give the baby up for adoption; also you work to find an adoptive home for the baby within the neighborhood.

38. WHAT DO YOU WANT ALICE TO DO?
    A. accept her situation and begin to think of you as a friend.

B. decide, with your influence, to give the baby up for adoption.
C. obtain help from an agency which has the facilities to help her.
D. marry the father if possible; if not, accept her situation.

Case T

For three months, you have been working after school with a group of young boys from the ages of six to eight. You have been helping them with various projects, and teaching them some games and crafts. One six-year-old, Tommy, has not joined into either the activities or the talks of the group. Although you have tried to get him interested in joining the group, Tommy usually stands apart from the group. When Tommy does say anything, he does not make sense. You talk with his first grade teacher and learn that he is also like this at school. He does not cause any trouble, but does not seem to know what is going on in the classroom. You decide to visit with Tommy's parents to see if they can help you work with Tommy. When you talk with Tommy's parents, you learn that they are worried because Tommy does not act at all like their other three children. He seems to live in a world of his own. They ask you how they can help Tommy.

39. WHAT DO YOU DO?
    A. refer Tommy and his parents to an agency or clinic which has the facilities to find out what is wrong with Tommy and to help him with his problem.
    B. tell the parents that you will do the best you can to help Tommy. You want him to think of you as a friend and as a person who can help him.
    C. work with the parents, and try to get them to think of you as a friend; try to help them to accept the fact that Tommy is not a normal little boy.
    D. tell the parents that you think they should ignore the fact that Tommy seems different than their own children. He may be just seeking attention.

40. WHAT DO YOU WANT TOMMY TO DO?
    A. you want Tommy to begin to think of you as a friend who can help him; until this happens, you cannot help Tommy.
    B. you want and expect nothing from Tommy. You are interested in working with Tommy's parents so they can help Tommy.
    C. go to an agency or clinic with the facilities to find out what his problem is and to give him help with his problem.
    D. you expect Tommy to gradually change his behavior when his behavior no longer brings him any attention from his parents.

APPENDIX D

ROVING RECREATION LEADER PROJECT GENERAL INFORMATION TEST

GENERAL INFORMATION TEST

Multiple Choice

Directions: Circle the letter that best describes your answer. For example:

History tells us that all nations have enjoyed participation in

    A. Gymnastics

    B. Football

    (C.) Physical training of some sort

    D. Baseball

    E. Basketball

CIRCLE THAT STATEMENT WHICH BEST DESCRIBES YOUR ANSWER:

1. The most immediate and critical function of the roving leaders is
   A. to reach the youngster as quickly as possible
   B. to know how to serve youth
   C. to establish rapport
   D. to plan activities immediately
   E. to plan athletic programs

2. The ultimate goal of a roving leader is
   A. to be liked by all
   B. to introduce many activities
   C. to be honored by the neighborhood
   D. to be no longer needed
   E. to accept people as they are

3. A roving leader is
   A. generally assigned to a specific geographic area within the community.

B. moves from neighborhood to neighborhood
C. concerned with recreation activity only
D. based at a recreation center and rotates among a number of stations within the center
E. moves from city to city

4. The most important factor that contributes to sub-standard housing is
   A. a lack of concern on the part of the Department of Housing and Urban Development
   B. a lack of citizen involvement in the planning process
   C. planners giving little consideration to this aspect of community planning
   D. the mayor having too much veto power
   E. not enough land available

5. An individual has complained to his landlord about rats in his apartment and has only been given promises of action. Which agency would you refer him to
   A. Unemployment Agency
   B. Board of Health
   C. Welfare Department
   D. Police Department
   E. National Association for the Advancement of Colored People

6. The philosophy of the roving leader concept points out that it is
   A. a police service
   B. an organized recreation program
   C. a parole guideline service
   D. a problem-oriented service
   E. a service for low income families only

7. The major health problem with which roving leaders contend are
   A. venereal disease
   B. drug addiction
   C. alcoholism
   D. T.B.
   E. all of these

8. Impoverished and hard-to-reach youth would generally be found at the
   A. school
   B. pool hall
   C. Boys' Club
   D. Police Athletic League
   E. Recreation center

9. The YMCA Roving Leader approach in St. Louis has been termed
   A. "gettin" the ghetto
   B. my boy
   C. outreach
   D. SPU
   E. "in" the city

10. The roving leader concept began as early as
    A. 1917
    B. 1848
    C. 1927
    D. 1907
    E. 1868

11. The basic form of communication among gang members is
    A. neighborhood meetings
    B. activity
    C. secret meetings
    D. groove chatter (inner-city language)
    E. attending city council meetings

12. The major objective of in-service training for the roving leader is
    A. to help leaders understand their roles
    B. to teach first aid
    C. to complete high school
    D. to learn more about Black people
    E. to learn how to shoot a gun

13. The major reasons why hard-to-reach youth do not participate in recreation activities is
    A. lack of opportunity
    B. boredom
    C. poor leadership
    D. not enough money
    E. too many activities being offered

14. The first organized Outreach (streetwork) Program was conducted in
    A. Chicago
    B. St. Louis
    C. Detroit
    D. New York
    E. Los Angeles

15. The Harlem Street Academy works with
    A. bailing kids out of trouble
    B. dropouts

C. teenagers only
D. dope addicts
E. senior citizens

16. Which of the following is most important for the roving leader to know
    A. the power structure
    B. the population of the community
    C. the authority lines
    D. the number of YMCA's
    E. A and C

17. The major requirement for a community to become eligible for funds from the Model Cities Program required that
    A. the mayor and council approve the program
    B. there was community involvement in the planning
    C. the community provide 10 per cent matching funds
    D. the money be distributed evenly throughout the city
    E. the county board of supervisors approve the program

18. The major objective of the roving leader efforts within the school system is
    A. to bridge the gap between the youth and the teacher
    B. to assist in coaching athletic teams
    C. to direct a noon-hour recreation program
    D. to encourage the development of programs which meet the needs and interests of youth
    E. A and D

19. The Office of Economic Opportunity is a Department in
    A. Housing and Urban Development
    B. Department of Health, Education, and Welfare
    C. Labor Department
    D. Office of Education
    E. none of these

Matching Question

Directions: On the line to the left of each word or phrase in Column A write the letter of the word in Column B that best matches the word or phrase.

Column A	Column B
1. ___ chicken scratch	A. squeal or to inform
2. ___ fink	B. sissy or male homosexual
3. ___ pansy	C. hypo marks on arm
4. ___ stick	D. head, leader
5. ___ the man	E. marijuana

True and False

Directions: Read the following statements. If the statement is true, circle the "T." If the statement is false, circle the "F." For example:

(T) F Richard Nixon became President of the United States in January, 1969.

1. T F An effective community attack on problem gang delinquency requires cooperation between the police and the roving leader personnel.
2. T F Delinquent youth tend to "act out" feelings or express themselves more through activity rather than through verbal exchange.
3. T F It would be beneficial to the participants if each roving leader had a set pattern of dealing with youth.
4. T F A person who has a car, home, and job is one who has gotten all society has to offer.
5. T F In order to keep his program running smoothly, the roving leader must establish the limits of acceptable behavior.
6. T F The roving leader who has lived in the inner city can relate better to disadvantaged youth than people from middle-class backgrounds.
7. T F In his behavior with the group, the roving leader must be prepared to demonstrate his ability to analyze problem situations in the light of reality.
8. T F In attempting to solve the group's problem, the roving leader should collect all of the available facts, formulate a variety of alternatives, select the best solution and recommend it to the group for action.
9. T F After he has established a supportive relationship with a youngster, the roving leader should firmly and consistently expect that he conform to acceptable standards.
10. T F As part of his function, the roving leader must acquaint youth with the various community resources available.
11. T F The roving leader should report all violations to the police, regardless of the seriousness of the crime.
12. T T Only those disadvantaged youth who show that they want help and show gratitude for this help should receive assistance from the roving leader.
13. T F One of the major requirements for a city to receive funds from the Model Cities Program was that citizens in the community had to be involved in the planning process.

14. T F Research has revealed that agencies such as schools, churches, neighborhood groups have little influence on the development of an individual's behavior.
15. T F The agency sponsoring the roving leader program should not have a firm operating policy with the police department.
16. T F The roving leader should be free to set his own priorities as far as his responsibilities and work schedule is concerned.
17. T F There are some individuals who have never been successful in making a satisfactory place for themselves in any group.
18. T F One of the important functions of the roving leader is to bring about some workable relationships between the objectives of the sponsoring agency and those of the group he is leading.
19. T F In order to maintain the confidence of the gang, the roving leader should offer a solution to problems that may exist in the neighborhood.
20. T F A leader is primarily a person who enables the members of a group to do things for themselves.
21. T F Since there is a lack of organization in inner-city groups, the roving leader should encourage a minimum of self-direction.
22. T F The ability or the inability of a youth to conform to the rules and regulations is directly related to the subsequent ability or inability of the youngster to adjust in the community.
23. T F Delinquency is essentially the behavior of emotionally disturbed children.
24. T F The roving leader should not become involved in seeking jobs for delinquent or potentially delinquent youths. If he knows of job opportunities, it is permissible only to suggest them.
25. T F The chief agent of socialization in the very early and crucial years is the family, and in the vast majority of cases it does an adequate job.
26. T F Other agents of socialization such as schools, churches, neighborhoods, peer groups, and social agencies also exert an influence on the evaluation of behavior. Research has revealed that these institutions have not been very successful.

APPENDIX E

ROVING RECREATION LEADER PROJECT SELF-ASSESSMENT INVENTORY*

A wide variety of different kinds of situations calling for different sorts of skills are listed in the Inventory below. For the purpose of assessing your needs in training, we would like you to be as honest as possible in responding to the questions.

We have provided below four possible feelings you might have about handling the range of situations that develop in a group. For each situation encircle the number which most closely corresponds to how you would feel.

1. *Feel you couldn't handle it without first discussing it with someone more experienced in running groups.*
2. *Would feel more comfortable if you had someone there to support you.*
3. *Feel you would find it difficult but probably could handle it.*
4. *Feel that you could handle it without too much difficulty.*

Now let us go on to the Inventory:

1. Dealing with an excessive amount of disruptive side conversations in the group.   1   2   3   4
2. Getting the group to assume responsibility for its members.   1   2   3   4
3. Getting good group participation in discussion.   1   2   3   4
4. Dealing with a leader in the group who exerts a negative influence on the group.   1   2   3   4
5. Dealing with a group member who constantly tattles on other group members.   1   2   3   4
6. Getting the group to make and follow-through on decisions.   1   2   3   4
7. Planning and implementing a schedule of activities for the group.   1   2   3   4
8. Keeping the group focused on discussing issues that are sensitive to members.   1   2   3   4
9. Getting the group to reconsider an action which goes against the group's best interests.   1   2   3   4

---

* The Self-Assessment Inventory, here reproduced by permission, was developed by the Institute for Youth Services, Howard University, Washington, D. C.

10. Dealing with a group member who continually challenges your position in the group. 1 2 3 4
11. Meeting with the neighborhood group to discuss their involvement in Community Programs. 1 2 3 4
12. Dealing with a group problem in which you have obviously taken the wrong position. 1 2 3 4
13. Openly reprimanding a group member. 1 2 3 4
14. Holding meetings consistently meaningful to members. 1 2 3 4
15. A situation in which the group is openly hostile to you. 1 2 3 4
16. Getting the group to discipline its own members. 1 2 3 4
17. A situation in which the members are obviously baiting you. 1 2 3 4
18. Getting group members to assume leadership in group. 1 2 3 4

INDEX

A

ADC mothers, 73
Advisory boards, 43-44, 49, 91, 95 (*see also* Community control)
Advocacy in outreach work, 33-34, 37-39, 76, 164, 170-171, 182, 183
 dilemmas of, 47, 77-79
 federal, 79
 Mobilization for Youth, Inc., 39-47
 role of, 48
Agency-client relations, 37n, 40-41, 45, 47-48, 50, 59, 176
Alienation, of youth, 130-132, 133, 138-139, 179 (*see also* Juvenile delinquency)
Alinsky, Saul, 47
Analysis (*see* Problem-solving)
Animals, attitudes toward, 99
Argyris, Chris, 104
Attica prison uprising, 57
Automated systems, 148-149

B

Bannon, Joseph J., 25, 89n
Behavior strategies, 111, 126-127
Birth control information, 94-95
Black family, 64-68
Black language, 61-64, 86-87, 153-154
Black militants, 57
Black World magazine, 62
Body language, 86
Boguslaw, Robert, 148-149, 161n, 162
Bordua, David J., 40n, 75n
Boys' Club, 12, 73, 92
Boy Scouts, 12, 73
Broker role, 34-38 *passim*, 47-48
Bronner, Augusta, 8, 9, 10
Brown, Claude, 100
Brown, William P., 69n, 70n
Buffalo (N.Y.) Youth Bureau, 24
Burt, Ciril, 8

C

Case studies, 81-82, 87, 118-121 (*see also* Appendix C, 191)
Change-agent (*see* Advocacy)
Change, rate of, 154-156, 182
Chicago Youth Development Project, 179-180

Chisholm, Shirley, 35
Christeve, Jacqueline, 97n
Christian Action Ministry (CAM), 53-54
Citizen involvement, 41-44, 46-51, 91-92, 94, 95, 133-135, 174-176
City, prototype of, 145-166
Clark, Kenneth P., 45-46
Client-agency relations, 37n, 40-41, 45, 47-48, 50, 59, 176
Cobbs, Price M., 65n, 67n
Coles, Robert, 85n
Communications exercises, 115-117, 121
Community Action Guide, 42
Community Action Projects (CAP), 34n, 39, 40, 41-44, 49-50
Community change-agent (*see* Advocacy)
Community Chest, 12
Community colleges, programs in, 172-174
Community control, 41-44, 46-51, 91-92, 94, 95, 33-35, 174-176
Community surveys, 55, 175
Crime (*see* Juvenile delinquency)

D

Decentralization (*see* Community control)
Delinquency index, 15
Demonstration Cities and Metropolitan Development Act, 39, 42
Depression, human services during, 3, 8, 18, 33
DeQuincey, Thomas, 101
Detached worker, 23-24, 33, 74, 75, 104-106 (*see also* Roving Recreation Leader; Street-club worker)
Deviancy, 97
Dewey, Thomas, 18
Douglas, Milton, Jr., 98n
Dropouts, 72-73, 100, 152
Drugs, 25, 36, 60, 69-71

E

East St. Louis (Illinois), 89-90
Ebony magazine, 60
Economic Opportunity Act (1964), 39, 42
Education and juvenile delinquency, 11, 13, 25
 Black English, 63-64

minority groups, 71-73
need for, 169
recreation, 74, 149-150, 161
roving leaders, 78-79
street academies, 53-54
Enabler role, 34-38 passim, 47-48
Essence magazine, 60
Etzkowitz, Henry, 66n
Evaluation: of recreation programs, 95, 96, 98; of outreach training, 103, 108, 115, 117-118, 122-123, 124-126

F

Facility use, 73-74, 90, 92-93, 134, 171-172
Fantini, Mario D., 54n
Fast, Julius, 86
Federal funds, for social welfare, xiii, 41, 93, 134
Feedback: exercises in, 116-117, 121; in system analysis, 155
Fees and charges, 90-91
Flint, Michigan, 156
Ford Foundation, 39
Fromm, Erich, 155
Fun-and-games approach, 30, 31, 101, 130
Funding, 92, 140, 142
Fun wagon, 136-137, 139 (photograph)

G

Games, street, 4, 6, 97
Gangs
case studies on, 118-121
changes in, 19, 25
defined, 105
inner-city, 5-7, 18
outreach with, 20-24, 79
research on, 8-10
role of girls, 6, 21, 25
wars in, 19-20, 36, 69
"General Information Test," 87, 207-212
Ghetto (*see* Inner city)
Girls' Club, 12, 73, 93
Gleazer, Edmund J., 173
Glueck, Eleanor and Sheldon, 10, 15
Goldberg, Ira, 38, 39
Gray, David E., 170, 171
Great Depression, 3, 8, 18, 33
Grier, William H., 65n, 67n
Group dynamics, 113-114, 135

H

Hannerz, Alf, 66n
Harlem (N. Y.), 36, 55
HARYOU, 30n, 38n, 42, 45-47, 54-55, 60

Health, Education, and Welfare, U. S. Department of, xiv, 25
Healy, William, 8, 9, 10
Hentoff, Nat, 31n, 34, 56n
Human services
advocacy in, 170-171, 182
education for, 169, 170, 172-174
new careers in, 44-45, 49
outreach work in, 88-89, 103, 179
recreation, 94, 171
techniques of, 41
(*see also* Social services)

I

Illinois Crime Commission, 9
Indigenous worker (*see* Paraprofessionals)
Inner city
ethos of, xiv, 40, 54, 57-74, 76, 79, 83, 86, 88, 108-109, 131, 177-179
language of, 61-64, 86-87, 153-154
recreation, 175-177, 180-181
source of problems, 36n
youth, 68-74, 83, 104-105
Inservice training (*see* Training)

J

Jenkins, Shirley, 176
Jenks, Christopher, 72n
Jet magazine, 60
Job training (*see* Manpower development)
Juvenile court, 11-12
Juvenile delinquency
courts for, 11-12
history of, 3-8
procedures for, 104
prevention of, 10-13, 14-24, 30-31, 179-180
research on, 8-10, 13-14
roving leader program, 75-76, 179
Juvenile Delinquency and Youth Offense Control Act (1961), 39

K

Kammeyer Community Leader's Rating Scale, 87
Kansas, Topeka, 49-50
King, Martin Luther, Jr., 155
Klein, Malcolm W., 105
Knowles, Malcolm S., 111, 113
Kraus, Richard, 171

L

Labor, U. S. Department of, 44-45
Ladner, Joyce, 65
Laing, R. D., 29n

Laird, Dugan, 126-127
Language, changes in, 153-154
Learning techniques, 111, 162
Legal services, 34
Leisure
  changes in, 130, 132, 155, 170, 174-177
  education for, 95, 169, 170, 172-174, 181-184
  estimation of needs, 133
  services for inner-city youth, 89-90, 92, 96-101, 180-181
  unemployment, xiii, 31, 60, 135
Likert, Rensis, 146
Lindsay, John, 94

M

Malcolm X, 76
Mann, Horace, 23
Manpower development, 44-45, 71, 72-73, 74
Maximum Feasible Participation, 40-45 passim, 49, 50, 91-92
Middle-class values, *passim*
Middleton, Donald J., 94-96
Miller, Walter B., 105
Minority groups
  ethos of, xiv, 40, 54, 57-74, 79, 83, 88, 108-109, 131, 177-179
  family, 64-68
  language, 61-64, 86-87, 153-154
  racism and, 56-58, 60, 71, 95
  recreation for, 175-177, 180-181
  youth, 60-61
Mobile recreation programs, 94, 135-138, 139 (photograph)
Mobilization for Youth, Inc., 29*n*, 34*n*, 37, 39-47, 60
Model Cities Program, 39, 42
Mott Foundation, 156
Moynihan, Daniel P., 42*n*, 91-92
Municipal services, 32, 175
Myrdal, Gunnar, 56-57

N

Narcotics (*see* Drugs)
National Education Association, 149-150
National Forum on Careers in Parks and Recreation, 174
National League of Cities, urban recreation, 175-176
National Recreation and Park Association, xiv, 2
National Welfare Rights Organization, 35
National Youth Authority, 12
Neighborhood Service Pilot Program, 39

New Careers, 44-45, 49, 95
New Towns Project, 148
New York City, roving leader program, 79-80
New York City, Welfare Council of, 117-118
New York City Youth Board, 19-24 *passim*, 36
New York State Crime Commission, 9
New York State Youth Commission, 18-19, 20-24 *passim*
Nixon, Richard M., 34, 62, 93
Nonprofit agencies, 12, 29, 73, 92-93, 165-166
Nuclear family, 64-68

O

Office of Economic Opportunity, 42, 49-50, 93
Opie, Iona and Peter, 97
Outreach:
  advocacy, 33-34, 37-39, 46, 47, 76-78, 170-171, 182-183
  defined, xi, xiii, 33, 53, 82-83, 179
  education, xv-xvi, 53-54, 169-170, 172-174, 181-184
  establishing rapport in, 16-18, 20-21, 60-61, 74, 86-89, 117-118
  ethos of, 54, 57-58, 59, 61-74, 76, 79, 83, 104, 108-109, 131, 177-179, 180, 181
  history of, 13, 16-18
  Mobilization for Youth, 41-42, 45
  services for youth, 89, 91, 94-101
  staff resistance to, 140-142
  systems analysis for, 145-166
  tasks of, 58-59, 104, 132, 140, 179-180
  training for, xiv, 15-16, 24-25, 26, 87-88, 98, 103-117
  with paraprofessionals, 44-45, 47
  (*see also* Roving Recreation Leader)

P

PAL program, 99
Paraprofessionals
  prejudice toward, 140-142
  recruitment of, 47, 72-73, 96, 183
  roving leaders, 80, 104, 163
  use of, 44-45, 49, 95, 134-135, 136, 181-182
Partners, Inc., 165
Peralta Colleges (Oakland), 173
Planning
  citizen involvement in, 49-51, 91

recreation program, 85-101, 129-135, 138-142
training program, 106-107, 123
Police, interaction with outreach worker, 20-21, 22, 99
Poverty, culture of, 29, 42, 71n
Private agencies, 12, 29, 73, 92-93, 165-166
Problem-solving, 35-36, 69, 89, 103, 183
Programmatic approach, 41, 93-95
Program planning, 85-101, 129-135, 138-142
Prospect Park, 22
Public agencies, 40, 165-166, 175, 176
Publicity, 96

R

Racism, 56-58, 60, 71, 95
Reckless, W. C., 9, 10
Recreation and parks
  advocacy in, 37-39, 170, 183
  community involvement in, 174
  critique of, 129, 130, 132, 142
  delinquency prevention, 8, 46, 58, 59, 81, 140
  drug abuse, 36
  expanded role of, 89, 94-95, 141, 174
  facilities for, 73-74, 90, 92-93, 134, 171-172
  for minority groups, 175-177, 180-181
  funding, 90-91
  Harlem survey, 55
  higher education, 169, 170, 172-174
  outreach services, xiii-xiv, 33, 46, 58, 59, 81, 140
  paraprofessionals in, 45, 47, 80
  urban programs, 31-33, 85-101, 129-135, 138-142, 175-177
  use of systems analysis, 145-166
  with human services, 36-37, 94
Recreation programming, urban, 31-33, 85-101, 129-135, 138-142, 175-177
Referral service, 59, 71, 88-89, 92, 98, 114-115, 145-166 passim
Riese, Herta, 178
Rochester (N. Y.), 23-24
Role playing, 112-113, 122
Roving Recreation Leader
  detached worker (see Streetclub worker)
  history of, 16-18, 24
  programs, 53, 74-83
  role of, 98, 104
  training, 15-16, 24-25, 26, 87-88, 103-127
  University of Illinois Project, xiv, 25, 103
  youth work, 85-90, 92, 96-101

"Roving Recreation Leader Rating Scale," 87-88, 187-189
Rural youth, problems with, 30

S

Salvation Army, 12, 92
Schaflander, Gerald M., 66n
Schultz, William C., 114
Seale, Bobby, 58
"Self-Assessment Inventory," 87, 213-214
Sexual roles, 67
Shaw, Clifford R., 9
Silberman, Charles E., 29n, 36n, 55n
"Situation-Problem Exercise," 87, 191-205
Skinner, B. F., 148, 149
Social services
  advocacy, 33-34, 37-39, 170-171, 182, 183
  changing role of, 34-37, 40, 41, 47-48
  critique of, xiv, 11, 29, 30, 39-40, 54-56
  federal funds for, xiii
  recreation outreach, 169, 171
  systems analysis and, 147-166 passim
Social systems, analysis of, 145-166, 169, 171
Staff development (see Training)
Staley, Edwin J., 176
Street clubs and gangs
  gang wars, 19-20
  inner-city, 3-7, 18
  research on, 8-10
Streetclub worker, 20-23, 24, 25, 74, 103-106 (see also Detached worker; Roving Recreation Leader)
Street games, 4, 6, 97
Street activity, 3-5
Suburban youth, problems with, 30, 81
Surveys, 55, 175
Systems analysis, 145-166

T

Topeka (Kansas) OEO program, 49-50
Thrasher, Frederic M., 9, 13-14
Training
  planning for, 106-107
  problem-solving approach in, 103
  procedures for, 109-122
  programs, xiv, 15-16, 24-25, 26, 76n, 87-88, 98
  trainer characteristics, 108
  value of, 126-127, 141
Traveling Recreation Leader, 135-138 (see also Roving Recreation Leader)
"Turf," 7, 19, 22, 76
Twenty-four hour facility, 92

Index

U

Unemployment
  leisure, xiii, 31, 60, 135
  minority groups, 60, 177
  paraprofessionals, 44-45
United Way Fund, 92, 142
Universities, responsibilities of, 169-170, 172-174, 181-184
University of Illinois, roving recreation leader program, xiv, 25,
  etiology, 177-179, 180-181
  prototype of, 145-166
Urban areas, 81
Urban recreation programming, 31-33, 85-101, 129-135, 138-142, 175-177
Urban university, 169-170
Urban youth, unemployment, 31, 60, 177

V

Vandalism, 91
Volunteers, 134, 136

W

War on Poverty, xiii, 39, 50, 91, 93
Washington (D. C.), roving leader program, 25-26
Washington Heights, gangs, 22
Weinstein, Gerald, 54n
Welfare, xiv, 11, 34-37 *passim* (*see also* Social services)
Welfare colonialism, xiv, 35, 39, 56, 86
Welfare Council of New York City, 117-118
Welfare Rights Organization, National, 35
White House Conference on Child Health and Protection, 10
World War II, 18
Work, attitudes toward, 72, 155
Works Progress Administration (WPA), 12
Work/study programs, 100
Wright, Richard, 67, 68

Y

YMCA/YWCA, 24, 29, 73, 92
Youth
  alienation of, 130-132
  rapport with, 60-61
  unemployment of, 31, 60, 177

Z

Zoo trips, 99